TH
CS
RT
WV
SC
GH

Aug 21
Nov 21
Dec 21
Apr 22
Aug 22
Mar 23

COME FLY THE WORLD

The Jet-Age Story of
the Women of Pan Am

JULIA COOKE

HOUGHTON MIFFLIN HARCOURT

BOSTON   NEW YORK

2021

hmhbooks.com

Library of Congress Cataloging-in-Publication Data
Names: Cooke, Julia, author.
Title: Come fly the world : the jet-age story of the women of Pan Am / Julia Cooke.
Description: Boston : Houghton Mifflin Harcourt, 2021. |
Includes bibliographical references and index.
Identifiers: LCCN 2020034163 (print) | LCCN 2020034164 (ebook) | ISBN 9780358251408
(hardcover) | ISBN 9780358448990 | ISBN 9780358449355 | ISBN 9780358251385 (ebook)
Subjects: LCSH: Pan American World Airways, Inc.—History. | Pan American World Airways,
Inc.—Employees—Biography. | Flight attendants—United States—History—
20th century. | Flight attendants—United States—Biography. | Sex role in the work
environment—United States.
Classification: LCC HD8039.A432 U6323 2021 (print) | LCC HD8039.A432 (ebook) |
DDC 387.7/42092273—dc23
LC record available at https://lccn.loc.gov/2020034163
LC ebook record available at https://lccn.loc.gov/2020034164

Book design by Helene Berinsky
Maps by Lucidity Information Design, LLC. Adapted from the 1968 edition of *New Horizons
World Guide*. Used by permission of Pan Am Airways, Inc. Records, Courtesy of Special
Collections, University of Miami Libraries.

Letters of Lynne Totten, 1966–1975, used by kind permission of Lynne D. Rawling.
Letters of Karen Ryan, 1966–1974, used by kind permission of Karen Walker Ryan.
"The Air Hostess" by Army Warrant Officer Jim Reese used by permission of World Wings
International, Inc. Records, Courtesy of Special Collections, University of Miami Libraries.

Printed in the United States of America
DOC 10 9 8 7 6 5 4 3 2 1

For my father
and the window seats he saved for me

CONTENTS

CONTENTS

III: WOMEN'S WORK

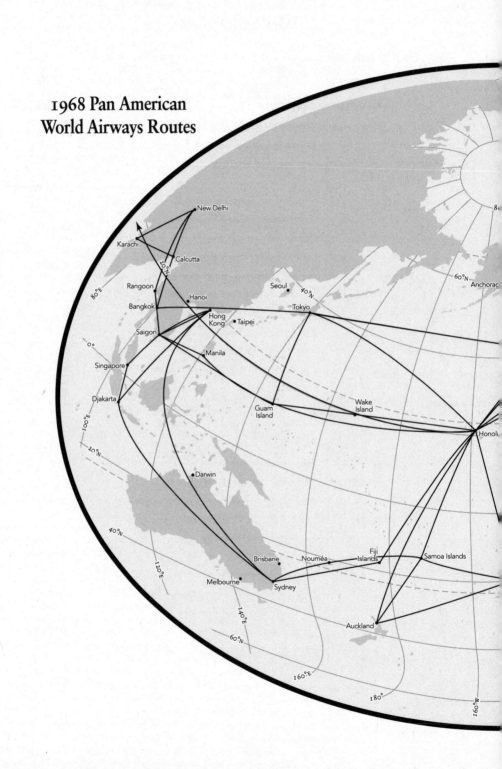

1968 Pan American
World Airways Routes

ARCTIC CIRCLE

40°N

20°N

20°W

airbanks
Juneau
Ketchikan
Vancouver
Seattle
Portland
San Francisco

Edmonton
Winnipeg
Minneapolis
Salt Lake
City
Boise
Denver
Santa Fe
Los Angeles

Montreal
Toronto
Detroit
Chicago
St. Louis
Oklahoma
City
Memphis
Dallas
New
Orleans
Houston
Mexico
City

Boston
New York
Philadelphia
Baltimore
Washington
Port-au-Prince
Tampa
Nassau
Miami
Havana
Mérida
Montego
Bay
Kingston

Bermuda

St. Thomas/
St. Croix
San Juan
Santo
Domingo
Curaçao
Caracas

St. Maarten
Antiqua
Guadeloupe
Martinique
Barbados
Port of Spain
Cayenne
Belém
Paramaribo
Georgetown

40°W

0°

Guatemala
San Salvador
Managua
San José

Tegucigalpa
Panama

Barranquilla

Cali
Bogotá
Quito
Guayaquil

Lima

Santa Cruz
La Paz

Brasilia
Rio de
Janeiro
São Paulo

Asunción

20°S

TROPIC OF CANCER

EQUATOR

Antofagasta
Santiago

Buenos
Aires

Montevideo

40°S

60°W

Tahiti
TROPIC OF CAPRICORN

60°S

80°W

100°W

120°W

140°W

LUCIDITY INFORMATION DESIGN, L.L.

1968 Pan American
World Airways Routes

Stewardess Wanted.
Must Want the World.

— PAN AM RECRUITMENT ADVERTISEMENT, 1967

PART I

THE WRONG
KIND OF GIRL

1

A Jet-Age Job

LYNNE TOTTEN STOOD IN THE DOORWAY FOR WHAT FELT LIKE a very long time, looking at the women sitting in rows in front of her. Only minutes before, she had walked confidently down Park Avenue to the Pan Am Building, an octagonal skyscraper of broad-faceted glass and concrete. As Lynne approached the fifty-nine-story building's shadow, she took in the enormous letters of the company's name at its crown. She'd walked through the Pan Am lobby and taken the elevator up to the offices above as if she knew where she was going and what she was doing.

Now Lynne stood facing bouffants and elegant French twists. As she headed to the front of the room, she saw the faces of the women who wore them—perfect eye makeup. Lynne, short and dainty in her brown suede skirt suit, with long dark hair down her back—she had not thought to pull it up into a bun—considered the reality of where she stood, waiting to be interviewed for a job as a stewardess.

"How can you change a world you've never seen?" a Pan Am magazine ad read. This was the yearning that had sent Lynne to the interview. On television, the same campaign asked, "Why don't you join the country club?" A golfer on a green field was quickly surrounded by people in varied international-looking clothing—men in the striped shirts of Italian *vaporetto* drivers or in baroque military jackets; women in Japanese *yukata*. "Big countries, small countries, old countries, new countries."

But another Pan Am advertisement frequently aired in 1969 might have sent Lynne walking away just as quickly as she'd come: a gorgeous woman with flawlessly applied eye makeup brushing mascara onto her lashes and then striding down the street as the camera panned up from the sidewalk, taking in the stewardess's perfectly cut blue suit, her tidy purse, her hair in precise waves under her hat. When Lynne considered how she must look to the assembled crowd of aspiring stewardesses, *country bumpkin* was the term that came to mind.

Lynne had grown up in Baldwinsville, thirteen miles outside of Syracuse, on the twisting Seneca River. In the summer, when the sun lit the streets long into evening, children came home only briefly for dinner, then went back out. Baldwinsville was an overgrown suburb with a quaint village of two- and three-story brick buildings, shade trees glowing orange and yellow on autumn afternoons, and church steeples of various Christian denominations rising above it all.

Until right now, Lynne had felt sure that this job was what she wanted. Her parents had worked hard to send her—the bright and promising student-body president of her small-town high school, obedient and optimistic—to college, the first one in their family to go. Lynne was grateful, but at college, her awareness of how lucky she was competed with a bone-deep disaffection for the lab work her biology major required. She was not always the only woman haunting the lab at the State University of New York at Oswego late into the night, but she rarely saw more than one other woman around. As far as she knew, she was the only female biology major in her year.

In the lab she barely glanced at the young men blending and separating compounds. Lynne paid strict attention to her own measurements; she harbored diffuse fears of blowing the building up. "Why are you here?" the men asked Lynne. It could have been intended as a compliment for a pretty woman under artificial lab lights, but the words had a hectoring edginess.

For Lynne, declaring a major was a promise, and she did not break her promises. She spent four years in class and in the lab and acquired two assistantships to keep herself afloat financially, including one working with soil samples for a palynology professor. Lynne was good at extracting hundred-year-old pollen from soil; it impressed her that pollen could not be destroyed and would always provide a map of the past. But beneath her commitment to her biology major, her gratitude to her parents, and her determination in the face of the subtle intimidation in the labs, Lynne had doubts. Sometimes she wondered what she was doing, what she was preparing for, especially as she learned about the world outside of upstate New York.

In Baldwinsville, around the dinner table on Sundays, when her parents closed the general store they owned to eat together as a family, international politics never came up. But at the coffee shops and diners in Oswego, Lynne's peers debated government policy ardently. Combat in Vietnam escalated throughout Lynne's undergraduate years and Lynne listened to her college boyfriend and his friends discussing the war. The first few times they challenged the decisions President Johnson and Secretary of Defense Robert McNamara were making in Washington, she felt uneasy. Who were they to question figures of authority? she asked.

They were male college seniors in the United States, they answered —their draft numbers and the end of their deferment upon graduation entitled them to question the government. Around the country and the world—in West Berlin, Sweden, Mexico City—students had begun to protest a war that, Lynne learned, had never been declared a war by Congress. Now she realized that covert American intervention in the region went back decades, to the Second World War and the decolonization that followed, separating Vietnam into north and south. Communism ruled in the USSR-allied north; a nominally democratic regime ruled in the south. American interest in the region centered on natural resources—Vietnam's tin, tungsten, and rubber—and the fear of what President Eisenhower had called a decade earlier "the 'falling domino' principle."

Between school and jobs, Lynne had little time to read newspapers. But she listened as her boyfriend honed his arguments, incorporating information gleaned from local and national newspapers and his political science coursework. He and his friends drained cup after stained coffee cup during heated debate. Two perspectives on the American troops that flooded into South Vietnam emerged. From one angle, American aid to the democratic half of a split Vietnam represented the nation's commitment to helping the residents of a small, poor country resist a Communist insurgency. From another, deteriorating conditions in the south—antidemocratic elections, political arrests that kept prisons continually stuffed, a hampered press, corruption of the military and government, and deepening poverty—demonstrated the essentially imperialist nature of growing American intervention. As one semester led to the next, Lynne's reluctance to second-guess national policy faded and grew into a conviction that she could do more in the real world than in a lab. In her scant free time, she glanced at the front pages of newspapers and magazines and saw names of countries she had never thought about before. *There's a whole world out there,* she thought, *and I need to get involved.*

As she walked across the stage at graduation, her parents clapping proudly in the audience, Lynne felt a sinking sensation over the choices that had narrowed her life. She was qualified to work as a research assistant or a science teacher, or, as many of her peers had done already, she could marry. Lynne was still awed by the intricacies of the natural world but felt drained by the isolation and intimidation of the lab. She had the extroversion for teaching but she had already spent much of her life in classrooms. Marriage eventually, but certainly not now. Graduation was the worst day of her life.

But a professor had encouraged Lynne to sign up for a college-sponsored painting course in Rome that summer, and she had taken out a small loan to pay for what her savings did not cover. A break from science coursework might be refreshing for her, the professor had said. For the first time in her life, Lynne was doing something for herself. She flew to Rome. The hot city was relatively empty, but the sepia-toned streets were alive with history. Lynne understood, after the heat and activity, why Italians slept in the afternoons.

The men in Italy were a trial. *Like flies or bloodhounds,* Lynne thought. "*Bella, bellissima,*" they whispered after her, though Lynne had never thought of herself as beautiful. She had to be downright rude to get rid of them. Once she retreated to the bathroom of a train station to avoid the men who harassed her.

Every day she took the bus from student housing on the outskirts of the city into Rome, going past the low outlying neighborhoods, winding through the tight old streets like a corkscrew. She would set up her easel on sidewalks. She had no talent for painting but that did not matter. She bought slides of the Vatican and Roman monuments to show her parents and snapped photographs of the "common things" that enchanted her: the shopkeepers and bartenders sitting on folding chairs in front of a trattoria with an ancient façade; Coca-Cola and Peroni logos on tin signs on the sides of markets; the women waving money toward piles of tomatoes and greens and citrus set atop fruit crates in the streets, red and green and lemon yellow against the old stone.

In Naples, Siena, and Florence, the alchemy of person, time, and place inspired not hesitation in Lynne but a growing certainty that the world was enormous and that she wanted to be out there, be in it.

In Baldwinsville, she told her parents about the plan she had hatched on her flight back to the States, and her mother was appalled. "You're nuts," she said. "We've just paid for four years of college." Her elegant, disciplined, educated daughter was not a stewardess. Stewardess duties revolved around serving others. Airline press releases and recruiting advertisements evoked training schools focused on fashion, hostessing, and helping women acquire a "first-class husband."

Stewardesses were bound to be insipid, and Lynne was intelligent and serious.

Then Lynne's father took her aside. After he had fought in the war, he'd traveled through Europe and Africa. He, too, was concerned about his daughter's new goal, but he told her he would convince her mother if Lynne would agree to fly with Pan Am, the only American airline that flew exclusively international routes. He would accept no domestic airlines.

Lynne sent in her application and waited for her interview. At first she had not cared which airline she flew for; her only goals were not being in a lab and having a job that allowed her to experience different places.

She would have wanted to fly internationally eventually, she later realized. Her father had intuited her dreams more accurately than she.

Working as a stewardess gave a woman the ability to see different places—and also to experience who she could *be* against those varied backdrops. This invitation to try out an unfettered version of oneself somewhere else had appealed to enormous numbers of women from the start of the commercial airline industry. "Sadie in New York," read a 1936 profile in the *Chicago Sunday Tribune* of a stewardess who had beaten out hundreds of other women for a spot on a United shuttle, "is a very different person from Sadie in Chicago." In Chicago, Sadie Ericson lived "a life of considerable dash," biking, swimming, roller-skating, and shopping. But twice a week, her job took her to New York, and New York Sadie was a different sort of woman. As soon as she arrived there, she bought two books—one fiction and one nonfiction—and a supply of magazines; she stocked her hotel room with a pound of chocolates and half a dozen apples and had her meals sent up as she read stretched across the hotel-room bed in her dressing gown.

A decade earlier, when air travel was raw and new, cabin attendants, in the established model of train stewards, had been men. But in 1930, a nurse and trained pilot approached an airline executive to convince him that nurses would make better cabin crew. The pitch worked. A nurse could more naturally reassure a fearful passenger, the executive wrote in a memo, or minister to airsick men. "The passengers relax," reported an *Atlantic Monthly* writer. "If a mere girl isn't worried, why should they be?"

In the mid-1930s, a stewardess had dragged two passengers from the burning wreckage of a Pennsylvania crash that killed twelve. Though she was injured herself, she ran four miles for help. Front-page articles celebrated her as a heroine. Profiles of other women and their crews, friendships, and habits appeared across newspapers and magazines. "Air Hostess Finds Life Adventurous," read one front-page headline in the *New York Times*. Indeed, Sadie Ericson was a model of the duality expected of stewardesses: she had social skills and self-determination, glamour and grit. The petite blonde looked "like a captivating French doll" and was "almost magically endowed by looks, temperament, and education to be outstanding" in a profession that required "poise and fearless capacity for action" and "grim courage."

The next two decades consolidated the view of the job as women's work. During the Second World War, women took cabin positions across airlines as men served in the military. Passengers began to favor air travel over ocean or rail in the postwar 1950s, due in part to technological advances such as a jet plane that sliced a trip across the Atlantic down to six or ten hours, depending on whether there were tail- or headwinds. Airlines competed for passengers by touting technical innovations, but only so many customizations to the new jet plane existed. Prices were stabilized by the government at four hundred or five hundred dollars to cross the Atlantic, so flying was too expensive to be a regular undertaking for anyone but the rich. Each airline tried to convince customers that it had the highest level of luxury and service, and the women who served a predominantly male clientele became a particular selling point.

On the ground, architecture and design contributed to image. In

New York City, Bauhaus school founder Walter Gropius designed the largest corporate office building in the world, and Pan American World Airways occupied more than a quarter of its space. On Park Avenue at East Forty-Fifth, it towered above the ornate beaux arts Grand Central Station, displacing it as the area's focal point. PAN AM, spelled out in fifteen-foot letters at the building's crest, visible from north and south, was the last corporate name permitted to top a Manhattan building's exterior so brazenly. "Marvel or Monster?" a *New York Times* headline asked readers of the wide, octagonal skyscraper. The building was polarizing but exerted a gravitational pull through midtown Manhattan.

In the sky, perks varied from airline to airline. On the President Special to Paris, Pan Am gave women passengers orchids and perfume and men cigars after a seven-course meal. TWA offered Sky Chief service with breakfast in bed. On Continental, passengers walked to the plane across a velvety gold carpet. Stewardess uniforms conveyed a unified brand with stylish panache. United Airlines hired industrial designer Raymond Loewy, the "father of streamlining," to design jet interiors and stewardess uniforms; the "Loewy look" in beige-pink wool featured softly rounded shoulders, a trim shawl collar, and hidden vertical pockets. Other airlines enlisted famous designers: Pan Am's stewardesses sported sky-blue skirt suits by "Beverly Hills couturier" Don Loper, and National Airlines crews wore Jacqueline Kennedy's favored designer, Oleg Cassini.

By the early 1960s, air travel, once new and uncertain, had become an American institution complete with industrial titans, frequent fliers, government oversight, and clamoring press. Celebrity executives Howard Hughes at TWA and Juan Trippe at Pan Am inspired invention and attracted attention. An upper crust of frequent customers were christened the "jet set" by gossip columnist Igor Cassini; they were a polyglot group dominated by "post-debutantes, scions of bigwigs in business and government or sons of just plain millionaires,

Greek shipowners' sons, people with titles (many of these spuriously used)." Repeat fliers, mostly businessmen and members of the jet set, constituted 64 percent of flight traffic. The Civil Aeronautics Board, which regulated prices and routes, supervised the increasing number of local airlines that connected smaller American towns and cities with the larger hubs that flew international routes.

In the 1960s, the appeal of the international was evident throughout high and low culture: James Bond and his jet-set espionage and the television show *I Spy;* Epcot and the International House of Pancakes; the popularity of the films *La Dolce Vita* and *Endless Summer*. At the Monterey International Pop Festival in Northern California, the Beach Boys and the Mamas and the Papas played alongside Hugh Masekela from South Africa, Donovan from Scotland, and headliner Ravi Shankar from India. Pan Am distributed a free bimonthly newspaper to teachers around the country, the *Classroom Clipper,* with features on individual countries. After the 1950s postwar stability, anything international held a waft of glamour, a counterpoint to the hum and drone of suburbs and nine-to-fives. When French-speaking Jackie Kennedy hosted a small dinner party at the White House, she was advised to "have pretty women, attractive men, guests who are *en passant,* the flavor of another language. This is the jet age, so have something new and changing."

A plane was an expensive piece of machinery moving among varied and changing jurisdictions, and it offered its passengers access to nearly all of them: to the countries of U.S. allies, to new republics across Africa and Asia, even to countries that were technically forbidden to Americans amid Cold War tensions. As Fidel Castro's new regime consolidated power in embargoed Cuba, planes heading to and from nearby Puerto Rico and Florida were hijacked by a dizzying zigzag of Americans and Cubans. Americans sympathetic to the Communist cause sought refuge in Cuba; Cubans hoping to escape an autocratic leader headed north. Hijackings as yet had little impact on passengers apart from the inconvenience. Flight crews plied those passengers with food and cocktails to pass the time.

In the United States, the cabin of an international airplane was a sought-after workplace for young, unmarried, mostly white women. Airlines in the early 1960s hired only 3 to 5 percent of applicants. Base pay was commensurate with other acceptably feminine roles: nurse, teacher, librarian, secretary. Perks included insurance, free air travel, paid vacation, and stipends on layovers. Layovers in themselves were extraordinary. A decade earlier, solitary international travel was rarely undertaken by a woman who could not leverage high social status to excuse her lack of a chaperone. And most women had married long before their mid-twenties: in the 1950s, only a third of American women were still single at age twenty-four; some years, more teenage girls walked down the aisle than attended the prom.

The women applying for stewardess positions in the 1960s had in the 1950s been forbidden to wear pants in high school and sometimes even in college. Now, during layovers, a stewardess could pull off the skirt of her uniform, put on slacks, and, chaperone-free, sashay around the museums of the sixteenth arrondissement; she could wear jeans and wander through Mexican markets. Flight routes, experience, and expertise varied by airline. But having a job on any plane was a reason for a woman to roam. What was revolutionary was the lack of *should* in this job, the plenitude of *could*.

Lynne had known her chances of getting the job were low, but as she faced the crowd of waiting women, it looked like hundreds were competing for one position. Intimidation became alienation. Now Lynne felt her desire to see the world was not only vague but a little bit vulgar. In a word, *selfish*.

Then the calculations began: the money spent on the plane ticket from Syracuse, the time spent walking down Park Avenue toward the

Pan Am Building, the pride she would swallow if she went back to the disapproving friend on whose couch she was sleeping and told her she'd been right.

"This is ridiculous," her friend had said the night before. "You should be going into social work or research and helping society. Teaching, at least, or having a family, if that's what you want."

Standing in the doorway now, facing women who projected such composed beauty and considered style, Lynne thought, *Do I really want a job where I have to be someone I'm not?* But she had an appointment. She took a seat.

When her name was called, Lynne stood and approached a small room to one side. She had nothing to lose, she thought.

A nice man sat across the table from her. What had she done in her life so far, he asked her, and why did she want to be a stewardess?

She told him about her time in college. "I've just spent four years in labs and research and I'm really tired," she said. "All of a sudden I go to Rome, and I find out that there's a world out there. I want to be in it."

He nodded. "Get out of the country, get into this world," the new Pan Am radio jingle went.

They talked about her foreign-language qualification—German, though Lynne knew that communicating with a German-speaking passenger would stretch her abilities—and the slight tightness of her suit. She had put on a few pounds in Rome, she said with a laugh when he asked if losing a bit of weight would be a problem. All that pasta. Then, since they were already speaking frankly, she told him about her hesitations. If Pan Am was looking for girls' girls, Lynne would not be the right fit.

At the end of the interview, the man handed her a clutch of forms and instructed her to fill them out. "Where did you get those papers?" one of the beautiful women sitting in the rows of seats asked Lynne, standing up to approach her as she walked through the waiting area. In the moment, Lynne did not register the fact that she hadn't seen anyone else exiting the interview room with papers. She had been instructed to fill them out and hand them to the secretary as she departed, and she assumed that they would then go straight into the trash. She descended from the offices and walked through the austere lobby with its square granite columns and contrasting tones of dark gray and sandy travertine. An eighty-by-forty-foot sculpture with the shape of a globe at its center dominated the west lobby. Hundreds of delicate stainless-steel filaments stretched from the gold sphere up and out in seven directions — one for each continent — and burst into what felt like every corner of the space, glistening, lit from below.

"How'd it go?" her friend asked when she returned from her day of teaching.

Lynne sighed and told her about the women. Coiffed, bubbly, invested in their appearance.

"Be real, Lynne," her friend said. "You're going to end up with people who aren't like you and you're not going to enjoy it at all."

Lynne agreed.

The next day, when her friend left for work, Lynne picked up a phone book and traced down the Ps. She called the listed number for Pan Am. She wanted her application pulled. The phone rang and rang.

2

Horizons Unlimited

THE GROOMING CLASSES SHE WAS RECEIVING AS A PAN AM RE-
cruit would have cost five hundred on the outside, Karen Walker
wrote to her mother. Hyperbole, perhaps, but Karen had never known
that blue eyeshadow de-emphasized her blue eyes—she should choose
a greenish hue—or that a hint of a bright white below the eyebrows
would highlight the arch. A grooming supervisor had reshaped her
eyebrows, and they now looked 100 percent better, Karen thought.
The trainees that spring of 1969 were among the first permitted to
keep their hair long if they wore it clipped neatly at the nape of the
neck; too bad, because Karen had just cut her blond hair into a bob,
the same efficient style she had worn when she worked for the U.S.
Army four years earlier.

Karen had arrived at the airline's Miami training school at the oldest acceptable age: twenty-six. She was a little suspicious of stewardessing. Already an experienced traveler, she was on board for that aspect of the job, but when she saw her fellow trainees standing together
on the hot-pink carpeting of the training school, they resembled something along the lines of a Mickey Mouse Club for sorority girls. But
the woman who had met Karen's class of twenty-four in the lobby of
the Miami Airways Motel had casually called out each of their names

from memory, and Karen's hesitation began to dissolve. In the course of the six-week training, Karen learned about the airline's history of technical pioneering and its contributions to American military campaigns. She observed the organization exemplified by her stewardess instructors as they delivered thorough, commonsense lessons in everything from deftly carving a rack of lamb to asserting authority during emergency procedures. The other women in her class were young but mostly quick, she thought. After they'd learned how to ditch the plane in a water landing and slide from an airplane's fuselage into a pool constructed for the purpose, Karen thought that this plane crewed by these stewardesses could handle anything but a bomb or a head-on collision. But just in case, she took out a twelve-thousand-dollar life insurance policy that would be paid to her parents in the event of her death.

The four pages of packing tips in the training manual addressed both the practical and the philosophical. The practical advice included "leave the extras at home . . . build your wardrobe around one basic color." Processed wools and linens shed wrinkles quickly. Drip-dry fabrics for lingerie and dresses meant less time standing over a hot iron, time that could be spent at monuments, in markets, or interacting with locals. The philosophical advice was "to enjoy a 'traveling job' like yours, do not spend all your energy on non-essentials . . . concentrate on people, places and ideas; don't spend your time dressing, changing and repacking." In capital letters, the last tip read, "WEAR COMFORTABLE SHOES."

Karen had always preferred hiking boots to heels, and she knew how to pack a suitcase for swift movement. Her earliest memories were of roaming. As a small child she used to wander away from her parents' house in Whittier, California. She remembered the sensation of it, watery memories of one wide suburban street nearly identical to her own and then another and another. Once, at about age three, Karen had toddled two miles. Her parents had called the police. They locked their screen doors after that.

Karen's family hardly ever left the state. Her father had been an athlete, and her mother had grown up on a farm in Lompoc, the daughter of farmers from Switzerland. Karen played beach volleyball and knew how to skim-board and when she spent enough time in the sun, her hair glimmered and her light brown eyebrows nearly disappeared. With her fluid body language, her arms taut from swimming and spiking, a mouth that usually hinted at a smile, Karen looked like the California girl of advertisements. But with the same devotion that other young women in her politically conservative part of the state directed toward God or marriage, Karen believed in the transformational possibilities of the rest of the world. After college—she had a degree in education from the University of California at Santa Barbara —she liked to sit on the misty cliffs around the area tracing the moon's rivers across the ocean. "I'm crossing you in style someday," Karen would repeat, the Johnny Mercer lyrics spooling through her mind as she drew vectors across the Pacific to Alaska, Japan, China, then a hop down to Tahiti, then Australia. She felt certain that a world rich with purpose and excitement waited for her past the borders of California.

Soon she found a way to leave. A girl from school had begun to work at a service club on an army base in West Germany. The enlisted men in peacetime required entertainment in the form of activities and outings. Karen's education degree qualified her to manage those programs. The pay was good; the experience was better. Karen cried her eyes out to leave her boyfriend, Alan—he was charismatic and athletic with full dark hair and an intense gaze, an avid hiker and backpacker and an intellectual too. But he would be spending the next two years flying navy planes around the world. Karen would not wait at home for him.

"I'm so happy I'm almost speechless," she wrote to her parents from the city of Ulm. The other two women who would run activities at the service club with her were "hang loose," and her living quarters encompassed a full suite: she had a bedroom, bathroom, and living room all her own. The club came equipped with board games, a pool table, guitars, and an outdoor patio overlooking the Danube. Surrounding the army base was West Germany; encircling West Germany was the rest of Europe. Within six weeks Karen had bought a used VW Beetle on credit and banked enough days off to embark on her first "great adventure": a trip to Salzburg, where she spent a night in a tent she assembled in the dark. When she woke, she found the fabric had collapsed around her. A circle of giggling Austrian hikers reconstructed the tent as she lay within it, cocooned in her sleeping bag. When she returned to Ulm she pledged to see everything within driving distance. She had been saving up for plastic surgery, but she decided she would not fix what she saw as her too-big nose just then. She wanted to buy skis and tour all of Europe first.

Karen took countryside drives and spent a weekend in Paris. She thought the *Mona Lisa* was underwhelming, but Parisian streets and people exceeded all her expectations. Here she was, like Sartre and de Beauvoir, observing the city from sidewalk cafés, nursing one coffee after another, overhearing French words with musical consonants she did not understand. She had moved through Southern California on automatic, unseeing. In Europe Karen observed details in an entirely new way. She described it in letters to her parents—the deep feelings, the rambling observations, the minutiae of her conversations. A street performer's plastic rat; the café table of Bolivian Communists whose dim view of America Karen tried to amend.

To the Bolivians, Karen had explained the "beauty of our system of checks and balances," but she had her own political doubts. In Germany, she stood amid a peacetime army—two hundred fifty thousand American troops had been committed to the country after the defeat of the Nazis. Back home, the civil rights movement demonstrated the hypocrisy of the army's task: 10 percent of the soldiers on West German bases were Black, symbolizing the ideals of democracy and equality, but Jim Crow laws persisted and violence against Black Americans spread through the U.S. despite peaceful protests. "I don't see how President Johnson can send troops to Vietnam—I don't see how he can send troops to the Congo—I don't see how he can send troops to Africa and can't send troops to Selma, Alabama," John Lewis had said, speaking to an assembled crowd in the southern city, his skull fractured by a police nightstick. No federal troops had been sent to protect the lawful marchers. Dozens were beaten by state troopers' clubs.

A Department of Defense report would later reveal the extent and pervasiveness of hostility toward Black GIs on American bases in Germany: cross burnings, Ku Klux Klan meetings among servicemen, and threatened boycotts of German business owners who chose to serve Black GIs were all documented. All Karen knew was what she observed: The way the men segregated themselves rigidly by race at social events. The young Black man who was stabbed in the torso and staggered into the service club but refused to report the incident no matter how hard she pleaded. The "ugly little lieutenant" who disliked how chummy the three women had become with the troops, including Black GIs. The five soldiers who beat up one Black GI. The bite marks on arms and necks after a game of football. "This damn Army is getting to me," Karen confessed to her parents in a burst of frustration. "I've never seen so many outright injustices in my life." She was fed up and she felt useless. She began to save money to quit and travel.

When she was young, Karen had flipped through her parents' copies of *National Geographic,* mesmerized by the color photographs. Now she was tantalizingly close to the places that had captivated her as a child. "Life is too short to waste even one precious year on dullness," she wrote to her parents. "Don't misinterpret this as Jet Set philosophy—please." She signed her letters with a tiny stick figure in a dress and a bobbed haircut, a suitcase hanging from one arm.

Karen spent a year and a half traveling. When her money ran low, she hitchhiked, then worked through the winter at a service club in the Alps. She picked melons on a kibbutz in Israel and camped out in a van in Portugal. When her stamina and money ran out, she went home, where she resolved to live a stable life. She got a teaching job at a high school and rented a shared bungalow by the beach. Her students loved her. "Hey, Miss Walker!" they shouted when they saw her biking around town on Sundays, their bodies halfway out car windows as they waved. But again, Karen's restlessness percolated.

When she told her parents she had been accepted by Pan Am and was going to Miami for training, they called her a quitter; she had quit the army, quit teaching, Karen the quitter. But everything she learned in her six weeks of training in Miami vindicated, at least to Karen, her choice.

"In our advertising, we use the slogan, 'World's Most Experienced Airline,'" read *Horizons Unlimited: An Indoctrination Course for Flight Service Personnel,* the most conversational and ruminative of the three texts used in training. "The key word of this slogan is 'Experienced.' The root of the word 'experienced' is from the Latin *peritus,* meaning a trial. To this has been added *ex,* so that the combined word means, 'out of trials . . .' Or, 'knowledge gained through one's own acts.'"

Karen had learned from her travels and the constraint she felt back at home. Wanderlust was not just a condition of her youth. But first, Karen discovered, she and the twenty-four other aspiring stewardesses who entered training that Monday—there was a new group every week, and in less than a year, Lynne would walk the same pink carpeting and sit in the same classrooms—had to earn admission to the world that they craved. An airplane, all of the stewardesses learned, could rotate in three directions around its axes. Those directions were the plane's roll, pitch, and yaw. Their training courses similarly pointed all aspiring Pan Am stewardesses in three directions: technology, service, and image. None functioned independently of the others.

Paragraphs of text explained the difference between thrust and drag —the forces that propelled an airplane forward and pulled it back— and the difference between a plane's allowable useful load and allowable cabin load. Diagrams demonstrated how to calculate each based on the principles of weight and balance and also located and named the various parts of the plane: brake spoilers, vortex generators, horizontal and vertical stabilizers, wing flaps, engine pods, ailerons. Such practical information contributed to good service; passengers were often curious and the stewardesses were expected to competently answer questions using "simple and direct" terminology. Stewardesses should "attempt to identify" the first-time rider, the manual advised, "and make every effort to make his flight most interesting and memorable." Keep conversation tactful, slang-free, oiled with eye contact, lightly logistical. Points of interest, location, meal service, ETA — such topics could alleviate the reasonable anxiety and fear of being trapped in a metal tube high above the earth.

Emergencies occurred very infrequently, but the women were trained to reassure a nervous passenger, and crews and airplanes were well equipped to handle any incident. Safety instruction during training included preparation for evacuation of the aircraft by land and water. Maps of each jet in the service manual — variations on the 707, 720, and others — showed the locations of ropes, rafts, first-aid kits, escape slides, and spare life vests. A stewardess's role in an emergency was mapped out according to her position on takeoff; evacuation by land dictated different responsibilities than ditching the plane in water did. Aspiring stewardesses practiced inflating and then tossing the enormous yellow raft into a ditching pool built specifically for the task. In an emergency landing, the chief stewardess would notify passengers with detailed but calm announcements over the PA system. "Establish firm passenger control and simultaneously issue instructions," the guide directed. The rest of the stewardesses were to follow her commands, identify competent passengers to help them throughout the cabin, and return to their crew seats at five hundred feet. Manuals would soon include sections on hijackings too. "As in any emergency situation, coordination and communication between members of the crew are essential," the manual read. Stewardesses should communicate with the hijacker, keeping him occupied with conversation and transmitting as much information as possible to the captain. The women were told to "become a neutral friend," to serve caffeine-free nonalcoholic beverages, and to try to lead the hijacker into asking to land the airplane. But they were also to keep such tactics confidential. Specific passenger questions about Pan Am's security measures should be "left tactfully unanswered."

The manual instructed stewardesses to use titles for the crew in the presence of passengers: "Captain" for the pilot, "Sir" for copilot and engineer, "Miss" for other stewardesses. "Intra-crew courtesy" contributed to setting a flight's tone, and only English was to be spoken among the crew. The stewardesses were given rules to follow outside of the plane too. The only permissible situation in which a stewardess in uniform could smoke on the ground was when she was seated after eating a meal. On a plane she could light up in the galley after meal service. General etiquette guidelines followed Emily Post rules; no discussion of politics or religion, ever. "Tact and diplomacy," the manual read, "are required when discussing topics relative to the customs and ideals of the passenger's country." The manual showed line drawings of the pins of various fraternal organizations—Elks, Masons, Knights of Columbus, Kiwanis, Optimist International—and encouraged the stewardesses to introduce two passengers wearing the same pin if both were agreeable. Military charters were "an excellent and lucrative source" of revenue for Pan Am; courteous service on military flights was of paramount importance. At the end of the course, the women were tested on how to properly address a U.S. senator, Catholic bishop, prime minister, ambassador, and rabbi.

The word *diplomacy* appeared over and over in the manual's sections about service; stewardesses would be called upon to interpret for foreign passengers, respond appropriately to different religions and nationalities, and control rowdy children. Even where that word did not appear, the concept threaded through. Stewardesses were taught to prepare Malayan chicken curry, to offer chopsticks as well as silverware roll-ups on any flight across Asia, to prepare Passover meals and know that the message of Passover stressed "the theme of human freedom and the sacrilege of human bondage." The airline's reputation as a "truly international airline" relied on internationally knowledgeable service. It also relied on stewardesses knowing how to prepare fluffy scrambled eggs in a pressurized cabin and how to mix an excellent cocktail. Stewardesses circled answers on quizzes to prove that they knew what to put into a highball first (liquor, ice, or mixer) and how to make a dry martini in flight.

Pan Am stewardesses learned that projecting the right image was essential to good service. Every flight began with an announcement that was read in English and the language of the destination, which was part of the reason why every Pan Am stewardess was tested on her language proficiency in her interviews. "It has been pointed out that in many cases all passengers speak English and there would seem to be no reason for non-English announcements. However, we have a second reason for making these announcements," read *Horizons Unlimited*. "That reason is showmanship. The announcements, needed or not, add a continental flavor which Americans love. Our passengers are starting out on an adventure and we are helping them to get the feel of it immediately. As the first cosmopolitan people they meet, our personnel assume greater stature in their eyes."

Along with their linguistic dexterity, Pan Am's stewardesses conjured the proper image with their physical attributes. Illustrations in the manual showed a variety of mouth shapes and how to apply lipstick to each to achieve a "more beautiful smile." There was posture instruction, skin-care techniques, makeup application, haircuts—grooming lessons took nearly as much time as first-aid training. Girdles, white gloves, and slips underpinned and accessorized every uniform, regardless of the weather in the plane's final destination. A "natural look" was outlined in the rules for makeup. Red, rose red, and coral were permitted on lips and nails. "Lavender, purple, orange, insipid pink, iridescent or flesh color" was not. Hair was to be cut above the shoulders or pulled back at the nape of the neck. No seductive or "extreme" styles were allowed. A 1959 memo circulated among stewardesses gave the rationale for banning more dramatic makeup choices. Psychiatrists explained that "outlandish" makeup reflected "unsatisfied personality need" or "emotional disturbance."

Pan Am's goal for its stewardesses was femininity and sophistication that stopped short of sexual availability; they were to be clean, pretty, ladylike, and uniform, their every angle enforcing corporate identity. "Grooming monitors" ensured that stewardesses maintained the look that each one had when training ended. Management's approval was required for a change in a woman's haircut or color; supervisors kept notes in stewardesses' employee files on the hairstyles they were allowed to wear. Some of the women, like outdoorsy Karen, welcomed instruction in how to achieve this professional look, even if they eventually strained at such oversight.

A woman didn't have to look like a model to become a stewardess, nor did she have to put overt effort into maintaining her appearance. The natural look that Pan Am favored could be attained with relative ease. But the job did require a woman to be born lucky, with symmetrical features, clear skin, height between five three and five nine, trim-ish body type. It required, too, a woman willing to adhere to the beauty norms set by a company run by men. Karen signed on, for now.

After training, Karen was assigned to Pan Am's New York base, flying out of JFK International Airport. In her first months she traveled the airline's routine flights—shuttles around the Caribbean and South America, out to London and back. She immediately recognized in the movement of a crew in the galley the easy camaraderie and physicality of her cheerleading squads—a hand on the small of the back, a "Behind you" as someone slid by.

She roomed with four other stewardesses in an apartment on Eighty-Ninth Street and Central Park West. The apartment was filthy; she cleaned and cleaned, and still strips of paint drooped from the walls. But Karen rarely spent more than a day or two at home every few weeks, and even when she was in New York, she was out seeing the city with the help of her copy of *New York on $5 a Day*—her bible, as she called it. On Sundays in the summer, when it seemed as if the city's overlay of taxis and pedestrians and hot-dog and pretzel carts had been peeled from the sidewalks and streets, Karen walked down the middle of the empty avenues. She read *One Flew Over the Cuckoo's Nest* and *The Confessions of Nat Turner* atop the boulders in Central Park. She walked into Elaine's once, the Upper East Side haunt of Norman Mailer, Mikhail Baryshnikov, and other famed authors and artists, though she had no money to pay for a meal.

Sticking to a budget at home meant she was able to make purchases in foreign countries. Karen met stewardesses who plotted their layovers around shopping—Italy for leather shoes, Paris for hose, Beirut for jewelry, a pearl necklace in Hong Kong. But there were also women who bid their flights—requested routes—around Elvis Presley's tour schedule, or graduate-school coursework, or adventurous exploration, landing near Mexico's pyramids or as close to Timbuktu as possible for their two weeks off. The cities of specific foreign countries were coordinates on each stewardess's personal map. Clothing, shoes, and jewelry became accessible, but they also became talismans of knowledge, security, and choice. What a stewardess wore when out of uniform served as a reminder that she was now living a life guided by desire and possibility.

On Karen's first flights, the faultless sophistication of the European stewardesses intimidated her. She had to remind herself that she too had access to what she saw as the source of their sophistication—she too could move with ease around the world and become familiar with places that normal Americans like her family might see once or not at all. Every time she stepped onto the corner of Central Park West to hail a yellow taxi for the Carey bus, standing on the street in her crisp blue uniform and her nylons and sensible heels, she nearly jumped out of her skin with excitement. She would go to John F. Kennedy

Airport and get on a plane, and when she stepped out of it, she would be in a foreign country. The independence of her new life was just right; she was living in New York City but she was gone more often than she was there. In the same way that she read approvingly about the anti-war marches in the city but did not attend and admired the feminist movement but was not active in it, Karen enjoyed half participation in the clubby airline life. She rarely went to crew parties on layovers. She preferred dinner on her own.

On one of Karen's first flights to Puerto Rico, the captain called her into the cockpit to look at Cuba below. The island appeared enormous. Karen observed green fields of crops. She saw what she thought was a missile site with trucks coming and going, then lush mountains of variegated colors and very few people as the plane continued on. It was no wonder that the hijackers always went to Cuba—airplane skyjackings had risen into the dozens every year, and nearly all of the hijackers had directed the planes to Havana; "a true democracy," said one skyjacker. Karen left the cockpit to finish the drink service.

When the plane had passed over Haiti and the Dominican Republic and was approaching San Juan, the captain again called Karen up to the front. "Strap in," he said, gesturing at the seat behind him.

She sat down as he narrated how he would land the plane. The copilot and flight engineer chimed in, describing the function of different instruments, how the steering mechanism and gauges worked. As the plane descended ever lower, the ground rising toward the cockpit windows, the captain took his hand off the steering yoke and pointed at different sights—the good hotels, restaurants, and bars he had come to frequent while in Puerto Rico. The copilot and flight engineer followed the captain's finger. The cockpit was now close enough to each of the buildings that Karen could make out window dressings and pedestrians walking into doorways. She felt the blood slide out of her cheeks. The men's focus snapped back to the task at hand and an instant later the plane was on the ground and the men were laughing at Karen, the new girl startled by a simple landing.

3

A Woman in Uniform

THE SKIRT OF THE PAN AM UNIFORM HUNG AN INCH BELOW Karen's (and every other stewardess's) knees. The long white blouse fit snugly around her waist and tucked into the skirt so that even when she reached into the compartments above, it would not pull out of the waistband. The jacket, introduced in 1965, was boxier than the Don Loper–designed 1959 uniform; Pan Am called it the "easy" look.

Each stewardess was measured at training so that the pale blue worsted-wool suit fit her body perfectly. Its tailored shoulders imitated the lines of executive suits on Madison Avenue. Blue pillbox hats with white piping pulled the jacket and shirt together. In Paris a century earlier, the writer George Sand had traded her heels for men's boots and written that in such solid, freeing shoes, "it seemed to me that I could go round the world." The Pan Am uniform made many of the women feel equally capable.

Several years before Karen arrived at training in Miami, the sixty-odd stewardesses who worked on Pan Am's military charters, flying GIs from Vietnam battlefields for five-day R&R stints, had felt intimidated by the soldiers' eyes on their uniformed bodies as they crewed their first flights. Young men with identical haircuts sat three by three in rows stretching all the way to the back of the plane. They wore

identical military green shirts. Hundreds of eyes tracked each stewardess's movements. The older DC-6 propeller planes had been relegated
to these shorter flights, and as the women walked down the aisle—all
economy seats, a single long cabin with the roaring propellers on either side—the number of men looking at them sped their heartbeats.

At some point, after two flights or five, the men's eyes began not
to frighten but embolden Clare Christiansen and the other stewardesses who had volunteered to staff these new shuttle services. The men
looked at them like they were movie stars. Some women enjoyed this
newfound sense of their own glamour. Others did not enjoy the feeling
but appreciated that here, beauty could be useful. Clad in an authoritative uniform, beauty conferred control.

A stewardess had to have control over her cabin so she could keep
her passengers safe from the many things that could go wrong on
any of Pan Am's international flights. Around the world, airplanes
skimmed over and sometimes into violent conflicts on the ground. In
Nigeria, a coup and countercoup in 1966 had launched a civil war. Six
years after the nation's independence, tensions over who would rule
a sovereign Nigeria sparked along the lines of divisions cultivated by
former British colonizers. Power struggles escalated until massacres
took place at airports and train stations, in streets and homes.

Throughout West and Central Africa, other countries used seizing civil aircraft as a vehicle for "hard diplomacy"—a foreign minister marched off a KLM plane at gunpoint in the Ivory Coast, a
government-orchestrated hijacking of a plane on which a Congolese
rebel leader was traveling to Spain. Still, there was no modification to
Pan Am's flight routes across West Africa through Abidjan and Lagos.
The stewardesses were trusted to keep passengers bound for the next
destination aboard the plane when it stopped on the tarmac to load
more people.

Locations across Southeast Asia also posed varied dangers. In In-
donesia, a brutally anti-Communist ruler was in the process of kill-
ing up to a million Indonesians. The violence was indiscriminate and

unpredictable. Pilots told stewardesses not to stand too near the door when American diplomats exited the planes in Jakarta. In Vietnam, the airspace, one pilot coolly told a reporter in 1966, remained "the only place I know of where a passenger can sit back sipping a martini and watch an air strike going on below." An ex-navy pilot saw more enemy fire flying R&R shuttles than he had in his two years in the military.

The men on their way to the war in Vietnam did not appreciate the below-the-knee cornflower-blue worsted wool on Clare or any of the other women who crewed the Hong Kong R&R service. Tall, statuesque Clare had modeled. One of her crewmates, Pamela Borgfeldt, had been a Miss USA 1964 semifinalist; she had clear blue eyes and a slightly crooked smile. On other airlines, stewardesses wore less clothing. Braniff sent its stewardesses into the air wearing yellow coats; after two outfit changes, the women concluded flight service in leopard-print leotards with a sheer overlay. In Braniff advertisements, a model languidly unzipped layer after layer of costumes in what the airline called the "Air Strip." On Western, stewardesses served dinner in pajamas. American Airlines introduced uniforms of minidresses and fishnet stockings in the spring of 1967, but polls revealed that passengers across all demographics expressed distaste for the fishnets. Executives swapped them for neutral stockings but kept the dress length short despite the fact that some passengers—women of all ages and middle-aged men—objected to that choice too.

Only young men, the demographic that had always approved wholeheartedly of the short skirts on American, sat on Pan Am's flights to Vietnam. But Pan Am kept its stewardesses' skirts longer. One group of GIs circulated a petition to alter the situation. A soldier mailed it to the Pan Am Building on Park Avenue in New York. "If we are going to fight for American womanhood," the petition read, "we would like to see more of it."

Across all airlines, executives had agreed with these GIs on the importance of a stewardess's appearance and availability. Vetting began in
hiring. "Attractive appearance will be foremost in importance," read
a 1963 American Airlines supervisor handbook, the sentence under-
lined for emphasis and elaborated on in excruciating detail: "We can
sometimes pretend a person is attractive, if we admire them for some
other reason. [Hiring such people] should be avoided." Round faces,
close-set eyes, scars, and moles were undesirable. Pan Am's "philosophy and techniques of stewardess selection" focused on physical appeal
plus personality, education, language skill, and hip size, since a stewardess's hips moved at a passenger's eye level. Supervisors in charge
of hiring assessed granular details of physical appearance, limning the
factual and the subjective in cool commentary: "Needs to have teeth
fixed. Model-cold, passive . . . Pretty smile, no personality. Dumpy—
head small for body . . . Theatrical, too much eyebrow. Pretty eyes, no
girdle."

Youth and marital status were monitored by rules that allowed
for dismissal at a woman's thirty-second or thirty-fifth birthday, depending on the airline, or upon her marriage. A married woman, management feared, would miss work too often, gain weight, or have a
husband who often called to complain of her absence. Besides, a suffi-
ciently nurturing and attentive woman would not abandon a husband
at home. Marriage signaled a woman's investment in the traditional
values that institution implied. In the mid-1960s, the average U.S. airline stewardess worked for 32.4 months. "If that figure ever got up to
thirty-five months, I'd know we're getting the wrong kind of girl. She's
not getting married," said a personnel manager at United in 1965.

To the airlines, a stewardess's eventual marriage was as important
as her temporary singledom. It made her retirement either likely or inevitable, leaving an opening for someone younger and unattached; she
would accrue no pension and require minimal insurance expenditure.
And as fare regulation continued, stewardesses' availability and attrac-
tiveness provided an essential lure for a largely male flying clientele,

especially for airlines with no other venue by which to project the full glamour of the jet age. Pan Am had stylish hotels frequented by international royalty—by the mid-1960s, its InterContinental hotel brand was the second-largest international hotel chain—and celebrities like Barbara Parkins and the Beatles posed for paparazzi alongside its jets. The airline retained the right to terminate a stewardess after she had been married for six months, though its managers rarely exercised the option, since enough women quit on their own to render the few openly married stewardesses acceptable. Other airlines relied nearly entirely on stewardesses to set their brands apart.

For decades stewardesses had tried to disentangle their work in flight from their unmarried status. "We *don't* fly for love," one stewardess said in a 1938 *Popular Aviation* article. The fact that a third of her cohort quit each year to marry "does not mean that all of us sit on a perch in the sky waiting for Dan Cupid to soar by and take a pot shot at us." She and her colleagues worked as "sincerely and efficiently" as "regular businesswomen."

Slight shifts in women's roles and moments of permissiveness had come and gone in the past—the New Woman of the turn of the century, the flappers of the 1920s—but by the early 1960s, the American perspective on women's sex lives had begun to undergo an irrevocable change. "Sex is neutral, like money. It's the way you use it that counts," one woman told journalist Gloria Steinem for a 1962 *Esquire* article. Another echoed the voices of those who believed that "people who have no share in the consequences should have no share in the decision." A new birth control pill had been approved in 1960, though it was still legally limited to use by married women. A poll of college students revealed that nearly everyone agreed that sex, for men or women, was "something you have to decide for yourself."

Stewardesses—young, beautiful, single women in great numbers with access to movement around varied geographies—were now, often unintentionally, in the thick of the culture wars.

A rising chorus of celluloid stewardesses suggested that love—or at least sex—formed an essential part of the job's opportunities. *Play-boy* featured its first stewardess centerfold in 1957, interspersing photos of the "brown-eyed beauty" from Dayton in white panties with images of her in uniform, a version of the X-ray vision plenty of airline customers imagined when they boarded planes. By the early 1960s, sexy, servile stewardesses were a feature of the pop-culture landscape in books and plays all written by men. A British novel, *Girl on a Wing,* depicted a group of stewardesses hunting wealthy husbands. A French play, *Boeing-Boeing,* sold out in London's West End. Both were soon bought by major Hollywood studios. In *Boeing-Boeing,* Tony Curtis plays a man with bubbly rotating girlfriends who fly for Lufthansa, British Airways, and Air France. The film based on *Girl on a Wing, Come Fly with Me,* used the advertising tagline "Three airline hostesses with the mostess' of fun in mind!"

Around no single group of people did so much anxiety about new sexual mores cohere more easily. The book *Coffee, Tea, or Me? The Uninhibited Memoirs of Two Airline Stewardesses* came to encompass the overarching societal perspective on airline stewardesses; it flew off shelves from the moment of its 1967 publication. After a month and a half, it went into a second printing and the film rights were sold. Trudy Baker and Rachel Jones—not the real names of the Eastern Airlines stewardesses who spoke as the book's authors even though they had not, in fact, written the book—spoke on radio shows throughout the autumn.

In reality, *Coffee, Tea, or Me?* was not a memoir but a novel authored by a young PR executive at American Airlines. After meeting two stewardesses one night at Toots Shor's Restaurant in Manhattan, one of whom he characterized as a "blowsy blonde who knew every four letter word," he realized that he could write a book embellishing the anecdotes they told him. He saw the stewardesses twice; they told him about their training, the apartments they shared, the men who sought stewardesses as trophy dates, and the men they pursued. The book outlined work culture and airline terminology as well as the sexual and romantic habits of different nationalities and professions —Englishmen and engineers, Danes and doctors. And though many current stewardesses rankled at the book's terms—the apartments they shared were "stew zoos" complete with "stew bums," men who slept with various compliant stewardesses at once—the former stewardesses who promoted the book charmed the journalists who interviewed them, male and female alike. "The way she describes them, her six years as a stew sound more like she was the self-appointed mistress of ceremonies of a sky-high vaudeville act," a *Chicago Tribune* columnist wrote of Rachel Jones. "Fun was compulsory." Soon *Coffee, Tea, or Me?* became a fixture on paperback-bestseller lists. In 1968 alone, members of the American reading public purchased 1.25 million copies.

Airlines picked up where pop culture left off. The industry saw no reason not to capitalize on male fantasy, which saw stewardesses as a new sort of woman in uniform, sexually empowered but a little buttoned up, with evident investment in male comfort and pleasure. The most louche advertisements and uniforms often came from smaller, domestic carriers—international airlines had their respectability around the world to consider. A miniskirt would not read the same in New Delhi as it did in London, New York, and Paris. Still, the tone of a 1965 Continental advertising campaign became the norm. The advertisement featured an image of a pencil-skirted rear end leaning away from the viewer. Text alongside the photo read, "Our first run movies are so interesting we hope you're not missing the other attractions aboard."

4

Pipeline to Paradise

R OUGHLY THREE HUNDRED THOUSAND AMERICAN MEN HAD poured into Vietnam in the year and a half since the Tonkin Gulf Resolution in 1964. And as the American military presence in Southeast Asia swelled, so did yearly takeoffs and landings at the Tan Son Nhut air base near Saigon; 20,880 in 1964 had grown to a monstrous 379,000 in 1965. A combination of regularly scheduled commercial flights and U.S. military air traffic clogged the tarmac as Saigon, a city of two hundred thousand inhabitants, grew to over two million people, many of them refugees and short-term residents. The foreign press corps, charity workers, academics, diplomats, and businesspeople from international corporations with business interests in South Vietnam at war—Bank of America, IBM, Pan Am—milled through the city.

Arguably, Tan Son Nhut was busier than the world's busiest airport, Chicago's O'Hare. For safety reasons, 95 percent of its flights arrived and departed during daylight hours. Even so, potential danger was not limited to military flights. In the mid-1960s a bullet ripped through the oil line of a commercial Pan Am 707 en route to Singapore. There were no injuries; the pilot landed the plane safely. Reporters speculated that the intended target was Defense Secretary Robert

McNamara, scheduled to arrive in Saigon on a commercial 707 the same day.

More planes were on their way. It was in the first months of 1966 that the Department of Defense committed to sending each soldier on five days of rest and recuperation during his twelve-month tour of duty. The only barrier standing between a GI and his respite from combat, officials reported, was a lack of transport planes. Pan Am president Harold Gray, in an act of corporate magnanimity that the company's PR executives ensured would be well covered in newspapers, offered the U.S. government a bargain. For four months, Pan Am would fly eighteen hundred military passengers from Vietnam to Hong Kong and back and twelve hundred from Vietnam to Tokyo and back for just one dollar per month.

From the start, the media vaunted Pan Am's involvement in the war effort, though twelve other carriers also supplemented military aircraft with charter passenger and cargo flights to and from Southeast Asia. To every woman who crewed any airline into Vietnam, the U.S. government issued a slip of paper that designated her a second lieutenant in the U.S. Armed Forces. Every stewardess was to carry her Geneva Conventions identification card at all times in case she was captured by enemy forces; it ensured that she would be treated as a prisoner of war.

You are an ambassador of the United States of America, Pan Am instructors had drilled into each stewardess in her six weeks of training in Miami. *You represent America,* they said. *If you don't want this job, a hundred women are waiting to take your place.* Every stewardess who had signed up to move to Hong Kong had, as evidence of her ambassadorship, the eagle wings of the U.S. Department of Defense crest watermarked across her name, rank, service number, and date of birth on her Geneva Conventions card.

The significance of this assignment reflected a natural progression for Clare Christiansen. For years she had kept herself keenly aware of opportunities for advancement within Pan Am. She was determined to rise. Clare, tall and composed, knew her stately bearing inspired confidence.

Clare had known she would love working as a stewardess since she was a teen. "Aviation is the most exciting thing in the world," the character played by Jane Wyman said in the 1951 comedy *Three Guys Named Mike* when she interviewed for a position on American Airlines. "God didn't mean people to be strangers, and with commercial aviation, people all over the world are becoming neighbors." After seeing the movie in her small Ohio hometown, Clare had stuck her head through the cardboard cutout of Wyman's uniformed body in the theater's lobby. Even as a teenager she'd had to lean down—Clare was five foot ten, an inch over Pan Am's limit. Still, she hoped. She had always wanted to do something interesting with her life.

She wrote a letter to Pan Am in 1955, after two years of studying theater at college. Pan Am had garnered headlines for ordering a fleet of forty-five new jets, the largest single purchase in the history of commercial aviation. "You're ordering great big new airplanes," Clare wrote, "will you take a taller woman, too?" A month later she opened an envelope that contained an application and a form letter telling her that interviews took place in New York.

But there the company reps told Clare the application was a mistake, that she would never be hired; she was too tall. She met the weight requirements, though, and her composure and high cheekbones did not hurt (her other interview in New York had been with Eileen Ford's new modeling agency), and since she was there anyway, they said, they would interview her.

Her mother and sister cried when her acceptance letter arrived in Ohio. Stewardesses, they believed, were loose and immoral. Clare pointed out the flaw in their logic: she was neither loose nor immoral and she would be a stewardess. Plus, her travel benefits extended to her mother and sister.

By 1965 Clare had been flying for nearly a decade. She participated in the rollout of the first 707 jets, watched her flight-shy mother take full advantage of Clare's travel benefits, and flew Richard Nixon just after he lost the California governor's race. She tried to find another job within the company as her roles of stewardess and then purser—the chief stewardess, who oversaw safety procedures, flight manifests, any necessary reports, and the rest of the crew's assignments—grew rote. Clare applied for three ground positions: grooming supervisor, recruiter, and crew supervisor. In the first instance, she lost out to another woman who had waited for years for this single management position customarily filled by a woman. In the latter two instances she was neither rejected nor accepted. *No openings* was all she heard back. So she moved around, climbed as high as she could as a stewardess, and leveraged her seniority to switch bases and fly different routes. Still, with enough repetition, even once-thrilling trips became routine.

In Tokyo in 1965, she experienced something different. Her plane was rerouted; no one explained why the aircraft ran empty to Saigon or why, as it approached the city, fighter jets pulled into the surrounding clouds. Clare's excitement grew as she watched army planes moving against the clouds. Wheels hit the tarmac; the plane coasted to a stop. After a while, General William Westmoreland and Maxwell Taylor, the ambassador to Vietnam, stepped aboard. A line of passengers followed.

Thank you, they said to the assembled crew before exiting the plane, *for taking our families home.* Clare understood that each passenger she greeted and helped into a seat was leaving a city on the verge of war. Anti-American demonstrations in Vietnam had escalated and the embassy feared that any violence against families of State Department employees would be politically catastrophic. Ambassador Taylor wanted the approximately twenty-three hundred dependents shuttled out of the country before the real fighting began.

Clare had never participated in anything so overtly political. She believed fervently in her country, its goals, and its leaders. Years earlier, as she shook Mr. Nixon's hand, she had told him gravely, "I'd vote for you whenever, sir."

When the call sounded for volunteers to be based in Hong Kong for the R&R shuttles, Clare signed up immediately. Layovers in Hong Kong always lured her to Pacific routes. She was drawn to this city wrapped around a harbor, encircled by green mountains, its verticals theatrical, its colors bright. Clare loved the city lights from the rooftop restaurants, the precision tailors, the variety of fantastic foods. She could stretch the monthly foreign-station allowance of three hundred dollars to cover housing, transportation, food, and a tailored dress or a trip within Asia. Her paycheck itself went straight into her bank account back home; the mounting sum would buy her future independence. Living in Hong Kong would be luxurious—apartments were spacious and usually came with an amah or a houseboy, so Clare would not have to do the cleaning herself, which pleased her very much—and the job held a tang of danger and purpose.

The U.S. military in Vietnam would stop Communism from spreading around the world. Participating in that effort, Clare thought, sounded wonderful. Here was representation on a higher level than dinner service; here was a kind of ambassadorship—unscripted, sophisticated, and largely unsupervised.

As its dollar-a-month R&R deal drew to a close in July 1966, Pan Am presented the U.S. government with a bill for four dollars. The company estimated the value of the services rendered at $2.8 million and announced that future R&R flights would be charged at cost. Deals had been struck and destinations expanded to include Taipei, Taiwan, and Honolulu. The airline would increase non-R&R flights to Saigon from twenty-three a week to thirty-eight to meet the demand for carrying military cargo and civilian passengers. Pan Am also contracted cargo and technical assistance and leased aircraft maintenance to Air Vietnam. The airline bought two 727s, and Pan Am provided interim crews to fly them. A ticket office in Saigon catered to foreigners and American servicemen, aiming to solidify the Pan Am brand among the many expats in the city. By the spring of 1966, Pan Am founder and CEO Juan Trippe reported the airline's first profits since 1956, when U.S. government subsidies had ceased. Needing more planes—the old DC-6s in Hong Kong were no longer sufficient to handle R&R operations—the airline scheduled 707s from San Francisco International Airport and a new Los Angeles base to fill in. In a press release at the start of the year, the airline announced that it expected to fly 375,000 men around the Pacific.

"No army has ever had anything quite like [the R&R program]—but then there has never been a war quite so frustrating as Viet Nam," began a *Time* article on the "absolutely free" vacations it called a "five-day bonanza." Nor were military airlift command charters quite like regular flights. The army provided one meal: steak with milk and vegetables and ice cream for dessert for all soldiers. On arrival at Saigon, Cam Ranh Bay, or Da Nang, the pilots usually dropped sharply toward the tarmac to avoid any possible fire from below—a surprise to most of the stewardesses on their first flight. Occasionally a pilot would ask a stewardess to sit on a jump seat wearing a spare set of headphones so the captain had another pair of ears listening in on radio information.

Even on an uneventful flight, a plane full of soldiers was nothing like a customary cabin. The men—eighteen, nineteen, twenty-two—appeared staggeringly young even to stewardesses in their twenties. They read *Archie* comics; they asked for second servings of ice cream. On flights to Vietnam, whether after R&R or on their first flight into the country, they talked for the first, second, third hours, but the cabin's ambience became quieter and thicker the closer to Tan Son Nhut they flew. Even enthusiastic conscripts—men who had grown up playing soldier, men who viewed their service in this war as a way to live up to their fathers' victory against the Nazis—went silent one by one. When the soldiers stood to disembark and file off the plane, they were mute.

As the men walked past the stewardess at the door and down the stairs, they glanced at the file of soldiers waiting to take their seats. In their dank and dusty fatigues, these men looked like ghosts, like dead men, each with that thousand-yard stare.

Well, here's the war, one soldier thought as he stood at the top of the steps, feeling the heat across his face, smelling fuel and animal dung. Then he and the rest of the soldiers got off the plane.

Even as they were reminded of the possibility of danger, the stewardesses often felt a sense of separation from the worst consequences. "If you look to your right you can see the Viet Cong," Clare sometimes heard the captain say over the loudspeaker. Captains usually pointed out what there was to see below: bays, mountain ranges, cities, firefights. "Down and over to the left you can see a napalm drop," she heard once. Plenty of planes had come under fire in flight. The tarmac was pitted and rutted, a reminder of how close the war hovered; airports were primary targets for North Vietnamese aggression. Over the duration of the war, North Vietnamese forces would hit U.S. and South Vietnamese air bases with mortars and rockets nearly five hundred times, an average of four times a month. Almost four hundred aircraft were destroyed and twelve hundred damaged. The big commercial planes bounced like frogs on the battered runways as they came down.

Once, following a landing in Saigon, the flight engineer called Clare outside. He had done his walkaround; all passengers had marched across the tarmac. Now he pointed to the underside of one of the DC-6's four engines.

"What's that?" Clare asked, eyeing the hole.

"He was probably standing in the field over there and took a shot at us," the engineer said. "Small-arms fire. Probably a rifle. Never could have downed a plane." A patch could cover the hole and the flight would take off in short order. At each base, Pan Am provided station kits with materials for the most commonly required fixes: aluminum speed tape for bullet holes or wear and tear around the cargo doors from careless baggage handlers; spare wheels for a hard landing on rough tarmac; small instruments. The goal was for flight engineers and ground maintenance to get a plane patched up and turned around safely and quickly. The plane then hopscotched to bigger stations with more repair capacity, like London and Frankfurt, until it reached a base in New York, Miami, or San Francisco.

If a repair could not be made, the logistics team back in New York would hop on the line and locate the nearest necessary component and get it moving to wherever the plane was grounded, whether outside of Vietnam or in-country. Sometimes a crew would be stranded for a day or two due to a plane's mechanical failure or structural damage. Military passengers were sent back to barracks, while the airline crew billeted wherever they could find room. It was hardly ideal to repair a plane while it was in Cam Ranh Bay or Da Nang, but when it happened, the women slept in the barracks too. During one stewardess's overnight in Da Nang, she dozed on a cot in the V-neck men's undershirt someone had handed her. It came nearly to her knees. When she woke, the pantyhose and gloves she had left next to her bed were gone. She looked around and the men just grinned. When she arrived back in Hong Kong, she said nothing to the supervisor who gave her a knuckle-rapping for her inadequate uniform.

R&Rs expanded well beyond Tokyo and Hong Kong. Married soldiers boarded one of forty-five monthly flights to Honolulu, where wives and, sometimes, new babies waited for them. The unmarried GIs flew to Hong Kong, Kuala Lumpur, Tokyo, Taipei, Penang, Bangkok, Singapore, or, eventually, Sydney. Newspapers back home called the cities "Bachelor Paradise," an impression emphasized by the advice local R&R centers offered to incoming soldiers. From Taipei: "Keep out of the buses or you may lose your wallet. Do not purchase the company of a girl for more than 24 hours at a time; they seldom look as good in the morning."

For the soldiers, the R&R program was a "Pipeline to Paradise" from its very first moment. As one article observed, "The first pleasure is climbing into big Pan Am planes, complete with tilt-back seats, pretty stewardesses and 'refreshments.'" In the black-and-white photo spread, women with brown or blond bobs under their pillbox hats lift trays above the clipped hair of a row of GIs or hand an officer a washcloth with delicate tongs. A smiling stewardess arranges a lei on the chest of a soldier at the bottom of a flight of stairs. He smiles winningly back at her. Behind him, nearly a dozen dazed-looking men stand arrayed on the steps, having just arrived in Hawaii at night. Dark circles can be seen beneath some of their eyes. One boyish soldier appears, with his crushed hair, to have slept in his seat. A few of the soldiers look at the stewardesses. More of the men, receding into the dark at the top of the stairs, gaze into the distance, past the camera, at a place where there is no war.

Articles also detailed the R&R flights from the stewardesses' point of view. "Stewardesses Love Their Job, but It Punishes Them Emotionally," read one headline. The headline captured a truth, but both the love and the punishment were, for many stewardesses, part of the complex brew of personal fulfillment. Another article gave the endeavor a flirty veneer: "Sixty very happy young girls fly in and out of here every day with what could be the young maiden's dream . . . planeloads of nothing but young men."

Journalists struggled to explain why Pan Am reported a waiting list of female flight personnel eager to serve in Vietnam, especially when the planes were so visibly and dangerously American. Pan Am planes were not supposed to remain on Vietnamese tarmac long enough to become a target, but if there was time, some of the women liked to visit with the men in the terminal. When Clare's galley had extra ice cream, she and another stewardess piled a tray with the Dixie cups and circulated them among the men waiting to board. The men were dirty, occasionally bloody; a sheet could cover a wound, but the red seeped through. Clare cried sometimes as she walked back to the plane. The soldiers knew it too. They watched stewardesses' smiles falter and their eyes fill with tears as they walked through a group of wounded men. The sympathy felt good.

Some stewardesses brought rolls of homemade chocolate chip–cookie dough to bake on board; some lent money to the GIs or mailed letters for them. Flying R&Rs had "made Good Samaritans out of many of the girls," one article declared. The pleasure Clare took from performing a demanding job was real. But she and her fellow stewardesses were not Florence Nightingales or Mother Teresas, nor were they maiden flirts eager to meet young soldiers; they were multifaceted professionals living independent lives in Hong Kong. Clare and another Hong Kong–based stewardess traveled to Kashmir to see the Kolahoi glacier, known in the Himalayas as the "goddess of light." And if sometimes they danced cheek to cheek with their dates at a rooftop bar above the city lights, such outings were hardly the end goal of the work.

For many stewardesses, their memories of access to the world's hazards as well as its opportunities could not be put on a shelf. In the New York suburbs a group of former Pan Am stewardesses began a club to keep in touch after they had quit to marry and have children. Soon their newsletter included entreaties for social connections as often as birth announcements. The 1967 directory of the Manhattan chapter recorded a salient new fact: of forty members, twelve women listed themselves by their maiden names, and five specified office phone numbers instead of home phones.

Most of the soldiers had been planning their R&R trips since they'd arrived in Vietnam. On their way out, they asked the stewardesses for shopping recommendations—servicemen on R&Rs spent about two million dollars each month in Hong Kong alone. They brought the comfort of R&R back to Vietnam in the form of tape recorders, cameras, and tailored suits for after a tour was over. Clare played tour guide for two lieutenants for a day; after loading up on presents for their wives, they took her to lunch.

Nightlife was the first thing on most of the men's agendas. The neon signs of rooftop clubs in Hong Kong—DIAMOND'S KITCHEN, HONG KONG PLAYBOY CLUB, SUZIE WONG BAR NIGHT CLUB, PUSSYCAT, HOT PANTS—made a variegated carpet of light below. At ground level —under the open windows and laundry lines and hanging plants of second-floor flats—neon martinis, bunny ears, and TOPLESS in capital letters lit the humid night air with promises of erotic exploits. On one flight to Hong Kong, Clare overheard a group of three GIs—especially young, she thought—talking big about the bars, the women, their plans. When she opened the door on landing, the sergeant who usually stepped on board to relay any special instructions over the PA told her to read out the name of one of the three boys. He had a message waiting.

"I hope it's not bad news," Clare said to the sergeant as they stood at the front of the plane watching the passengers file out.

"It could be," the sergeant said. "His mother and aunt have flown out to surprise him."

Clare watched the boy's face drop as the sergeant spoke to him. His two friends looked stricken on his behalf. Clare and the other steward-esses waited until they were out of earshot to laugh. But nearly every single person on an R&R plane was young, and they understood the soldier's disappointment.

While on R&R service, the stewardesses did what they could to make the flying fun for the soldiers, listening to their stories, laughing as they crouched on coolers in the galley together in this casual cabin. One stewardess, suffering in the Saigon humidity, shimmied out of her slip between loads of passengers. It was expressly not allowed for stewardesses to go slip-less. But the wave of damp heat that had come sliding under her uniform as soon as she opened the plane door over-rode regulations. Once or twice during the flight to Hong Kong, she saw a soldier exiting the lavatory with a broad grin splashed across his face. She had left the slip hanging on the lavatory hook, she realized as her cheeks reddened. Then she considered the men she looked at, where they had come from, where they would return after R&R. They deserved the thrill, she thought.

To Clare, the Hong Kong landing felt more harrowing than descending to Saigon's airfield. A single runway jutted out into Victoria Harbor, with high towers of glass and white concrete all around—a challenge for any pilot. The landing had acquired the nicknames "Kai Tak Heart Attack" and "the laundry line." When a plane swooped in to land, a stewardess could play voyeur, glimpsing people eating a meal or taking off their shirts in the windows of the apartments with the best views. At ground level, buildings served as backdrop for exuberant red-fringed banners—red was the Chinese color of happiness, joy, celebration, youth, health, and fortune. Even as hundreds of thousands of Chinese refugees jammed into informal settlements climbing the city's hills, Hong Kong earned comparisons to Monte Carlo for its setting and its luxury. As the months in Hong Kong ticked by, Clare could not believe her luck. Every woman with whom she worked had achieved a measure of the goal that had led her to accept the pseudo-military position in the first place: financial security, easy travel through Asia, a higher-ranking position, or, for one Chinese-American stewardess, the opportunity to polish her Cantonese.

One day, when Clare had been in Hong Kong for a year and a half, the airline called her and the rest of the stewardesses to a luncheon with General William Westmoreland. "Thank you for your service," the general, with his widow's peak and his sloped shoulders and the many-colored bars of commendations on his chest, said to them. It was the second time Clare had heard more or less the same words from his mouth.

The vice president for Pan Am flight operations was there too, with news no one wanted to hear. The airline was closing the Hong Kong base, the assembled women were told. It would transport servicemen on R&Rs via the larger 707 jets that flew out of Hawaii and California rather than on the aging DC-6 propeller planes out of Hong Kong; the base had fallen victim to the program's success. Crews out of San Francisco and Honolulu would staff the flights. San Francisco–based stewardesses had already been flying some of the routes. "Stewardesses with high seniority, which would enable them to take the truly plush intercontinental runs, keep coming back time and again to fly such missions," a Defense Department representative told *Air Force* magazine in an article about the continued R&R service. "The fact that a Pan American jet was hit by Viet Cong ground fire on its approach to Saigon shows what may occasionally be expected of our civil crews," he continued.

"HKG Crews Return for Reassignment," the company newsletter's headline read; the article detailed the bases that would absorb the nearly two hundred crew members in Hong Kong. Most moved to New York or San Francisco, with a few going to Miami or a new base in Los Angeles.

Clare and the rest of the stewardesses in Hong Kong had grown accustomed to the danger of flying into enemy territory. They had learned to strap in early for the too-steep descent into Vietnamese airspace and not to think about the coffins that were sometimes loaded into the belly of the plane from the mortuary the military ran at Tan Son Nhut, where the casualties were stripped of their fatigues and dog tags and photographs of girlfriends, the very photographs many had shown the stewardesses on their way into the country. Clare and her fellow stewardesses had acquired the habits and routines that cut their fear and sadness: they gave a hero's welcome to each serviceman as he sighed into his seat; they bade farewell to the soldiers with a cheery "See you next year"; they ate the perfect French onion soup at the upstairs restaurant at Tan Son Nhut airport.

Over the year and a half of R&Rs and troop transport, the Pan Am newsletter reprinted appreciative letters from soldiers. "Your stewardesses are to be complimented," read one man's note. "They served us in an efficient, but completely friendly and almost personal manner. They also served as a reminder that a beautiful girl still exists to give us something 'extra' to fight for." Another soldier had composed a poem in pentameter on his homeward flight. "You also serve who smile and fly / With cute face and pert figure high in the sky," he began. He typed the lines and mailed the poem to someone up the hierarchy.

Yet often and clear during the course of my year
Came the vision of my air hostess so warm and dear.
She is mother, sister, lover, and warm, true, friend
For countless thousands that never seem to end.
The last American woman that some will ever see,
As they go to guard liberty and keep the world free.

Flying for Pan Am was an honor, the best job in the world, and it delivered a paycheck that made Clare pinch herself. Now in her mid-thirties, she knew that if she'd worked for another airline, she likely would have been dismissed already; most airlines enforced their age limits and no-marriage rules in an industry that prized youth and beauty. Clare was lucky. She was reassigned to work in New York as a purser, the position she'd forfeited to go to Hong Kong. She had her pick of routes.

But even with all the seniority in the world, after Hong Kong, Clare was not sure if she wanted to live in New York and fly the same planes on the same routes she had flown for a decade. She had experienced more in her job and now she wanted more.

5

Foreign Service

THEY HELD A GLORIOUS DINNER PARTY THAT NIGHT, THE CEN-
terpiece a roast turkey the stewardesses had flown, frozen, from
New York to West Africa. They did this sometimes, brought party
fixings from New York. Roberts International Airport, the three-day
rest stop for crews flying east and south across the African continent,
sat alongside the Firestone rubber fields of Liberia, which meant a
raucous collective of expatriate company men far from home, which
meant parties.

Stewardesses who had peeled off to marry Europeans generally
stayed in close touch with their former coworkers. To Robertsfield, as
it was known, New York crews brought new records—the Beatles, the
Monkees, the Supremes—or flour or sugar to make up for shortages
on local supermarket shelves; they brought turkey from New York,
beef flown in from Nairobi. Everyone took turns hosting. Former
stewardesses living overseas often had household staff, so the flour
and sugar quickly became a cake, and the night's mess would be gone
by morning with no effort from the hostess. Single men threw parties
too, with panache, at company houses on the beach or with a dock
and waterski jump on the river. Guests included flight crews from the
United States as well those working for KLM Royal Dutch Airlines,

Swissair, and British Caledonian. Sometimes the crews put together a celebration at the hotel across the street, recently built of cinder blocks and furnished with Craftsman-style tables and chairs. Wallpaper made of wine-bottle labels and hand-drawn cartoons evolved with the passing months. No excuse was too small for festivities in a dedicated crew room with refrigerators stocked with leftover caviar and cheeses.

All of the New York stewardesses knew about Liberia's capital city, Monrovia. Africa trips were long—ten days, including the long layover at Robertsfield—and paychecks were calculated on a per-hour basis when stewardesses were away from their stations. The high pay, along with the safaris and jazz bands at the Equator Club in Nairobi, the thrill of airports consisting of little more than a sandy airstrip, the boisterous parties, and the vivid local markets, made Africa competitive. The route was limited to only the most senior stewardesses, especially those willing to embrace the Robertsfield experience—parties unlike anywhere else and, in the jungles around the airfield, worms as big as snakes and snakes as big as tree trunks.

Torild Werner had never seen a turkey before that night in October 1966. There were no turkeys in her native Norway, and this October had been only her fourth month living in New York working as a Pan Am stewardess. Her presence in Monrovia was a fluke. Her previous trips had been limited to entry-level New York–based flights: a Bermuda route one month, military charters out of Frankfurt the next, regular London flights. All were new to Tori.

On October 26, at the tail end of a month on standby—"in the pool," as stewardesses called it—the scheduler had called Tori's apartment and asked if she would go to Africa. She packed a bag and left quickly, arrived within the necessary hour and a half, and considered herself lucky. In Monrovia she felt even luckier when the crew invited her to the beachfront home of an English accountant.

After dinner, giddy with wine, the party of eight stewardesses and expats left the house for the beach. The air was soft and balmy in Liberia, not at all like the snap of autumn in New York. In the moonlight the gently sloping beach looked glossy leading down to the moving surf. Sunlight would have revealed brown sand, the occasional low palm tree on a hump between house and ocean, and a barely populated beach on the busiest of days. Laughter punctuated the crashing waves. They all stripped down and launched themselves into the water.

Tori had splashed in with the rest of them, but now she could not get back to shore. Nearly as soon as she'd begun to swim, she was pushed and pulled by the waves. With each ineffectual stroke, she slid farther out. Her thoughts fuzzed with an unfamiliar sensation: panic.

The others, too, thrashed against the dark water. Phyllis, a 4-H star from Illinois and a poor swimmer, had meant to dip in only up to her knees but slid off the sandbar and was now wailing for help. Elke, from landlocked Frankfurt, was more daring than Phyllis but found herself struggling in the undertow as soon as she submerged herself. Elke was a few years older than the others and had been flying for three years already; she had staffed presidential charters, flown to Tokyo, Africa, and across Europe and India. She knew the good day trips to take from Pan Am's bases in Africa; she had been among the organizers of this evening, and she was the connection to John, the accountant. Elke remembered hearing a rumor that Tori was an Olympic swimmer. *The new girl will be okay,* she'd thought in the ocean between prayers and goodbyes to her mother.

Rather than continuing to struggle, Tori swam farther out and floated. Overhead, the moon gilded the silver tops of the waves between her body and the shore. She kept herself oriented to the ribbon of lights on the coast. Paddling with her hands, she drifted gently in the calm water beyond the crashing surf. She would be fine, she thought, as always.

One by one, the party reassembled on the sand. The tide had constructed several shelves of sandbars with shallow water, and two of the women found purchase there. Tori heard them calling her name like birdsong. She was not an Olympic swimmer but she had spent every summer at her family's yellow cottage on the Oslo fjord, splashing in the water with her older cousins. In the worst scenario, she thought, she would continue to float and one of the men would commandeer the small fishing boat she had spied at the house next door to rescue her.

Time felt elastic in the water, but Tori could not have been out there long. No boat came for her; no flares lit the air. When she felt strong again, she began to swim, and this time, the ocean cooperated. Distance receded in the pushing and pulling of her breaststroke and finally she touched ground. Phyllis lay farther up on the sand, the water lapping at her feet, murmuring about how stupid she had been. Tori was standing in six inches of water when she heard someone shout her name. And then she felt her knees give out.

A tan had led Tori to Pan Am the previous year. A Norwegian friend from high school had become a stewardess; while Tori was in college practicing Latin declensions and setting her sights on a foreign service career, her friend had been flying from New York to the Caribbean. She sounded happy. She looked tan. Nobody looked tan in Norway in late autumn. The two women had lunch together one week, and days later Tori heard that the Norwegian Foreign Service Academy had different entry requirements for men and women. A woman would not be admitted without a master's degree. Fifteen years earlier, Norwegian women had not been allowed to serve in the foreign service at all. Around the world, few women worked in the official diplomatic corps. Rather, they served as quasi-professional partners for ambassador husbands—hosting, gathering information, and representing their countries even as governments argued against women working in professional capacities. In the United States, women made up 1.5 percent of the Foreign Service. The rare woman who did pass the exams and obtained a position was required to retire upon her marriage.

Tori's latest goal now spun out of reach. The two previous jobs Tori had dreamed of, radio operator on a merchant ship and archaeologist, both chosen for the travel they entailed, were vetoed by her parents. A merchant ship was no place for a good girl, they said. Archaeology was a pastime for someone with money. Tori needed work that paid right from the start, one with no graduate school involved, a husband neither required nor forbidden. She did not want to have to quit if or when she married.

Tori sat in the university cafeteria that week, deflated. A friend shouted that he had found the job for her. He held up a newspaper advertisement looking for people to interview with Pan Am, the United States' only exclusively international airline. Every time a plane's doors opened after a flight, the stairs descended into a new country.

"It's perfect," other friends insisted, "you can travel!"

Tori dismissed the idea outright with her light but logical manner —a stewardess job was not serious enough for her—but her friends continued their campaign. On a sheet of notebook paper, half a dozen of them wrote one sentence each detailing Tori's competence and extroversion, her wit and composure. She excelled at board games, crossword puzzles, games of strategy, and telling jokes. She was competitive. Someone pulled out a sheaf of photos from a recent party and drew arrows pointing to Tori in the group picture. Blue eyes, broad cheekbones, a smile that hijacked her whole face.

It had gotten everyone laughing, and then they tore the paper out of the notebook and stuffed it and the picture into an envelope. Tori was surprised when she got a phone call two days later.

"We received a very interesting . . . application," the man on the line said. "We'd like to send you a real form. Or, better, why don't you come into the office to pick it up?"

He gave an address downtown, just across a plaza from Oslo's city hall. The thought *I want to travel, I want to travel* kept running through her head. As she walked down gray cobblestone streets in the dim light of the approaching winter, her desperation to get out of town built.

Good thing I don't want the job, Tori thought. But she did want to see the places that had acquired mythic possibility in her imagination from books read as a child, Latin classes taken in college, and a year spent as an au pair in France.

Tori had never chafed at living with her parents before she took time off from college to go to France. She had taken the au pair job to perfect her French and ended up doing secretarial work at NATO in Paris too. Her parents knew nothing about this, but she had fallen in love with a Frenchman and they planned to elope. An entire life sprang up in those months away. Mild weather, rich wine, stone walls across easy parcels of countryside on weekends, starting up a consequential career at NATO—Tori would live forever in France. Her parents would be upset, she knew, by her marrying so young, before finishing her university degree. It was better to declare a fait accompli than to ask their permission, she thought. Ten days before the civil ceremony, her fiancé died in a car crash.

Devastated, Tori returned home to Oslo. At least she could still pursue the NATO job later. Then President de Gaulle moved to withdraw French troops from the alliance, citing disproportionate American influence. NATO would soon move to Belgium. Brussels did not hold the same attraction for Tori as Paris, a city she knew and loved. In Oslo, nothing was materially different but everything had changed —Tori's old life no longer fit in the one she'd proved could be wider.

In Oslo, Tori crossed the plaza, ducked around the enormous gray stone columns of the building in front of her, and entered the modern Pan Am ticket office. The man at the desk handed her an application form and asked a few polite questions about her studies. He told her to wear a skirt and heels to the interview in December. *Heels in Norway in winter!* she thought.

After her December interview, she carried her pumps back to the bookstore where she worked every Christmas break. In the dull winter light, the book-lined windows glowed. Her English was rusty. Her face was bare of makeup; she had been aiming for something of an intellectual look while working at the bookstore. The Pan Am interviewers said they would call after the holidays, but Tori was not holding her breath. She said yes when an acquaintance at the French embassy offered her a position filling in for six months at the student center. Maybe the job would lead back to France.

In mid-January, someone called to tell her that her papers for working in the United States were incomplete. Tori would need a physical before her visa could be processed. She could go to training over the summer. She would finish school later, she told her parents, and in June of 1966, she packed her bags for Miami.

The crew's chatter still revolved around the midnight swim two days later as the women gathered in the hotel for the flight's continuation to Ghana and Kenya. They talked about how Elke had washed in so far down the shore from the house, how Tori might have drowned in six inches of water had someone not heard the sound she'd made as she fell. The women were no longer new to one another.

But in two days, the story's dangerous edges had been sanded down to a neat anecdote. *That time we almost drowned* — that's what the evening became as the women recounted the tale. After the swim, Tori had been up until daybreak, filled with adrenaline, alive with gratitude. The women had hugged and talked as the sunrise painted magnificent colors above the water.

Now they advanced past the gate as a group and walked across the tarmac toward the plane, a cluster of crisp-shouldered uniforms moving as one. The women wore their required white gloves and blue hats, their hips trim beneath girdles, square blue bags hanging from their shoulders. Instructions suggested they carry with them extra hose, fresh gloves, a clothes brush, hand lotion, lipstick. Comfortable, sensible heels too — they would be on their feet for hours.

The ground agent approached Elke; as the flight's purser, she checked the manifest for special needs and VIPs. Now she saw that this load of passengers included three political delegations: state representatives from Senegal, Liberia, and Guinea were all headed to a meeting of the three-year-old Organization of African Unity in Ethiopia. It was an important group, she noted as she prepared the plane. They would require no flight modifications, only the bit of extra attention and deference owed to government functionaries.

As decolonization swept the continent throughout the early sixties (seventeen nations had claimed independence in 1960 alone) the OAU had become a venue for competing visions of postcolonial Africa —united entity or separate nations; political and economic alliances with rising Communist powers or with the United States and former empires of Europe. The Ghanaian president's lean toward the USSR and China had become more pronounced as the decade continued. That year, he talked of unification as inevitable. "The emancipation of Africa could be the emancipation of Man," he thundered.

The next year's conference was held in Accra, the Ghanaian capital. But half of the organization's membership did not attend. The country harbored "subversive elements" aimed at assassinations and government overthrow, said delegates from Niger and the Ivory Coast. Ghana's new grand modernist conference complexes were evidence of financial mismanagement, and inflation and dissent spread across Ghana. There was a rumor, too, that Ghanaian troops would be sent to fight for the Communists in North Vietnam.

In February 1966, there was a military coup while the Ghanaian president visited Hanoi. His entourage abandoned him. The USSR sent a plane to bring him back to Africa, to nearby Guinea, where the Guinean president, another Soviet ally, named him co-president of the country. Flight routes did not show it, but relations between Ghana and Guinea had grown brittle to the point of breaking. Now, as delegations from across Africa moved toward the meeting in Ethiopia, the OAU conference could measure the temperature of the rest of the continent.

One stewardess took stock of the galley—cocktail shaker, water pitcher, tureen, coffeepot, serving trays, cabinet after full cabinet—as

Tori and the others directed important-looking passengers to their seats. Tori was used to diplomats. She smiled as she pointed them down the aisle.

Diplomacy appealed to Tori for its international social life and essential purpose amid the tensions of the Cold War and, now, of the changing globe. Tiny, neutral Norway had been under Nazi occupation the year she was born. The king had fled to London as Oslo's citizens grew potatoes and cabbage in city parks in the midst of famine, and hundreds of underground presses had distributed news from the BBC Radio. Tori grew up on stories of the five-year occupation. Lying north of Sweden and Finland, her country shared one hundred twenty miles of border with the USSR. A Communist grade-school teacher's strident political lesson plans had infuriated and frightened her parents.

The Oslo Tori knew was evidence of the tangible effects of diplomacy. National sovereignty depended on international agreements, on NATO and the United Nations. She was a child of the war; her memories, education, even reserve among the German women in the new Pan Am crew were of a piece. She did not trust many West German women yet, though she liked Elke.

Something looked wrong to Elke as soon as she opened the front door of the DC-8 on the ground in Accra, the first leg of the flight. At the top of the stairs, hulking over the shoulders of the Pan Am ground official, stood a man in a military uniform. She heard the man inform the crew that Lieutenant General Ankrah needed to see the Guinean passengers.

Elke turned and knocked on the cockpit. In an instant, the captain emerged. "Absolutely not," Elke heard him say to the soldiers now crowding the airplane door. They disregarded this directive and shouldered into the plane, asking for passports. "My plane is American soil and I'm in charge!" The pilot was furious. "This is a scheduled flight of a commercial airline," Tori heard him protest moments later.

As the soldiers made their way through the plane, the captain strode off to the terminal to find the station manager. Some of the passengers followed. There were vendors inside, and there was shade, and regardless of Ankrah and his plans, the day had only just begun. The flight would continue on to Nigeria and then to Nairobi, Kenya. The political delegations would continue on a smaller regional flight up to Addis Ababa. Rather than waiting on an overheating airplane, some of the crew marched across the airfield toward the tiny terminal behind the passengers who had been allowed off the plane.

Tori did not. The new girl remained with the Guinean delegation, nineteen people, all of whom had stayed in their seats. Tori sank into one of the wide chairs in the front lounge of the DC-8.

Tori heard the captain's voice from below on the tarmac. "American embassy," she heard him saying, presumably to the station manager. "Scheduled flight . . . delay for no good reason."

She waited. The climate would be coolish in Nairobi, at just over five thousand feet elevation. The crew would stay the night in Nairobi, the end of the line. Pan Am's *New Horizons* guidebook highlighted the city's "handsome modern architecture" and urban sophistication —city dwellers ate dinners no earlier than eight, and top restaurants included the Lobster Pot, the Topaz Grill, and the Pagoda for excellent Chinese—but noted that the savanna was still exotically close. Leopards and hyenas raided the chickens of residents on the edge of town. Nightclubs switched between local acts and international pop; Elvis Presley and Harry Belafonte had toured just a few years earlier during Kenya's independence celebrations. As the sun set, local teenage dancers at all-day "boogies" gave way to whiter, international crowds drinking sixty-three-cent martinis. *Jambo,* the guidebook said, was an all-purpose greeting.

A scream burst from the back of the plane. Tori stood and turned toward the sound.

The angle of the machine guns relative to the straight-up-and-down of the seats struck her first. She saw one gun, slung across the body of a uniformed man moving quickly down the aisle, and a muzzle poking out behind him—then more men. Her eyes continued to absorb the movements of their bodies coming toward her. She turned to the front door and saw more soldiers crashing up the stairs. She shouted to the captain.

"Lock yourself in the cockpit," she heard him yell as he moved toward the stairs.

Tori did just that, and for a single beat of time she was surrounded by cold, steady machinery, the familiar knobs and dials and lines and cool rivets alongside the glass windows. But the cockpit doors were flimsy, meant to be able to be broken by a five-and-a-half-foot stewardess in case of a crash landing, and these soldiers pushed it in with ease. A man's frame filled the doorway.

The way they carried their machine guns frightened Tori more as they came closer. They wore uniforms but they had no uniform bearing. The guns swung and swayed differently on each man.

"Make an announcement," the soldier said as he reached for her. "Another passport check."

The soldier held her forearm as Tori picked up the PA system and ad-libbed according to his instructions. "There are officials on board," Tori said, as if the men were not already visible to anyone who remained on the plane. "Please take out your passports for a routine passport check," she continued, as if a previous check had not already been done. She did her best to muster calm. She reached out for the safety bar alongside the door. In training she had been instructed not to let go of this bar in an emergency.

Looking down the aisle, Tori watched as soldiers glanced cursorily at passports and then waved the Guineans out of their seats. As passengers began to stand with the awkward movements of stiff bodies, the soldiers herded them toward the front of the plane. Tori held on to the bar.

One woman began to shout and reached her arms out toward the seat on each side for resistance while a soldier pushed her down the aisle. The eighteen others passed in a confused shuffle. As the woman neared the entrance, screaming, she grabbed Tori's arm. Tori gripped the plane's safety bar as the woman gripped her and for a second all three—Tori, the woman, and the soldier—were connected.

Then the soldier must have pulled harder because the woman's fingers released Tori's flesh and the soldiers herded the nineteen passengers onto an open-door truck that peeled off down the tarmac. Tori stood at the top of the stairs, catching her breath.

On October 30, the *New York Times* ran an article headlined "18 Guinean Officials and Minister Seized by Ghana at Airport." By the time newspapers began to run stories about the incident, Tori and Elke and the rest of the crew had arrived in Nairobi. Late and exhausted, they retreated to hotel rooms to sleep before they went back across the continent to Robertsfield.

The passengers who boarded the plane in Nairobi the next day probably did not know what had happened in Ghana. How could they? No tangible evidence remained. The plane was fresh, pillows puffed in orderly threes in the open overhead container, the accordion blinds across the windows pinned back to offer a view of the tarmac's bustle and hum. The fuselage arched overhead, lights in a straight line down its middle. Passengers heading to economy class would pass through the front lounge with its midcentury-design tables and chairs and a mural depicting jaunty hot-air balloons.

Most flights were a practiced ritual of enforced sameness. When a flight went as planned, Tori served meals on the same gold-rimmed china, laid the same tablecloths across trays, and poured coffee into the same delicate cups and reliably dry martinis into the same long-stemmed glasses. Only the territory onto which the cabin doors opened changed.

But not every flight went as planned. On this day there was one significant difference in the flight pattern: the plane would not stop in Accra on its way to New York. The Guinean hostages had not yet been released; the incident remained unresolved. In Ghana, the general

who'd assumed control after the coup insisted that he would free the
Guineans only when his conditions were met. The Guinean president
responded by putting the U.S. ambassador and Pan American Airways
station manager in the Guinean capital, Conakry, under house arrest.
Movie theaters, dance halls, and bars across the city would close for
the day to "show solidarity of the people in the face of the act of ban-
ditry perpetrated by the U.S. puppets of Accra." Anti-American mobs
fifty thousand strong assembled in the streets.

The initial cool and distanced tone of news reports began to reflect
the chaos of the event. The Ghanaian head of state said that the Guinean president was "just being stupid." In an emergency meeting at the
OAU, an Ethiopian spokesman called the hostage situation an "act of
madness." It was "piracy," said the Egyptians.

In the face of Guinean criticism, the U.S. embassy in Senegal now
contradicted the pilot's assertions that he was in charge and declared,
"It is a fundamental principal [sic] of international law that a state is
sovereign within its own territory and that . . . it has full jurisdiction
over persons and property within that territory. The Pan American
aircraft flying to Accra came within the jurisdiction of Ghana as soon
as it entered Ghana's air space," read an aide-mémoire. The Guinean
government alleged that the plane and its crew—including Tori, Phyllis, and Elke—had allowed and possibly even enabled the kidnapping.
The basis of the claim was an understanding of Pan Am as an arm of
the U.S. government. "The fact is," read the State Department memo,
the Pan Am pilot—an employee of a private company—could not
possibly have assured the total security of his Guinean passengers. The
pilot and crew had, "moreover," gone above and beyond their specified
roles. The law did not back up the pilot's confrontation of the Ghanaian officials at the door of the aircraft or the crew's protesting "the
involuntary removal of any passengers and object[ing] strongly to the
entry of any armed Ghanaian security agents into the aircraft."

When Tori's stepfather heard about the Ghana hostage incident
back in Oslo and understood, days later, that she had been aboard

this particular flight, he urged her to quit. In Norway, Pan Am's name evoked images of fashion shows the airline sponsored at luxury hotels. Tori's stepfather had not envisioned machine guns and soldiers in proximity to her. He reminded Tori that she had a good job waiting for her back in Europe. Two, if she wanted them—there was the position with NATO, and the French embassy had also extended a full-time offer as a liaison for Norwegian students heading to France. Both were in safe offices where she could do something for her country. But Tori did not want safe office work just yet.

Her plane made its way back across the continent from Nairobi to Liberia for a second three-day layover at Robertsfield. When Tori arrived at Robertsfield, John, the English accountant host of the earlier dinner party, sent his driver out to the tarmac to pick her up. She walked across the airfield to the hotel to retrieve the envelope of local currency Pan Am provided as a stipend, and then she sat back in the car as it drove on red dirt roads among anthills so large and sandy, they gave the appearance of drippy sandcastles.

At John's house Tori let the flirtation with the Englishman bloom into a romance. She spent several days sunbathing and reading alone —the beach was nearly always empty. On the sand, she met other stewardesses driven in on an airline crew bus that ferried them between hotel and beach. Blue eyeshadow worked just as well as sunscreen on the tender nose of a woman who forgot to buy her own. Tori spent evenings at parties with John and other European expatriates, acquaintances she would come to know better in three-day installments every few months. On that trip, as Tori flipped from front to back on her towel on the Liberian beach, she thought fleetingly of the woman who had gripped her arm and wondered what had happened to her.

As the skin of Tori's bruised arm darkened, the Guinean delegation remained in custody in Ghana. The OAU conference had opened in Addis Ababa without its presence. U.S. embassy staff in Guinea were under house arrest. One diplomat's wife suffered a nervous breakdown and was evacuated. From oceans away, China weighed in on the ongoing situation, condemning the "American imperialists." The Guinean delegation was eventually released from custody. The Guinean president released the American diplomats but continued to insist that Pan Am bore the blame for the incident. The airline had a juridical responsibility, he said, to assure the safety of its passengers.

In Addis Ababa, an American diplomat—Alison Palmer, an analyst and Africa specialist who was approaching a decade in service—requested a promotion. Of fifty diplomats at a government executive-development course, she had been the only woman. A State Department newsletter reported that "promotions came this year to a large proportion of the many mid-career Foreign Service officers" who'd participated in the executive-development courses. She was not among those promoted. She knew that she would have to retire from the Foreign Service should she ever marry. She also knew that some ambassadors did not want women in political positions; she had recently learned confidentially that the ambassadors to Ethiopia, Tanzania, and Uganda had denied her reassignment and requested a man instead.

Six months before Alison Palmer's executive-development seminar, Tori had returned to New York following her dramatic trip through Ghana. Airline management had instructed her not to speak with any reporters waiting for the crew at JFK. She headed back to the apartment on Twenty-Eighth and Third that she shared with four American stewardesses—three brass single beds in one large bedroom and an infrequently used queen sleeper sofa in the living room. The Nordic stewardesses she knew had chosen to room together, but Tori had chosen American roommates because she was determined to acquire full fluency in English. That all of the women in her apartment wore more or less the same dress size offered a side benefit—the clothes at home could be worn by any of the five.

Around the apartment hovered a sense of disheveled glamour from the rotating roommates, the dresses in the closet, the reruns of 1950s sitcoms Tori watched on her days off so that she could understand the pop-culture references her roommates tossed around, the fact of being home at all during the day. In a year she could apply to be a purser and make a decent living.

All of the apartment's kitchenware bore Pan Am branding. The stewardesses who had lived in the apartment before Tori had spirited dishes and silverware off planes. Every time Tori opened a kitchen cabinet, the plates mortified her, symbols of graft. Whenever she had the money, she bought her own teacups and saucers, part of a set that could be purchased month by month at the department store; they had a pattern of gray branches and delicate roses.

Tori went to work at a stylish new airport of poured concrete, steel, and glass. The original blueprint for John F. Kennedy Airport, conceived in the mid-1950s when the airport was called Idlewild, centered on an international arrivals building and an eleven-story control tower facing a park with fountains and pools. The overarching design had been overridden as airlines constructed their own terminals. Architecture critics applauded the 1962 TWA terminal, shaped of bright white concrete into the curves of a bird in flight; it was, in the word of one critic, "exhilarating." Inside, swooping arcs and bows poured out and up toward the sky, a feat of twentieth-century engineering. In Pan Am's terminal, passengers and staff moved through a crystalline space walled with twenty-seven-foot panels of glass under the vast ellipse of a 175,000-square-foot cable-hung roof that dramatically cantilevered out above planes. *Vogue,* which used the recently completed terminal as a set for a 1960 fashion spread, called the UFO-like building's roof a "pale, floaty umbrella." During the day, an external catwalk around the glass terminal offered vistas on one side of moving planes and, on the other, of the lines of passengers who would soon fly on them. Boarding was an event. The airline called its terminal the Worldport.

Tori lived her New York City life amid the entirely new phenomenon of single women living together. Nearly eight hundred thousand singles lived on the East Side of Manhattan, and the city began to adjust to meet the unprecedented needs of this unprecedented "convergence," as one urban planner put it, of huge numbers of unattached strangers. Singles parties, resort weekends, and apartment complexes all catered to the new demographic. On the Upper East Side, the first bars ever to beckon specifically to female patrons opened—clean, brightly lit spaces with curtains and ferns and Tiffany lamps. It was no coincidence that the pioneer of the bunch sat two blocks from a fifteen-story apartment building occupied almost exclusively—90 percent—by stewardesses. During Tori's first summer in New York, on Friday nights between eight and midnight, police barricades shut down the stretch of First Avenue separating these new bars as thick crowds of singles mingled outside.

In four months flying, Tori had visited Frankfurt, London, the Caribbean, and Africa. She liked her coworkers; even the German girls were nice. She walked to the United Nations headquarters in New York and volunteered to help in whatever capacity she—a young woman proficient in five languages with erratic but plentiful time off —could. Maybe they would give her translation work. Certainly her last trip had been an anomaly amid the day-to-day tasks of flight and the predictable sightseeing, shopping, beaches, restaurants filling the layovers. But even that more routine work, Tori reasoned, would entertain her for a while longer before she embarked on a real career.

6

Pan Am Was the American Flag

PAN AM WAS NOT AN ORGAN OF THE U.S. GOVERNMENT. ALL the same, the company's loyalties were hardly exclusive to its shareholders. During the first half of the century, as European nations linked empires with homelands through national airlines, the United States used what Pan Am founder Juan Trippe referred to as the "chosen instrument," an international air company that could serve the national interest in ways the American government could not. Even as competition grew amid the expanding field of the 1960s international air industry, Pan Am operated within its own proprietary tangle of private and public interests and funds, parallel to American power from the start.

Trippe began the company in 1927 with mail and passenger service across the hundred-mile stretch of sea between Key West and Havana. Expansion was rapid; within two years, Pan Am routes circled the perimeter of Central and South America. Trippe bought out smaller airlines in countries along the way. Soon the airline flew a single plane, the China Clipper, across the Pacific from island to island. In little more than a decade, Pan Am had sliced the time to cross from the United States to Asia from six weeks by boat to six days by air. In 1939 the airline introduced passenger service across the Atlantic—Long Island to Lisbon in two days.

Along with World War II came Africa. With the fall of France, the Roosevelt administration feared that Axis powers could use the French colony of Senegal to launch an attack across the Atlantic to South America. Though Winston Churchill asked President Roosevelt to establish air and naval bases in Africa, the United States demurred; America did not want another war. In 1940, by a secret contract via the War Department, the president called on Trippe to secure control of the Americas; a new subsidiary of the airline was funded from "the President's kitty," as the secretary of war called it. In 1941 a public-facing loophole for this deal with the airline appeared in the form of the Lend-Lease Act. Pan Am, President Roosevelt announced, would provide "direct and speedy delivery from the 'arsenal of democracy' to a critical point in the front against aggression." With twenty million dollars in government money, the company created two more subsidiaries to direct the construction or reparation of eighteen air bases in Africa. Pan American Airways–Ferries flew lend-lease supplies from South America to Africa, while Pan American Airways–Africa hired thousands of local employees and began to build bases. Its Accra headquarters, akin to a military base, would eventually employ seven hundred workers, and its facilities included an electric plant and water tower, an amphitheater, Protestant and Catholic chapels, and a private road to the beach.

With these new routes, Pan Am became the first—and, for decades to come, the only—commercial airline to circle the globe. As the act of connecting the world's cities like pearls on a string captured the public imagination, so did the airline that had orchestrated the expansion. Listeners on four continents had tuned in to the nine radio networks broadcasting the first flight across the Pacific a decade earlier. The movie *China Clipper*, starring Humphrey Bogart, dramatized the Pacific crossing as "the most heroic adventure of the twentieth century!"

Though no airline officially represented the United States, many collaborated with the government in various ways, sharing infrastructure and more—the CIA at one point controlled or was involved in the operations of thirty-odd small airlines in addition to its alliances with Braniff, Pan Am, and Continental. Corporate airline structures lent themselves to the carrying out of international surveillance; the established operations and regulations allowed penetration into foreign bureaucracies. In its resistance to government use of a single airline, an international "flag carrier," the United States was unique; other global powers established their own airlines, instruments of the national interest, such as the British Overseas Airways Corporation (BOAC), Air France, and the USSR's Aeroflot. For smaller countries, an airline was a way to prove itself deserving of a presence on the international stage. The world was changing; as vast swaths of the globe declared independence from colonial powers, empires became commonwealths. Countries across Africa and Asia established their own airlines rather than relying on connection via British Airways or Air France; Ghana Airways, Air Algérie, Central African Airways, and Royal Air Maroc were launched.

Pan Am's iconography spread rapidly and pervasively through the 1940s and 1950s. The airline's first logo featured a winged globe with the recognizable landmasses where its routes had begun: the Americas and the Caribbean. In the 1950s, a new logo, a blue circle with horizontal lines curving gently toward each pole, hinted at the airline's expansion and dominance. The logo appeared in far-flung corners of the world it depicted. "Pan Am was the American flag, for all practical purposes an extension of the United States government," said one CIA officer. "Even before there was Coca-Cola in some places, there was Pan Am." Private businessmen often sought out the airline's employees on the ground before going to the U.S. embassy. Company offices served as a shadow State Department. Thirteen of the top twenty-five world airlines were based in North America, but among the ascendant international airlines, Pan Am had the best fleet. In 1958 it had initiated the first jet service, albeit with an asterisk—really, BOAC had sent a jet across the Atlantic a month earlier, but the Boeing 707 was bigger and went faster than BOAC's planes, and so with its New York–to–Paris route on October 26, 1958, Pan Am claimed the trophy. The first jet age had begun.

Around Pan Am were the so-called Big Four domestic airlines: United, American, TWA, and Eastern. Though Pan Am remained the country's only exclusively international airline, it was not the only airline to fly internationally; TWA flew to Europe and Braniff to South America. The Civil Aeronautics Board issued permits and controlled routes, prices, and competition. Scrabbling at a level below the major "trunk airlines" were the supplementals: World, Universal, and Saturn, operating out of bases in Berkeley, Nashville, and Ypsilanti, respectively, accruing revenue from tour charters and military contracts. Thousands of small airlines began with war-surplus planes after the Second World War, but only a handful remained by the start of the jet age. Tightening government regulations eliminated the fly-by-night operations, the mom-and-pop "airline" that was essentially a man with two rusty planes and four women eager to fly passengers from one location to another. Each airline that persisted crafted its own internal culture, seen by the public through the ranks of employees who wore its uniforms.

At the top of the industry, titans and visionaries spurred legends and gossip. Howard Hughes, the polymath, penthouse-dwelling Hollywood producer, engineer, and record-setting pilot, was forced out of his own airline, TWA, over the course of the 1960s. Pan Am's Juan Trippe, the strategic visionary with Wall Street credentials, was "the most fascinating Yale gangster I ever met," according to Franklin Delano Roosevelt. Ed Daly, the rebel at tiny supplemental World Airways, was said to have won the fifty thousand dollars with which he purchased the airline in a game of poker (in reality he had borrowed the money from a small trucking company). The twenty-seven-year-old Daly launched World with a few retired Pan Am flying boats and built his "mostly benevolent dictatorship" through small U.S. military contracts: airlifting Hungarian refugees in 1956, flying passengers to and from nuclear test sites in the Marshall Islands, and delivering the military's newspaper to its one million readers in Vietnam.

In 1966, with mounting combat in Vietnam resulting in lucrative government contracts, profits rose in the industry; experts projected a 200 percent increase in passengers by 1980. Juan Trippe, forever eyeing expansion, ordered thirty-three Boeing 747s, the largest jet ever made, for $750 million. The plane had room for 550 passengers; it held twice the passenger load, was four times as expensive, and flew just as fast as jets half its size. The main cabin had eight-foot ceilings, like a real living room, and double aisles. Cargo space increased profit margins. The initial financial commitment Trippe made in 1965 equaled the previous year's full passenger and cargo revenue. And now he customized the huge new plane with a stateroom and cocktail lounge on the plane's second floor and an elegant spiral staircase connecting the two.

Pan Am's order for the industry-changing 747s heralded the start of the second jet age. As the time for the new plane's launch neared, the airline needed to hire more stewardesses like Lynne and Karen to join the ranks of women like Tori and Clare. If luxury and image mattered as much as technological innovation, the airline had just placed an enormous bet on both.

7

Unequivocally in the World

WHICHEVER WAY A FLIGHT BEGAN — HEADING WEST ACROSS the Pacific from Los Angeles or east across the Atlantic from New York — round-the-world flights moved crew and passengers far from where Pan Am's stewardesses lived. Pan Am Flight 1 flew from Los Angeles to Honolulu and then from there to Tokyo, Hong Kong, Bangkok, and Delhi. In Delhi, Pan Am Flight 1 took one of two paths, either south to Karachi or north to Tehran. In any case, its next stop was Beirut, and from there the plane continued on to Istanbul, Frankfurt, London, and, finally, New York. Pan Am Flight 2 traced the same route but in reverse; it began in New York and ended in Los Angeles. Other cities appeared and disappeared from the paths of Flights 1 and 2 over the years, but the basic loop around the globe remained.

In either direction, the airplane crossed oceans, islands, and landmasses. A middle segment of the voyage traversed the immensity of Asia, tracing a line south of the Caucasus, the Himalayas, and the Kunlun ranges. "I must pinch myself to realize my whereabouts," Amelia Earhart wrote in a letter just before her disappearance, noting the visual similarities between the arid mountain ranges and deserts of North Africa and the American Southwest: sandy gradations of tan to red punctured by dark cracks, rough-edged rivers and canyons, and tufts of vegetation above pale brown soil. From the sky, a landscape can be subjective, a canvas for the anxieties and yearnings of the person in the airplane above.

The twice-weekly postcards and letters delivered to Lynne Totten's family's mailbox in upstate New York featured images of hotels that looked nearly alike. Beneath each date in the upper corner, Lynne added in her orderly script *I think*. She knew what the date had been when she left home and she knew how many flight hours had passed, but how those hours added into the twisting of the earth as she moved around it took too much effort to track.

The cities were fascinating, her coworkers friendly, and Lynne slept quite a lot. Sometimes she slept through an entire city, staying in bed for twelve hours, startling herself when she woke. Flight service was demanding. She had never seen so many eggs in her life. She prepared lamb chops for 122 passengers. "Only wish we could stop flying long enough to enjoy places," she wrote on the first of a trio of postcards from one trip. "Stopped here for 45 min," she continued. "Wow are we tired and being flown to death."

Directly after training in Miami, Lynne had moved to Chicago with another stewardess, Betsy. They lived with one other woman in a bare apartment—beds were their only furniture—with white walls that Lynne hoped to paint. She wanted to sew drapes too. She asked her mother and father to pack and send her possessions along. Pan Am would reimburse freight up to three hundred pounds. At the airport she bought her parents discounted tickets to Europe in thanks.

She never painted her apartment walls. Instead, she flew to Europe. She also handled a twelve-hour flight delay during which the airline sent all 306 passengers to the races at one of Chicago's six racetracks. She and Betsy had requested transfers almost as soon as they arrived in Chicago, and soon those transfers, to Pan Am's recently opened base in Los Angeles, came through.

California. By day three Lynne could not understand how or why anyone would ever live in the cold Northeast when Southern

California, with its daily sun and dry, comfortable heat, existed. She and Betsy rented a bungalow in Manhattan Beach, neither a suburb nor a city but something all its own. If a culture could be character- ized by specific combinations of sensation and landscape, Southern California had made of itself a new sort of republic, one described by swooping highways and crashing surf. The bright sunlight was softer near the ocean's spray, where Lynne drank in the blue and beige of water, sun, and sand, punctuated by the colorful clothes of the beach denizens. The sounds of this new republic were the Beach Boys and the Byrds; Joni Mitchell; Crosby, Stills, and Nash; the Association—opti- mistic harmonies, ballads of individualism and action (surfing, driving, flying), or ascension to a higher consciousness.

Manhattan Beach, unlike much of the Los Angeles area, had sprung into being for the sake of aerospace rather than film. Between the U.S. Air Force base just north in El Segundo and the three beach cities along the coast—Manhattan, Hermosa, and Redondo Beaches—the residential population had more than doubled since 1950, going from 60,000 to 125,000. In Manhattan Beach, new Californians worked in engineering and manufacturing at TRW, Douglas, Lockheed, and Hughes. They sent their teenagers to school at Aviation High and made small talk at the laundromats and supermarkets and bars built to serve them. Airline crews chose the beaches for proximity to the airport and for the easy days of sunny standby among the area's combination of beach bums and avid professionals.

Lynne and Betsy stepped into their new lives. The ocean offered an immediate respite from the exhaustion of Lynne's job. The bungalow they shared with two other stewardesses sat in the low, lean blocks just off the beach, a few casual steps past scrubby grass, enough to shake a bit of sand from one's feet on the walk home. On her days off, Lynne liked to sit and look at the tableau of water and sand—the long pier stretching straight into the ocean, the volleyball courts in gridded succession, the players leaping, setting off tiny sandy fireworks with each dive.

In her first month in California, Lynne completed three Honolulu turnarounds, then flew to London and Tokyo. She and Betsy began to bid their flights together so each of them could explore new cities with a friend. But the pace was draining. She must have picked up a sleeping disease somewhere, Lynne joked.

Then a new opportunity presented itself. Amid the push to staff its 747s, Pan Am had hired too many stewardesses, and now the administration asked some of them to take brief unpaid leaves. Lynne and Betsy bought tickets to South America and planned an itinerary through the continent that allowed them multiple days in each place, enough time, finally, to both see things and sleep, rather than having to choose between the two. They would end the trip in Argentina, where Betsy had lived during college. In Guatemala they watched the Volcán de Fuego belch steam clouds opaque with ash while grilling dinner with a friend of a friend. In Panama, an American canal guard took them to dinner at the air force base after giving them a tour of the canal, restricted locks included.

The best part about working for Pan Am, Lynne thought, was the safety and access conferred by the new network of airline friends. They were businessmen and soldiers, Pan Am ground employees and women who had once been stewardesses and were now settled but keen to stay in touch with the women who were still flying. They were all eager to help reveal the best of a place. *There's a whole world out there,* Lynne had thought in college, back when foreign countries were just headlines and abstractions. Now the names of countries called up previous experiences and future plans. The pace of the knowledge she acquired would slow when she began to fly again. She fit brief excursions into scant layover time, but still, Lynne was unequivocally in the world now.

In even its remote outposts, where just one weekly flight let off a single-digit passenger load, Pan Am employed station managers, travel agents, and public relations representatives. Advertising campaigns and pamphlets in foreign countries also promoted travel to the United States: *The Pan Am Planning Guide to Travel in the U.S.A.*, printed in five languages, and *A Woman's Way to See the U.S.A.* It was an extravagant network for travelers, and, in fact, President Johnson became concerned about all the travel Americans were doing outside of the country. Foreigners did not match it with their visits to the United States. In 1968 he raised the alarm on what he called a "travel deficit" of two billion dollars.

The national deficit was so steep that one economic adviser told Johnson the administration's goal should be "to get through 1968 without an international financial crisis." On New Year's Day, the president asked American citizens not to leave the country for two years. Patriotic Americans who wanted to help the national economy and, by extension, the economic health of the free world, he said, should stay home. "Americans, traveling more than any other people in history, took $4 billion out of their country last year in travel costs," he said. Now, airplane tickets for travel outside the Western Hemisphere would carry a 5 percent tax, and daily expenditures would be taxed at 15 to 30 percent. An African safari, a night in an English hotel, a meal in an Italian trattoria, a ticket to scale the Eiffel Tower—each one of these experiences snatched funds from American tour operators, hoteliers, chefs, and national monuments.

A decade earlier, Americans had been charged with keeping Europe stable by spending their tourism money in all sixteen of the Marshall Plan countries. International travel had been seen as diminishing the need for expensive government-aid programs, and prototypical American tourists—he with his cigarette lighter and briefcase and affability, she with her crisp clothing and even smile—were ambassadors for capitalism. Now the same travel was cast as unpatriotic.

Discouraging travel abroad would not solve the deficit, so under emergency authority, Johnson set limits on American private investments abroad too, the first time in history that such controls had been put in place. But Johnson's travel policies rapidly became, in the words of one administration official, "probably his most thoroughly unpopular legislative proposal in Congress." Politicians called them "unbecoming" and "undemocratic." Newspapers in Indiana and Massachusetts implored the government to look across the Pacific for cash rather than at American tourists: "Save money by getting us out of the mess in Vietnam instead," wrote one. Another critic pointed out that Europe offered an essential respite from the racial struggle and violence that consumed the nation. "*Really* seeing America first could get us arrested or even killed . . . for those of us Black Americans who can occasionally scrape together enough money to go, a trip abroad is not just a vacation, it's an urgent necessity," he wrote. A *Chicago Tribune* editorial highlighted the 1958 Supreme Court decision that had established the right to travel as, in the words of Justice Douglas, "the very essence of our free society, setting us apart." Freedom of movement, he said, lent meaning to "knowing, studying, arguing, exploring, conversing, observing, and even thinking."

"Fly American" was Juan Trippe's public counterproposal to Johnson's travel embargo. He pointed out that only half of the Americans who flew to Europe in 1967 had purchased tickets on American carriers, while 80 percent of Europeans used their own national airlines for travel abroad. In private in 1966, the president had asked the captains of American industry to exercise restraint in capital expenditures to help forestall the impending crisis, but Trippe had convinced him that the new 747 reflected a worthwhile investment—the planes would sell to foreign airlines, provide a reserve airlift capacity for the U.S. military, and carry double the freight load of present aircraft, Trippe said. Further, if the United States did not build a jumbo jet, the French or the British would. Johnson had approved the endeavor, but now his plea to the public depressed airline traffic for the first six months of the year, with contracts approaching one and a half billion dollars' worth of 747s in production.

Overall, 1968 had been "somewhere between weird and wild,"

soon-to-be Pan Am CEO Najeeb Halaby told the assembled managers at an end-of-year meeting. News had been bad, good, and unclear.
In the last category, Juan Trippe had retired. Trippe had been the final
founder still at the helm of an American airline. At May's annual
meeting, after blue-suited stewardesses had shown shareholders to
their seats, Trippe went through the financial details of 1967, a good
year, if not as good as 1966, a high for profits. He spoke of the pending jumbo jets and the challenge of filling seats as current demand for
long-range flights to Europe and Asia decreased. Unlike other airlines
—the supplementals had gleaned huge profits from cargo and military contracts—two-thirds of Pan Am's revenues came from its commercial passengers. Then Trippe had announced his departure and
named his successor, Harold Gray. He would last only a year and a
half before stepping aside due to illness and handing the leadership
to Halaby.

In the good-news category, the airline had been granted permission
to fly across the United States, connecting West and East Coast hubs
in a consecutive string. Its Los Angeles base offered a second portal to
Asia from the West Coast. And 1968 would see the launch of a historic
first: direct flights between New York and Moscow.

The airline had been chasing a Moscow route for years, albeit with
some hesitance. In 1966, hoping to gauge Moscow's interest in reaching some sort of agreement with Washington while waging indirect
war in Vietnam, President Johnson revived talks over an international
air accord. Since 1961 the agreement had been held in a limbo of cas-
cading Cold War disputes. "Peace will not dramatically appear from
a single agreement or a single utterance or a single meeting," Johnson
said in a speech that summer of 1966. "It will be advanced by one
small, perhaps imperceptible gain after another, in which neither the
pride nor the prestige of any large power is deemed more important
than the fate of the world." The air agreement had been a single gain,
a way toward potential agreements on space treaties, nuclear war, and,
possibly, Soviet mediation of peace in Vietnam. Though Juan Trippe

had known that the route would be a financial loss for the airline, "Pan Am does what's best for the country," he said.

"With this great instrument of friendship and understanding, the airplane, we were able to open up the heart of the Communist world," Halaby said. Aeroflot, the Soviet national airline, signed a ten-year lease for a two-story building in New York City on Forty-Fifth Street just off Park Avenue and took out a full-page ad in the *New York Times* touting the finest vodka and black caviar and low prices on its transatlantic flights. Expectations were high, if uncertain; the USSR hoped for dollars. "We want tourists, and we expect to carry about 50,000 a year from the U.S. within a few years," said a Soviet Ministry of Civil Aviation chief in a colorful eight-page spread in *Life*. Both Aeroflot and Pan Am professed the hope that air service might soften relations between the two world powers. The flights were "more symbolic than whole coveys of heavenly doves," a reporter for a Pennsylvania newspaper wrote.

"Blue Skies, Champagne and Caviar Make Cold War Seem Lost to Oblivion," *Newsweek* proclaimed even as other headlines about the latest Soviet spy ring uncovered in West Germany and the threat posed by lagging North American nuclear detection cast the claim in a dubious light. Nuclear war felt less like an existential threat than it had a decade earlier. Still, Pan Am management struggled to lure Russian language–qualified stewardesses to crew the new flights. And potential travelers weighed the allure of vodka and caviar against memories of duck-and-cover drills and cinder-block family fallout shelters. A ticket to Rome carried no such associations.

"Military business, and I think most of you would say 'thank god' as well as 'damn it,' is coming down," Halaby summarized. The landscape of the war had changed dramatically over the previous year; just before the Tet Offensive, General Westmoreland had predicted that the United States could begin to withdraw victorious troops from Vietnam in two years. "The enemy's hopes are bankrupt," he had said. Then, early in the morning of January 31, coordinated strikes by an estimated eighty thousand North Vietnamese soldiers began. In Saigon, the American embassy, the presidential palace, and Tan Son Nhut were attacked. Thirty-nine of South Vietnam's forty-four provincial capitals and nearly every allied airfield soon came under fire. Over two thousand American soldiers died in what dragged into a month of sustained fighting. North Vietnamese casualties numbered much higher, but the mere fact of the offensive—and the degree to which its coordination had surprised U.S. and South Vietnamese leadership —shocked the public.

"What the hell is going on? I thought we were winning the war!" said Walter Cronkite when the first bulletins buzzed into CBS headquarters. He flew to Saigon. After weeks of reporting, he addressed the American public with an hourlong bulletin that ended in a rare moment of subjectivity. "It seems now more certain than ever," he said, "that the bloody experience of Vietnam is to end in a stalemate." A chorus of voices rose in agreement with a war-opposition movement that had been led largely by intellectuals, students, and civil rights leaders before. Senator Bobby Kennedy called the war a "swamp"; Muhammad Ali and Beach Boy Carl Wilson refused draft induction and were indicted and sentenced for their resistance. Dr. Benjamin Spock pleaded with parents to keep their sons out of combat. Dr. Martin Luther King Jr. called the United States of America "the greatest purveyor of violence in the world today."

That fall, Richard Nixon squeaked into office, with a margin of about 1 percent of the popular vote, by promising to end the draft and the entire war. He would bring the half a million American soldiers in Vietnam home, he said. Twenty-one airlines shared the almost half a billion dollars of the government's war contracts over the course of 1968, and Pan Am claimed 17 percent—the largest single fraction— of that total. Twelve percent of the airline's fleet of long-range jets was assigned to military support services. But Pan Am would lose enormous sums on its commercial service to Vietnam the next year.

As 1968 ended, other airlines challenged Pan Am's international dominance. TWA had, with a new route to Tokyo, launched round-the-world service. British Airways, Air France, Lufthansa, KLM, and Japan Airlines had all ordered Boeing 747s. A growing crowd of American airlines flew internationally, and with increasing style and logistical connections. Braniff had opened the "Terminal of the Future" in Dallas, its halls decorated in lush reds and purples with furniture by Ray and Charles Eames, to service an array of South America routes. Its recent "End of the Plain Plane" campaign vaunted jets designed by Alexander Girard and uniforms by Emilio Pucci, though sometimes its stewardesses wore "something a little more comfortable," high-necked silky dresses.

Competition snuck into the field and Pan Am had to play. "We must add to [our excellence] 'a new dimension'—that is, emphasis on what pleases people. And I know of nothing that pleases people more," Halaby said in December of 1968, "than female people."

8

One, Two, Three,
What Are We Fighting For?

THE NEW 747, LYNNE WROTE TO HER PARENTS ONCE SHE HAD flown in it, was "just beautiful . . . like 7 of our houses one right behind another." A year passed as time and place swirled together amid the new routines and rhythms of flight.

The relief of a hotel, after the total unmooring of Lynne's body from any kind of normal twenty-four-hour cycle of day and night, was sheer balm. The Phoenicia InterContinental in Beirut was her favorite; she loved the grandiose marble lobby with its discrete sitting areas and the young men who served Turkish coffee from long-spouted brass pots as she walked in. Upstairs Lynne watched the boats bobbing in the Mediterranean beyond the doily-like screen of her balcony railing, eating fresh yogurt and reading the day's paper as the cars zippered along the corniche below. Here the hotel staff treated her just like any other hotel guest, and other guests at this particular hotel, she had heard, occasionally included Frank Sinatra and Brigitte Bardot.

Some hotels were like this, wired with the energy of potential sightings of royalty and international stars, perhaps found by the pool with its lounges and umbrellas, individual spaces meant to be visible. In the bar in the Beirut hotel's basement were wide windows looking into the very water itself; you could sip a drink while watching anonymous arms and legs drifting through the bluish-green translucence.

Other hotels the crew stayed at were less plush, catering to the Western businessman. To Lynne these hotels were no less gratifying. In even the blandest hotel lay satisfaction—an uncluttered desk, crisp sheets washed by someone else, crowds of people who were all committed to leaving one another alone. On some routes stewardesses shared rooms, and on others they were given their own space. Soon a private hotel room would be standard across the airline industry, but in this in-between time, Lynne wrote her letters in bathrooms while her roommates slept.

Across the world, the cities Lynne had grown to know were changing. Magazine articles referred to Beirut as the city that global aviation built, halfway between East and West both physically and metaphorically, a city in which tourism tripled and then doubled again and continued to rise as flight routes on all major airlines stopped off there. In Bangkok, tourism had increased sixfold in a decade. On streets that had until recently been flowing canals, newly imported Toyotas and Buicks clogged the city and brought traffic to a standstill for hours each day. Beginning in 1961, five major U.S. air bases were built in Thailand, and then came infrastructure spending around them —a tenfold increase in American spending. The swarms of American soldiers on R&R stayed in new hotels that housed military men exclusively; there was the Chaophraya, with 230 rooms for officers, the Trocadero, with 170 rooms for sergeants, and many more.

On one trip around the world, Lynne received a cable nearly as soon as she entered her room in Bangkok. Her stay at the hotel would be brief. The next evening, after her FAA-mandated rest time, as the last of the light bled out of the sky and as the cars that crowded Bangkok's streets lit into thick columns of white and red down each avenue, she would board a crew bus to the airport to ferry a flight to Cam Ranh Bay to pick up a planeload of American troops.

Lynne could hardly believe that American men were still fighting in Vietnam. Back in college, Lynne's boredom with her lab work had combined with her growing interest in politics to make her an unlikely anti-war activist. At the coffee shops in Oswego, Lynne had moved from silent observer to occasional, measured participant in policy debates as troop escalations and mounting protests urged her involvement. When the National Mobilization Committee to End the War in Vietnam announced an enormous march in Washington in November 1969 — the Moratorium to End the War in Vietnam — Lynne knew she had to go.

Together with her boyfriend and friends, Lynne drove to Washington, DC. Around the country, protest had risen to a fevered, violent pitch. Sit-ins at Columbia and Howard Universities shut down classes, and students took administrators hostage. At the Democratic National Convention in Chicago the previous year, the police and National Guardsmen had kicked their way through the mass of people with such force that the retreating crowd shattered the plate glass of the Hilton Hotel's ground-floor window.

President Nixon pleaded with neutral and hawkish Americans to speak up: "To you, the great silent majority of my fellow Americans," he had said in a speech, "I ask for your support." And he had received it; cars drove around Boston Common during a peace protest with American flags wrapped around the hoods of VW Bugs and signs declaring I SUPPORT OUR BOYS IN VIETNAM. A West Virginia chief of police who organized a parade of armed and uniformed policemen said, "We won't creep around in the dark with candles like these traitors do." Young Americans for Freedom prepared for confrontation. "It's our anticipation that we're in a long, drawn out struggle — almost a war," one representative said. On the day of the moratorium, Nixon was described as being "feisty." "We've got those liberal bastards on the run now," he said.

But an enormous, diverse crowd from across the United States gathered in Washington. They climbed on buses at colleges in Kalamazoo and carpooled down country roads toward the nation's capital. The marchers moved in unison and Lynne felt proud to move with them. She saw children and grandmothers, young men and women, Black people and white, a wide economic and social spread of Americans. They were not, as Vice President Agnew had called them, "effete snobs" or "rotten apples," nor were they "traitors."

"'All we are saying is give peace a chance.'" People sang John Lennon's new song over and over. Their clapping hands warmed their bodies. They stamped their feet to keep the blood flowing as they stood on cold asphalt pathways or nearly frozen ground. Not far from Lynne, someone burned an American flag. Within minutes, tear gas tendriled among the protesters. The nine thousand National Guardsmen waiting in federal buildings sprang into action. Lynne and her three friends raced out into the streets radiating from the Mall with the rest of the dispersing swarm. They had planned to find a restaurant where they could sit and exult in having changed the world, but the cafés around the Mall were filled with tear gas too. Instead, they found their car, got in, and began to drive.

She was fine, Lynne told her mother when she got home. But something about the day's end felt off—the readiness of the National Guard, the disjunction between the terrible act of burning an American flag and the patriotism she had felt from every single protester she met. In the morning, the numbers cited in the newspapers felt off too; "250,000 War Protestors Stage Peaceful Rally in Washington; Militants Stir Clashes Later," read one front-page headline, but the crowd had felt much bigger to Lynne (later, it was revealed that the crowd had been twice as large).

The week before the moratorium, a full-page ad covered the back page of the *New York Times'* Sunday Review section: 1,365 servicemen on active duty at seventy-nine bases in the United States and 200 men stationed in Vietnam had signed the ad's demand to end the war. "Bring us home now," it implored. In Vietnam, soldiers wore black armbands in solidarity with the marchers, some of whom would head to Vietnam soon themselves. They would go to fight; they would go as NGO workers and reporters and Donut Dollies.

Lynne had not made a conscious decision to avoid marches and protests when she began to work for Pan Am. Rather, the logistics of her life no longer accommodated her participation in the broader movement. She still considered herself fervently anti-war, still allied herself with the hundreds of thousands of students across the country who had halted classes over the Kent State killings during her first months flying on Pan Am and with the four million students who demonstrated against the war in the days immediately after the slaughter, which had left four dead and nine wounded. She admired the one thousand veterans who arrived on the National Mall the following year, stated their names, ranks, regiments, and the awards they had earned, then threw those very medals toward the Capitol, across a fence erected to keep them out. "Purple Heart, army commendation medal, eight air medals, national defense and the rest of this garbage," a uniformed young veteran screamed into a microphone, "doesn't mean a thing."

Military duty was stitched into the idea of manhood with which Lynne had grown up—her father's service, her college boyfriend's looming draft notice—and compliance with that service was equally sewn into the concept of womanhood. Now, as Lynne faced her first war flight, her personal and political ideals were at odds. On the hour-long passengerless flight she took from Thailand to Vietnam to pick up the men, she imagined asking the soldiers on the next flight if anyone was a member of Vietnam Veterans Against the War and offering them information. But Lynne knew that she received biweekly paychecks to provide courteous service—the dignity of a calm flight and a friendly face—to any passenger.

Lynne felt the stress tightening in her chest as the plane approached Vietnam. Someone pointed through the window to the puffs of smoke rising from the base of a green mountain. On an empty flight Lynne could sit and observe the landscape, watching blue dunes sift and fall under the skin of a shallow sea or the texture of the mountains beneath a plane's wing. Now she stood at a window on the plane watching mortar fire in the war zone below.

On the ground in Cam Ranh Bay, Lynne felt the tautness across her shoulders wind tighter. As the plane refueled, an officer invited the stewardesses to tour the facilities. He showed them his machine guns and held up a .38. Back at the plane, Lynne helped the soldiers board. The plane taxied down the runway, and the men were silent until the wheels lifted off the tarmac, then they began to cheer. Their next stop would be Yokota Air Base just outside Tokyo, six hours north, and then a series of flights across the Pacific Ocean toward home. She looked around as the men eagerly ate their military rations, drank their milk and coffee. The coffee was good and thick, one soldier told Lynne as she served him, his voice full of gratitude. The flight held so much compressed joy and relief that it might have been, she wrote to her parents, the best flight she had ever staffed.

What followed, her letter continued, was the worst. On the ground in Yokota she was assigned a full load of new draftees who were heading into Bien Hoa the next day. As the young men boarded the plane, Lynne wondered how many of them would not return. And what would they have died for? She boiled inside.

A soldier talked to her in the galley when the plane leveled out at altitude. He held up an eight-by-ten glossy photograph of a sweet-faced young woman. His new wife, he said. A second soldier told her he planned to marry his girl as soon as his twelve months were done. The men appeared to Lynne to be frozen in high school. She saw them as the boys she'd dated, the friends she'd made, the men from Baldwinsville with whom she'd grown up.

A third soldier approached. To Lynne he looked like her younger brother, Bob. She excused herself. She would have taken Bob to Canada rather than let him set foot on the plane on which she now rode. In the lavatory, she splashed water on her face, glared at her red eyes in the mirror.

Every corner of the plane contained men in uniform—sitting, standing, in the seats and galleys, leaning into rows and walking down the aisles. "Captain, I've forgotten something, can we turn this bird around?" Lynne heard one man yell as she walked to the jump seat just outside the cockpit.

One of the soldiers sat down next to her, asked what was wrong. The cigarette smoke on the plane irritated her eyes, Lynne told him. A few others approached Betsy, also on the flight, to ask what had happened to Lynne. She had been having personal troubles, Betsy said.

Lynne had never been a good liar. The soldier next to her put his arm around her shoulders. "It's really nice," he said, "to see that some-one really cares what happens to us."

Nothing, absolutely nothing, can be worse than this flight, Lynne thought.

PART II

YOU CAN'T
FLY ME

9

What Do You Women Want?

AROUND THE WORLD, SIX HUNDRED MILLION PEOPLE watched Neil Armstrong, "Buzz" Aldrin, and Michael Collins land on the moon live on television. Soon newspaper front pages in every country would carry the same images: the pocked surface of the moon, the white peaks of lunar mountains, the men's faces above the wide circular necks of their suits.

On an airplane somewhere over the Pacific on July 20, 1969, the stewardess had just served dinner when the pilot announced to his plane full of U.S. Marines on their way to Vietnam that Neil Armstrong had taken his first step on the moon's surface. The stewardess prepared, in the silence immediately after the announcement, for a bright, loud cheer. Instead the quiet stretched.

An older man set his food on the floor, folded up his tray table, and stood up.

"'O beautiful for spacious skies, for amber waves of grain,'" he began.

One by one the others set their food on the floor and stood, all 164 of them. As the minutes ticked by, the men stood and sang. They went through all the patriotic songs they knew and ended with the Marine hymn: "'From the Halls of Montezuma to the shores of Tripoli . . . In the snow of far-off northern lands and in sunny tropic scenes, you will find us always on the job, the United States Marines.'"

When the stewardess walked down the aisle she saw the tears on the men's faces. They were heading to someplace they had probably never heard of, she thought, to die for a confusing, likely doomed cause, and still, they had stood up to sing about America. She thought the purity of the moment set against the backdrop of the war the men would soon enter would never leave her.

Karen sat cross-legged on the floor of her New York apartment. Today, she was the only one home. The afternoon sun flared through the windows onto the dingy walls. Tears streaked her cheeks as she watched the grainy images of the moon on TV. It was the same moon she had gazed at as a teenager on the cliffs of Santa Barbara, eager for experience, the moon that had pointed her toward Asia, the moon that represented all the places she had already seen and those she had not. "There's such a lot of world to see," the Johnny Mercer song went. Now uniforms hung in her closet, a vinyl bag with the Pan Am globe below them. Karen could bid flights to anywhere now, any city Pan Am serviced, anywhere on the globe above which Aldrin and Armstrong stood.

In Rome, Lynne and a friend planned to head to the American Academy for its television. Soon after she woke up on July 21—her birthday—Lynne knew that the astronauts had already made it, but she dressed and climbed aboard a bus to go to the American Academy anyway. The two women walked into the academy's library to the three televisions showing the rebroadcast. Lynne thought the news might be dubbed in English but it was florid Italian that rang out from the recordings. Lynne, surrounded by old, rare books, listened to the

Italian narration of the American astronauts' buoyant jumps across the moon's surface, and wept.

Tori had flown in from Tokyo that morning and wanted to watch Armstrong's first steps, but the man was taking forever to exit the capsule. She fell asleep on the couch, then was jolted awake by the scratchy sound of the astronaut's voice coming from far above the sky where she had just been flying. Her eyes closed again; she woke up again. *Come on,* she thought, *get on it—get astral!* In her apartment the gold shag carpeting and avocado-green appliances gleamed in the noon light. Waiting for an event so surreal and so exciting, while drifting between waking and sleep—the moment was like a dream.

This dreamlike version of reality held up a strikingly accurate mirror to Tori's life. Aldrin, Armstrong, and Collins had ridden to the moon in a capsule whose instrumentation appeared familiar to any observant stewardess. The ship used the same basic principles of propulsion that sent Tori into the air every few days of every month of every year. Her job, too, broke her away from earth's gravitational pull.

Over the course of two years of flying now, she'd had many such experiences that once might have struck her as surreal. Once, Tori had sat in a rented bus in Nairobi National Park, watching the sunrise around a watering hole, still wearing the dress she had put on to go dancing hours earlier at the Equator Club. The Nairobi nightclub required black tie on Saturday nights but never turned the more casually dressed stewardesses away. A rented bus had picked the women up outside as the party wound down and driven them the four miles out of the city and into the park. Tori had forgotten her camera. She watched antelope, a zebra or two, and monkeys. She impressed the image upon her memory: the negative-space silhouette of the animals in the rising light, the dark outline around the water, the long, low plain farther back. Acacia trees shot up and then out with wispy branches.

Thick grasses on the ground feathered the horizon line. As the day brightened, the women were driven out of the park on gray roads that sliced through the brush like any country road anywhere, except that here monkeys might be spied knuckling their way alongside their van.

Another time, Tori had been scheduled for Flight 281 to San Juan, but at Kennedy she was told to wait for the next flight, so she sat and read in the airport until her new plane arrived. Once she was on board, the pilot called her into the cockpit to tell her what he'd heard over the radio. Flight 281 had flown toward Havana. "Lucky you," he had said. *Unlucky,* Tori thought. *I wish I'd been there.* Skyjackings were still mostly regarded as an amusing novelty. Magazines published cheeky tourist guides to Havana, like one titled "What to Do When the Hijacker Comes." "It was great," said pro golfer Barbara Romack of a diverted flight. "I got more publicity out of this than when I won the Women's Open." A skyjacker on Flight 281 had given .32-caliber bullets to passengers as souvenirs. Tori had always wanted to visit Cuba.

On yet a different one of Tori's flights, across Africa to Johannesburg this time, emergency vehicles had raced across the tarmac toward her plane as soon as it landed. Ground crew attached stairs to the plane and Tori heard a man outside question the purser through the opening door. "Are you okay?" he asked. "Didn't you get the cable in Kinshasa?" The flight engineer emerged and walked down the stairs with the ground crew. Tori and the rest of the stewardesses continued their work. Tori learned later that bullets had penetrated the plane millimeters away from the steering wires. Nigeria was engaged in a civil war with newly seceded Biafra, and the Nigerian army stationed at the end of the runway in Lagos had fired at her plane as it lifted off. Airplanes represented Biafra's primary link to the outside world. Planes from Iberia, TAP Air Portugal, and Air France were covered in fresh coats of paint and given false tail numbers, and a ragtag group of Israeli restaurant owners and retired U.S. Air Force pilots flew food and arms to the starving refugees in Biafra. Nigerian radar-guided antiaircraft fire christened planes with dozens of bullet holes as they chased the same route as the commercial Pan Am flight from Lisbon to Lagos. Many flights did not make it past the Nigerian artillery. Still, Pan Am made no changes to that route.

Airport authorities in Lagos had sent a cable to Kinshasa, but Tori's plane had landed and just as quickly left. In Johannesburg, Tori walked across the tarmac, boarded the crew bus, and was taken to the hotel, all actions she had performed, at this point, hundreds of times before. She heard about the incident only after she and the rest of the crew were safe from its consequences. As she learned what happened, she stayed calm. She stood safe on the ground. Still, she thought, maybe her time flying frequent Africa routes should end.

Enough time flying recalibrated a person's concept of excitement and danger. For a certain sort of woman, the repetitive thought, applied to repeated murky situations—*Maybe this is a bad idea*—created an unlikely sense of security. In public, the people Tori had begun to refer to as the "Pan Am family"—the pilots and stewardesses, station managers, and public relations agents in various ports of call—maintained an attitude of safety-minded responsibility. One of Pan Am's popular guidebooks, compiled of surveys from the wives of employees and expatriates around the world, told readers not to swim off the coast of Liberia. "Strong currents make boating and swimming too hazardous to be much fun," read the entry on Monrovia. Yet few of the Pan Am women Tori knew considered anything hazardous enough to ruin their fun. One stewardess had almost lost an arm waterskiing on a moonless night in Monrovia when the boat's driver had not seen her fall. Another, a former stewardess married to a Firestone employee and making a home in Liberia, became so good at waterskiing off her dock that she barely got wet anymore. Tori herself had almost drowned swimming on that ecstatic first night there. She was fine.

Tori would do nearly anything once. Her competitive streak aligned with her opinionated nature. And she never knew when a particular crew would next be in a particular place. Routes changed rapidly outside of Europe and North America. Expanding markets for

Pan Am flights and political volatility around the globe meant that a route might shift in days or weeks, removing a destination from a map entirely. Amid the rotations of crews, each group of pilots, engineers, and stewardesses created its own fleeting chemistry. The individuals of each group crafted their own balance between responsibility and audacity. These were the sort of people who arrived on time or early but rarely said no to a dare. An airplane was no place for anyone too reckless. But at the same time, the world around which it flew was no place for anyone too fearful. Crews worked together and then split apart and reassembled with the easy sociability of camp friends.

In New York, Tori's living situation settled. Her roommate's sister, who had lived with them while her husband was deployed, moved out. So did the one flaky roommate. Now only four stewardesses shared the apartment, meaning that there was a bed for every woman—not that they were often at the apartment together. In New York Tori went on dinner dates with men she met through friends of her European friends or with the younger pilots just out of service in Vietnam; she had platonic dates with an affluent, older gentleman she'd met through the woman she'd au paired for in Paris. She preferred talking to dancing, and the formality of dating appealed to her. A dinner date could be romantic or casual, a one-off or a frequent meeting. Tori was picky, and women in New York did not go out to dinners together. Dating the right man offered one-on-one conversation and the chance to be out and about in the city.

If Tori had arrived in New York even five years earlier, she might have lived in one of the city's many women's hotels, where young women's parents allowed them to stay because there, as Sylvia Plath wrote in *The Bell Jar,* "men couldn't get at them and deceive them." Now apartments shared by single women fizzed with new autonomy amid a historic loosening. Respectable, middle-class Americans were no longer as invested in a woman's virginity as they had been a generation earlier. In 1962, Helen Gurley Brown had published *Sex and the Single Girl,* arguing that sex could be enjoyed by unmarried women.

"Good girls go to heaven. Bad girls go everywhere," as Brown's favorite saying went. The nation's first topless bar had opened in San Francisco in 1964. Pan Am's stewardesses had already spent considerable time in cities where topless bars were not unique. Many knew how to party hard. In the crew's party room at the Monrovia hotel, the outline of one stewardess's naked body appeared on the wallpaper. She had drenched herself in red wine and made a print of her own form among the bottle labels and hand-drawn cartoons decorating the wall. The image remained a feature of the room long after the stewardess had continued on.

Tori's brief romance with the English accountant in Monrovia had ended when she stopped bidding Africa routes after her flight to Johannesburg. Now Tori flew to the Caribbean or flew round-the-worlds to London or Karachi. In New York she was taken for cocktails and dinners to Le Club, to the former speakeasy 21, to La Grenouille. The men she dated wanted to impress her, though she never had a say in where they ate. Whichever roommate had a date brought back a doggie bag to save whoever else was home from another night of spaghetti. The roommates had non–Pan Am dishware now too. Tori had bought a full tea set, roses on white china.

Tori hoped to volunteer with the United Nations in her time off. Dozens of new skyscrapers had appeared not far from the UN headquarters in midtown, where stone and brick town houses and aristocratic mansions had been reduced to piles of rubble and then replaced by new glass-and-steel offices. As a volunteer, Tori knew she would not immediately be interpreting for foreign dignitaries in one of these buildings. At first she stuffed envelopes at the Biltmore Hotel, two twenty-six-story towers across from the Grand Central terminal with the Pan Am skyscraper looming above. Tori had sat in a windowless room of the hotel folding paper leaflets for one program or another. A fine place to begin, but Tori sniffed when she understood that her job for the foreseeable future would involve envelopes.

The federal Equal Employment Opportunity Commission had

recently found in favor of the female State Department Africa specialist Alison Palmer, the woman who had requested promotions for nearly a decade. A 1969 memo recommended that "Miss Palmer's personnel file be documented to show that her career has been affected by prejudice against women officers—this documentation can best be done by placing a copy of this memorandum in her file." The memo was not placed in her file. Instead, Palmer received a letter. "Your career prospects could be damaged by inclusion of this reference in your file to this grievance procedure," it read.

Women in the State Department still had to retire upon marriage; the performance evaluation of male officers still included a section on the behavior of their wives. Among thirteen task forces recently set up to evaluate changes to the State Department's rules, none considered the role of women. A working group of eleven women held public meetings and soon grew to include two hundred members. "Just what do you women want?" the undersecretary of state asked them. Alison Palmer had still not received a promotion, and now she demanded an outside investigation into her case.

Tori finished the shifts she had volunteered for with the United Nations and declined further assignments at the Biltmore. She walked into the Pan Am Building instead. The first time she sought information on the company's pension plan, she was too young to begin one, but at age twenty-four she could start to save for her eventual retirement from the airline. She no longer thought that a shift to another career would come soon.

Tori had accrued enough seniority to take a thirty-day vacation, her first extended time off. With her 90 percent discount for passenger flights for her family and her employee rate at InterContinental hotels, she brought her mother on a vacation to Thailand. The Siam InterContinental, among the hotel group's newest, was decorated with gold-shot Thai textiles and motifs inside a starkly modern frame. Sitting at its blue pool at the center of the grounds, surrounded by a lush spray of palm trees, Tori attracted attention from a wide range of suitors, though she credited the attention to her beautiful blond mother.

Now, as a result of flirtations begun around the Siam InterContinental pool, three marriage proposals floated toward Tori. One of the men had been a joker, but two stayed in touch. The Texan businessman fell off as Tori's interest in him waned; the other, a Western Airlines pilot, stuck. She had a month of trips through Los Angeles, where he lived. They went to dinners at a piano bar in an old boat in Playa del Rey. He came to see her in New York, where they visited the Empire State Building and the Russian Tea Room. They vacationed together in Alaska when he had a short-term assignment in Anchorage. He kept a Cessna in LA and promised Tori trips to Cabo, which did not excite her—she felt more comfortable with four engines. After six months they decided to get married in Norway the following April, when they both had time off.

Tori was ready to be serious but she was not entirely comfortable with a marriage untested by daily life. She wanted to ask for a transfer to Pan Am's new Los Angeles base. If Pan Am refused to send her, she concluded, she and her fiancé would rethink the April wedding date.

Barely three months had passed when trouble emerged between them. Her transfer request had been granted, and she was set to move to LA. She and her pilot disagreed on minor points of their life together—like two kids versus three—but Tori thought they agreed on the broad strokes. They would wait two years for children and in the meantime enjoy the perks and flexibilities of crewing on an airline. Maybe she would fly in the Cessna and watch the Pacific Ocean scrolling up toward the dry mountains of the California coast on the way to Mexico.

But the pilot wanted Tori to get a ground position, a nine-to-five with the airline. Tori did not understand. Her nearly three years of seniority would transfer after a few months in LA. She had made purser the previous year; now she earned the highest paycheck available for a stewardess. She bid her own routes, made her own timetables, directed crews of four and then, on the 747, nine women as they attended to the needs of hundreds of passengers across vast oceans. On a geopolitical level, Pan Am was often a chosen instrument for the national interest, but in Tori's life it was the instrument of her own freedom. With that kind of ownership over her own time and schedule, she thought, she and the pilot could plan their work lives in tandem and together take advantage of the opportunities their jobs offered them.

The sixties had begun with a near-absolute norm for a woman of Tori's age: marriage. The age of women at marriage was young, the divorce rate low. Even if some of the numbers indicated fissures —separation was not such an anomaly—to most women, a good husband seemed the collective goal, marriage the only end point. But as the decade wound down, increasing numbers of households reported single women at their helms. The age of the women who walked down the aisles of churches and married in city halls rose. So did divorce rates, doubling the approximately 380,000 divorces granted annually between 1955 and 1960 to over 700,000 in 1970 and up to one million in 1975. The change happened in the United States and around the world; twenty-something-year-old women demanding, reassessing, and asserting themselves in ways that would drive the shift in countries with vastly different social, political, and religious contexts. In the United Kingdom, Poland, Uruguay, the USSR, Mexico, and Tori's native Norway, the divorce rate went up and up through the seventies. In another decade, 1.2 million couples would divorce in the United States.

The pilot did not trust Tori on layovers in Paris and Beirut, Hong Kong and Bangkok, she learned. A week before Tori's planned move to LA, her disagreement with him became a matter of commitment and control. *Hello,* Tori thought—if there's no trust, there's no basis for anything. What was he doing on *his* layovers?

10

I'm Okay, You're Okay

CLARE CHRISTIANSEN SAW HER REASSIGNMENT BACK TO NEW York announced in the company newsletter. Everyone with whom she'd worked in Hong Kong had scattered across old and new bases: New York, Miami, San Francisco, Chicago, Los Angeles, Boston.

Clare had aspired to do more than flight service before arriving in Hong Kong, and her time in the city flying R&Rs did nothing to dissuade her that stewardessing no longer satisfied. Other Hong Kong stewardesses also felt their ambitions shifting. One stewardess wrote a book of stories about soldiers. She had listened to the soldiers' tales in the unspooling tension of flights away from Cam Ranh Bay and Da Nang and accepted small gifts from them—an airman's pin, a Purple Heart, the armband taken off a dead Vietnamese fighter—talismans of combat that meant varied things to different men. She curled over her typewriter trying to capture these scenes in the irregular hours of her time off. One Chinese-American stewardess, a former ICU nurse who had signed up for Pan Am to ease her strained nerves and to improve her Cantonese, decided to go for a purser position and keep flying rather than return to nursing. The taxi drivers in Hong Kong still laughed at her American accent but she spoke passable Cantonese now.

The women had loved their time in Hong Kong—the meaningful work, the access, the lifestyle. And the social life too. In Hong Kong a stewardess could have two, three, five dates in a day if she wanted, and some of the women did. But they did not hunt for husbands. Anyone could get married, was the consensus among the Hong Kong crews. Not everyone could smuggle a newsreel from the war in Pakistan to Hong Kong for a journalist acquaintance or keep a cabin cool while coming under unexpected fire on a flight into Da Nang. To do that and then, later that night, after a date—because why go home at two?—to know the door code for the after-hours club where you could dance until the sun's light dimmed the glowing neon bar signs outside, to luxuriate in the company and the cocktails and the feeling of a young body, alive and all yours, moving passionately—that was the life they sought.

To Clare, anyplace else paled in comparison to Hong Kong. After the lush expatriate living and the duty and daring of war flights, flying regular passengers out of a domestic city in the same position she had held before felt like a demotion.

While Clare's two years in Asia had solidified her allegiance to Pan Am, they also sharpened her drive for more. In her earlier posting in San Francisco she had reported to a woman, the chief stewardess, and beneath her another woman served as the assistant chief. Clare knew that a position higher than purser for her existed somewhere, some-how. She was determined to fill that all but phantom spot. And yet, even with her loyalty and seniority, none of her three applications for positions in management went anywhere.

With a bank account relatively plush from her time in Hong Kong, Clare quit working for Pan Am. She spent a few weeks in Denmark and then enrolled in a language school in Lausanne. She could at least perfect her French while planning her next step.

Back in New York, management needed help. The enormous new 747 "Superjets"—hardly the catchiest nickname, but a 1969 staff con-test had yielded nothing better—required the airline to entice tens of thousands of new passengers to each destination, as Pan Am could now accommodate them. Some forty new InterContinental hotels opened in the 1960s, and the pace would increase through the 1970s. Customers could be lured on Pan Am planes to Accra, Quito, Lahore, Paris, and Manila, where, as in Beirut and Bangkok, luxurious accommodations featured local art and motifs in chic, modern forms. "When you've seen one, you haven't seen them all" went the InterContinental slogan.

And with these larger planes came hundreds of new stewardesses and new supervisory requirements. Executives had hoped that by setting up a scaffolding of restrictions around age, appearance, and marital status, stewardesses would always be young, beautiful, and single —because nothing pleased people more, as now CEO Najeeb Halaby had said. But the women were not content to merely go along with Halaby's plans.

The issue for stewardesses was not that they wanted the men on board the new 747s to avert their gazes from them or that they wanted to stop wearing makeup. The issue, rather, was that the women who had begun to work on airlines in their twenties did not want to stop when they got married or reached a certain age. In the early 1960s, eight stewardesses had hosted a press conference inviting journalists to "look us over" and determine if a thirty-something woman, single or married, looked like "an old bag."

For years, enormous numbers of stewardesses had rejected company rules in secret. They slipped subversive wedding bands on and off their fingers between flights. An estimated 30 to 40 percent of stewardesses hid their marriages from management and kept flying. They tailored their uniforms around widening midsections. One woman who did not want her name known told a reporter that her son had been born with 375 hours of flying time, about five months' worth.

A public venue by which to challenge age ceilings and marriage bans that were unequally applied on the basis of sex emerged in 1965 in the form of the Equal Employment Opportunity Commission

(EEOC). Among the first through the door were two American Airlines stewardesses. Others soon followed. Though protection from discrimination on the basis of sex had been a last-minute addition to race, color, religion, and national origin in President Johnson's Civil Rights Act of 1964, the stewardesses saw well-founded urgency regarding the dismantling of age ceilings. When they were fired, younger women filed in to take their place—graduating high-school seniors ranked the job first among future career options. In 1968—two years after Tori began to fly and one year before Lynne and Karen came to Pan Am—over 266,000 women applied for 12,000 positions across the American airline industry.

By October of 1966, the EEOC had collected ninety-two cases brought by stewardesses passionate about keeping their jobs. Some of the suits were more than a year old. None had seen rulings. Across industries, women's advocacy went unanswered. Discouraged, two dozen women—professionals, feminist activists, writers—founded the National Organization for Women.

Energized plaintiffs and attorneys plotted the points of prosecution in lawsuits against different airlines in district courts around the country. Delta put on a comprehensive defense in one of the first suits, filed by a stewardess who was terminated when her marriage was discovered. In another suit, United submitted an eighty-page brief detailing the reasons why only young, attractive women could address the "legitimate" business of meeting the social and psychological needs of its passengers: "Men *can* carry trays, and hang up coats and assist in the rare event of an emergency—they *cannot* convey the charm, the tact, the grace, the liveliness that young girls can—particularly to men, who comprise the vast majority of airline passengers . . . [men cannot] add to the pleasure of the trip, the loveliness of the environment or the ego of the male passenger."

Judges agreed. Over and over, they found in favor of the airlines in the first wave of lawsuits. One questioned whether sex discrimination was a viable subject of equal-opportunity law at all. Arbitrators waited for the EEOC to determine whether age and marriage rules violated its edicts. In the meantime, they seemed to approve of the role of a stewardess as written for a young, single woman—no possibility of gray hair, no specter of a husband waiting alone at home.

And yet, increasingly, bold activism was in the air. At the Miss America pageant in Atlantic City just after Labor Day in 1968, a few hundred feminists gathered with signs proclaiming ALL WOMEN ARE BEAUTIFUL. Laughing women tossed girdles, bras, and false eyelashes into a "freedom trash can" and agreed to interviews with female journalists only. At the Ritz-Carlton Hotel a few blocks away, a "curvy, hazel-eyed coed" won the first Miss Black America pageant. "Miss America does not represent us because there has never been a Black girl in the pageant," the newly crowned winner told a *New York Times* reporter. In Los Angeles, the National Organization for Women planned sit-ins at the Beverly Hills tiki bar Trader Vic's and the Beverly Hotel's Polo Lounge, which did not allow single women at the bar. At pubs and men's bars around the country, momentum was built martini by martini. In Manhattan Betty Friedan walked at midday into the Plaza Hotel's Oak Room. Two women sat down at McSorley's Old Ale House, where they incited hoots, alarm bells, and a mild brawl as they ordered beers. How far could a woman get in business, a letter from NOW to the EEOC asked, if she was legally prohibited from accompanying her male colleagues to a luncheon at the Oak Room or to after-work drinks at the Biltmore Hotel's Men's Bar or to any of the wood-paneled watering holes tucked around the corporate skyscrapers of midtown Manhattan?

In courtrooms around the country, airlines aimed to keep complainants tied up in legal battles in order to continue doing what they had been doing: hiring young, single, "pleasing" women to crew their flights. But the EEOC rolled into action at last. Age and marriage regulations applied only to female crewmates violated Title VII of the Equal Employment Opportunity Act, the commission decided in June 1968. Three separate cases soon confirmed the initial ruling. In one of these, American Airlines argued that part of the trouble posed by a married stewardess was the telephone calls her husband made to management. "However valid the airlines' arguments might be with regard to these women, there is nothing that distinguishes the husbands of stewardesses in this respect from the wives of pilots and stewards. Their spouses are also concerned about their mates' flight schedules," read one *California Law Review* summary of the case.

But in practical terms this meant only that a woman who had been fired for turning thirty-two or forgetting to remove her wedding band after June of 1968 could turn to the courts — often through one of the two unions that represented airline crews — to arbitrate her reinstatement. And airlines remained willing to use their considerable resources to fight in the courts, where certain judges expressed conservative perspectives on a woman's right to work. When it was still the case that the majority of stewardesses eventually left the job willingly — many stewardesses anticipated quitting when they had children, anyway — numbers were in the airlines' favor.

An international stewardess, at least, could always board a plane and fly away from the United States, where her allure was being dissected in courtrooms and pulpy novels. As long as she stayed young and beautiful, she could simply leave the American context in which the lurid characterization of her job had taken root. The *Coffee, Tea, or Me?* stewardesses had flown on Eastern, whose flight routes stayed in North America and the Caribbean. On airplanes and in crew hotels around the world — working hard on tired feet or bronzing their backs at the pool of an InterContinental — stewardesses waited for lawsuits to resolve. They wanted to keep flying. A crew, together, implied solidarity. If these women had not chosen to rock a cradle, many did not rock the boat either. Now they waited to see if they would face the choice of going quietly or waging battle in court.

———

Clare no longer worked for an airline. Her summer-school classes had ended; in Lausanne, she had her life savings with her. Maybe, she thought, she would stay in Europe.

A letter made its way from New York to Switzerland. "Would you be interested in coming back?" her former boss asked her. She offered Clare a position as supervisor, reporting to a new Manhattan flight service office. Management wanted closer supervision of its newer, bigger crews in Manhattan and Queens, where most of the stewardesses lived. Rather than requiring flight crews to travel to the airport for uniform changes, weight checks, and any necessary meeting with a supervisor, management would meet their needs closer to home.

Clare did not need to think about her answer.

The opulence and longing of the word *international* when Clare had begun to fly in the fifties—a word that conjured an alternative to the conformity of the postwar suburban straitjacket—had not dissipated. The implication of privilege of an evenly tanned body also remained. But as travel had become more accessible, as airlines courted new passengers, other images came along to join the airplane and the winter tan as signals of glamour. Magazine spreads and advertisements for clothing and perfume featured a woman in purposeful motion along a city street rather than a chic but languid couple in traveling suits standing alongside an airplane. In fashionable New York, the woman's pantsuit was ascendant. With her new job, Clare retained access to the airplane and the winter tan, but now she could wear her own groove into the Manhattan sidewalks too.

In New York and around the country, change spurred more change. A cascade of judges and juries across airlines and jurisdictions had begun to hand down verdicts. With new regulations, women with different circumstances—no longer exclusively young and single—would require more and different management in order to reflect a cohesive corporate image.

At first, state courts continued to rule against plaintiffs on the basis of new interpretations of the limits of the EEOC's reach. Sex *plus* marriage, one court found in a ruling for the defense at the end of 1969, did not violate discrimination laws; United Airlines had not fired the plaintiff because she was a woman or because she was married but rather because she was *both* a woman *and* married.

Two months later, a different United stewardess won nearly the same lawsuit in another court. Though the airline appealed, the next court only reinforced the finding, pointing to the source of the rule. "[The airline] was led to impose the requirement after it received complaints from husbands about their wives' working schedules and the irregularity of their working hours," the circuit judge wrote. "This is clearly insufficient." United was ordered to reinstate the defendant with accrued seniority, back pay, and legal costs.

For years, the two dominant airline-crew unions that represented stewardesses had negotiated with airlines over age limits and marriage rules, compromising their way toward agreements. Now, with courts upholding the same interpretations of the EEOC's rules and women increasingly emboldened to sue, the profitability of having age and marriage bans for the airlines dropped. The era of the age limit and the marriage ban was over. Stewardesses served on-board drinks with wedding rings on their hands. They filled out forms to extend airline health-care plans to husbands in graduate school. Staff turnover stalled immediately; in 1971, only one-ninth of stewardesses nationwide left their positions. By 1976, a job that women had performed for an average of two and a half years a decade earlier now kept women working for about six and a half years, and that number continued to rise.

Airlines had previously kept married women from flying, they claimed, due to the possibility of their getting pregnant, but now, the thinking went, if a stewardess could get married and keep her job, she could also get pregnant and keep her job. New regulations at Pan Am, responding to the specter of more and more married stewardesses, established a woman's obligation to inform the airline immediately upon finding out she was pregnant and take a leave of absence from that very moment until no less than sixty days after she gave birth but no more than ninety days; any longer than that, and she would be seen as quitting. She would under no circumstances wear a Pan Am uniform over a bulging belly.

All airlines agreed on the peril of a visibly pregnant stewardess. Beneath claims that a pregnant woman could not perform the duties of a stewardess, beyond stated fears for the safety of the fetus, there was the fact that a stewardess who was visibly pregnant would challenge both the aura of sexual availability airlines cultivated and the control over weight and appearance airlines still enforced. "By allowing a 'preggie' on board, management would obviously have to waive the weight restriction, right?" one stewardess asked in one of the many lawsuits that would stretch on for well over a decade. "And that would give away the name of the game, wouldn't it?" Within the thicket of appearance regulations that airlines enforced, women struggled to define ownership of their own bodies. They had wanted the legal right to be stewardesses *and* wives, to be older *and* beautiful. Now they wanted to be stewardesses *and* mothers.

The two airline-crew unions had spent years going back and forth between airlines and stewardesses. Legal battles over women's ages, bodies, and marital status revealed how essential it was for stewardesses to have a union of their own. Soon, pilots circulated handouts decrying the control that the "girls," who outnumbered pilots on planes if not in the union, might eventually wield over pilots' bargaining power. For their part, stewardesses had hugely different negotiation needs than pilots. A woman running for president of one of the two major unions, the Air Line Stewards and Stewardesses Association (ALSSA), wrote in her campaign literature, "This union is approximately ninety percent women, being 'led' by two men. How well do they represent the interests of the majority? Are we being well served?" The other major union was the stewardess division of the Air Line

Pilots Association, ALPA. In 1974, stewardesses split from the ALPA to form the Association of Flight Attendants, and ALSSA had begun to break down due to the different demands of its workers—domestic versus international airline stewardesses, pursers versus hostesses.

In the midst of this era of foment, Clare returned to work. Each supervisor would oversee novice stewardesses hired for the 747s—new hires like Karen and Lynne—as well as stewardesses newly permitted to continue working. Women now stayed on after they got married or had a baby, and some had returned to reclaim seniority years after they'd left to start a family, now that the lawsuits' resolution entitled them to do so. Clare would also steer two hundred or so stewardesses through fittings for new 747 uniforms (neither Clare nor anyone in her office called the plane a Superjet, no matter what the press releases said). Clare would review each employee's personnel file with her, parley with the union about grievances, and pass along accolades, all from an office near the Pan Am headquarters in the midst of Manhattan's skyscrapers.

As soon as she moved to New York, Clare learned that she could get a lot done in a week of nine-to-five days with a regular sleep pattern. She rented an apartment not far from the Manhattan flight service office. John Lennon and Yoko Ono's New Year message that year read, "We believe the last decade is the end of the old machine crumbling to pieces," but in Manhattan, at least, the machine hummed with activity. Every day Clare walked to her office among floods of neatly suited people, the yellow taxis gridlocking the midtown streets, and the glass office towers reflecting nearly identical buildings all around. Every afternoon at five Clare walked out of the office and into an evening's worth of free time.

The people in the office—seven or eight women and two or three male supervisors—got along well. They bought season tickets to the ballet to share. Every day the women dressed in business attire, the same clothing they expected of their stewardesses when they deadheaded (that is, when they traveled as passengers on a Pan Am assignment from one base to another) or flew for personal reasons on their airline passes: a dress, a skirt suit, or a pantsuit. One day Clare arrived at the office wearing slacks, a blouse, and a long vest, which led to a minor controversy. Did this count as business attire? How far could the definition stretch? Slacks and a vest, the women in the office decided eventually, was not business attire.

Clare and her fellow supervisors were the women who set such clothing classifications. If a stewardess arrived at JFK wearing inappropriate attire, the on-site manager pulled her aside, and she was sent to the crew room to change into something more formal, whatever was in her suitcase. Her look had to fit into the sleek lines of the Pan Am terminal, the Worldport (soon to be called the Spaceport as it expanded to fit the 747s). Stewardesses usually dressed for travel even in their time off, surrounded, as they might be, by tourists and the celebrities who favored Pan Am for both its routes and its excellent service. It was rare that a woman's personal attire landed her at the first step of a disciplinary action: a call to meet with a supervisor—like Clare —for a verbal warning. On anything resembling official business, the airline required a consistent image from its stewardesses. Uniforms were cut to hang the same way on women of similar body type. Every six months, stewardesses came to Clare's office for weigh-ins. If they were over the range dictated for their height, they received a written warning and were told to come in monthly for weigh-ins.

For some women, the weigh-ins were never an issue. Others ate hard-boiled eggs and tuna from a can for a month before each weight check. To Clare, the awkward unpleasantness of weight checks—no one enjoyed them—was mitigated by what she saw as reasonable disciplinary action around even the worst outcome. As long as a stewardess lost two pounds a month, she would keep flying.

Clare had no time to become bored by her Manhattan routine or frustrated with such supervisory roles, because she still traveled frequently for the new job. If a series of crews registered a persistent complaint about a single flight route or had a grumble about a crew member, a supervisor was sent to ride the route for a firsthand assessment. If a meal was too difficult to prepare in the prescribed time or if the air quality was bad on a longer flight, Clare would assess and report back, and management would take action. She still often flew out of JFK and worked on flights across the Atlantic or the Pacific and down to the Caribbean or South America. Now, though, she observed, examined, and assessed.

Among the first big projects Clare directed was the deployment of a new uniform. Pan Am had a new plane, the 747, for a new decade; the airlines representatives deserved a new look. All through 1969 rumors flew. "Stewardesses Get New Look at Pan Am," reported one article, detailing the shift in grooming courses from a "well-washed appearance" to instruction in the application of false eyelashes, eyeshadows, and wigs. Articles on new uniforms appeared in the *Manila Bulletin,* the *Auckland Star,* the *Osaka Mainichi Shimbun*, Berlin's *Spandauer Volksblatt,* and São Paulo's *Gazeta Esportiva*. Letters from patrons who preferred Pan Am's conservatism arrived in management offices. One frequent flier wrote directly to CEO Najeeb Halaby. "Do you really want to get rid of my business this much?" he asked. Halaby assured him that the coverage had been embellished and the natural look would prevail. Good, responded the letter writer. He would "continue to prefer Pan Am until my eyes convince me that you are becoming an airborne night club."

When Clare had begun flying, in the 1950s, training consisted of a few weeks of safety instruction in the Pan Am offices in Long Island City. No classes in makeup or the proper colors of nail polish, and no Miami training facility with its ditching pool to practice water landings. As a supervisor, Clare sometimes helped in the Pan Am Building with recruiting, and when she rose to manager, she traveled around the country and to India and Brazil to interview potential flight crew. It was something about enhanced lighting on the new 747s, Clare assumed, that required more attention to makeup and hair color. The airline still attracted the same type of applicants, women hungry to see the world, and still favored women with wholesome looks, foreign-language skills, problem-solving abilities, and friendly dispositions. But Pan Am dressed them differently now.

The new uniforms, designed by Evan Picone, reflected a departure from Pan Am's Tunis-blue suits. Stewardesses could choose dresses or skirt suits in Galaxy Gold or Superjet Blue. A bowler hat took the place of the pillbox. The dresses and suit separates could be modified for cold weather or the tropics, and the skirts were looser and shorter than previous uniform skirts. Now they could hit up to two inches above the knee if that was the wearer's preference. The jackets offered "a slimming, longish proportion above a softly moving skirt," a June 1970 press release read. Getting all stewardesses into the office for fittings was a chore. Clare called and called, left messages, coordinated appointments and pickups.

The office of *Wing Tips,* Pan Am's monthly company magazine, was on the same floor as Clare's office. A spring issue featured the new uniforms on the cover, and Clare composed an article for the feature detailing the ten-month process of creating a "uniform committee" with representatives from the Miami, San Francisco, and New York bases, gathering ideas from employees, hiring a designer, and defining the new uniforms. In her new position in management, Clare was among the first to see and approve the rib-cage-level faux vest of the dress, the single pleat running down the front left side of the skirt.

Sometimes Clare was sent to a training course, which she loved. Occasionally the entire office would close down for a morning for a group course built around the popular management principles of the day: I'm Okay, You're Okay; Discipline or Disaster: Management's Only Choice. In contrast to Trippe's top-down dictatorship, Halaby's leadership style leaned heavily on the current thinking out of business schools. He left six-minute ruminations and pep talks on a dial-in number for the company's thirty-nine thousand employees: "Fellow Pan Americans, this is Jeeb Halaby on the Pan Am line. Don't look upon youth fares as problems. Look upon them as prospects and love them. We need them." The reference was to a new program that offered discounted fares to passengers under the age of twenty-six; there was even a flight to Amsterdam that included organic breakfasts and rock music played over the sound system.

Clare needed no convincing to ensure her company loyalty. When she was a stewardess, she'd wanted to be a supervisor; when she was a supervisor, she'd aimed for manager. Once she was promoted to manager, she eyed a directorship or vice president position, on and up. Eventually the company offered her a director's position, but in a different city. By then she had married and needed a location that allowed her to stay with her husband, who was in the navy. Every position Pan Am offered her was in the wrong city. She bounced around for a decade and a half at manager level, directing supervisors, working in recruiting, handling union grievances. It occurred to her that if she had spent the previous two decades working for a company that was not as patently international as Pan Am, with its bases and directorships scattered across the United States and the world, she might have risen higher. But she never once considered interviewing with another airline or switching industries.

Over Clare's decades in management with Pan Am, her relationship to stewardesses would shift very slightly. A few former stewardess friends did not want to socialize with management. But during those first months of managing, she was not so far from having worn a uniform herself. She felt genuine enthusiasm for the new outfits stewardesses would wear on the new 747s. "Au revoir, figure-ruining boxy jacket and straight skirt!" she wrote to the company's thirty-five hundred stewardesses. "We're not at all sorry to see you go—and how we welcome your replacement!"

11

Open Skies for Negro Girls

N THE PHOTO ON THE COVER OF THE FEBRUARY 1969 SPECIAL
issue of *Wing Tips,* three women show off new uniform options as
they admire a model 747. Two wear the skirt-and-jacket outfit and
one wears the knee-length overcoat with its exaggeratedly pointed collar. Around each woman's face, bobbed hair curls gently. One of the
women is blond, another is of indeterminate Asian descent, and the
third is African-American.

Diversity among its stewardesses had been a company goal for
years, although within very limited parameters. A range of smiling,
eager-to-please women of varying backgrounds and from various cultures could reinforce the image of a global airline. In 1955 Pan Am began to hire dozens of Japanese-American women based in Honolulu,
its "Nisei stewardesses," ostensibly because they could speak Japanese
on Pacific routes. In reality, few of them spoke Japanese fluently. Still,
the women projected a corporate ideal—Najeeb Halaby hoped that
all stewardesses might be "more like Japanese geisha girls, prepared to
flatter and entertain the male passengers." For the stewardesses themselves, largely the children of recent immigrants raised in rural Hawaii,
travel presented both mobility and an opportunity to acquire the polish of upper-class America.

Such perceived exoticism did not apply to African-American women on Pan Am or any other airline. Black women attended the stewardess schools of the 1950s and early 1960s, unaffiliated training courses that promised to prepare aspiring stewardesses for successful interviews. These women watched as their white peers received offers from the small airlines that visited the schools while their own letters never arrived. Airline executives openly admitted that they feared losing their market share if the women who served mostly white passengers were Black. They were also concerned, as one *New York Times* article explained, that "existing and potential ranks of white stewardesses would dwindle fast if the 'glamor' of the job were 'down-graded' by the employment of Negro girls."

Lawyers with the NAACP and the Urban League built cases on behalf of the Black women graduating from stewardess schools with qualifications that should have guaranteed them jobs in flight service —they were educated, elegant, extroverted, and well within height and weight specifications. The lawsuits were widely covered in the American Black media. In the Soviet media, too, newspapers gleefully covered this visible iteration of capitalist racism. "Last year the State Department . . . was obliged to acknowledge that *Pravda* told the truth when it declared that bigotry barred negro girls from one of the most coveted careers open to women in this country," read a 1958 article in the NAACP's national magazine.

As lawsuits unfolded in courtrooms around the country, details about the extent of the racial bias against African-American women were splashed across newspapers nationwide. One applicant testified to her measurements on the stand: thirty-three, twenty-two, thirty-six, the feminine ideal. Another had been assessed as "too masculine" and having "an arrogant attitude," and in an especially acrobatic line of argument, the fact that she had brought a lawsuit at all was "evidence of an antagonistic attitude . . . such an attitude would constitute a lack of competence to deal with passengers on the airline."

Woman by woman, the aspiring stewardesses won their cases. In

The Pan Am Building rises above midtown Manhattan, looking austerely modern against the Chrysler Building, 1960s. *Pan Am Historical Foundation*

Stewardess wanted.
Must want the world.

This is a real want ad.
And the gal we want has to be someone special. Because she'll be living in the special world of the Pan Am® stewardess.

With a home base in San Francisco, Los Angeles, New York, Chicago, Washington, Miami or Seattle. And a second home all over the world. Europe, the South Pacific, the Caribbean, the Far East, the Middle East, Africa, South America.

She'll make as much as $550 a month after three years.

With food, housing and transportation paid for by Pan Am while she's away from home base.

Thirty days paid vacation a year.

Pan Am discounts after her first year. Up to 90% off on vacation travel for her and her eligible relatives.

And a great opportunity to see things, do things, learn things all over the world. It's a second education in itself.

But, back to our gal. How does she qualify for our Pan Am Stewardess training?

Well, if she's single, healthy, over 21, between 5'3" and 5'9", at least a high school grad with a knowledge of a foreign language, that's a good start.

There are more qualifications, but they'll require an interview. So, if you'd like to arrange one, just fill out our coupon. Or call a Pan Am ticket office.

Do it soon. The world is waiting.

Pan Am makes the going great.

Lynn Mechler, Hangar 14,
John F. Kennedy Airport,
Jamaica, N.Y.

I have the qualifications outlined above and would like to find out more about becoming a Pan Am stewardess.

Name
Address
City   State
Zip Code   Phone

"The world is waiting," a 1967 recruitment advertisement in *Time* told readers. *Pan Am Historical Foundation*

As low as $298* to Europe
and back by Pan Am Jet

*and you're
in U.S. hands
all the way!*

Not just pilots . . . but *Pan Am* pilots! U. S. airmen trained to exacting standards!

When it comes to U. S. ideas of comfort Pan Am stewardesses make you feel at home!

Wherever you go abroad, the U. S. is as close as the nearest Pan Am ticket office!

TYPICAL NEW 17-DAY ROUND-TRIP JET ECONOMY EXCURSION FARES

Boston–Shannon $298		Detroit–London $394
New York–London $360		Chicago–London $429
Balt./Wash.–Paris $413		West Coast–London $561

All-day Jet Economy Excursion fares good from October 1st through March 31st—lowest Jet fares ever!

PAN AMERICAN

A 1963 advertisement highlights American service across the Atlantic. *Pan Am Historical Foundation*

Lynne Totten as a newly minted Pan Am stewardess in her 1970 training photo *Lynne D. Rawling*

Karen Walker, center row, second from the right, training-class photo, 1969 *Karen Walker Ryan*

Karen Walker sits in the engine of a Boeing 707, early 1970s. *Karen Walker Ryan*

Tori Werner's training photo, 1966 *Tori Werner*

Tori Werner on a sightseeing trip during a layover in the Philippines, early 1970s *Tori Werner*

New stewardess Hazel Bowie in her training photo, 1972 *Hazel Bowie*

Clare Christiansen, center, along with six other former stewardesses, saw her promotion to supervisor detailed in the employee newsletter, 1969. *Pan Am Clipper, Vol. 20, No. 26, December 22, 1969. Pan Am Records, Courtesy of Special Collections, University of Miami Libraries*

Above: Cocktail service aboard a new Pan
Am Boeing 707, circa 1958 *Pan Am Historical
Foundation*

Right: In a *Vogue* photo shoot, models pose with
Pan Am bags at the new Worldport, 1960.
John Rawlings, Vogue © Condé Nast.

A 1964 class of
new stewardesses
amid the regular
traffic of the
Worldport
*Pan Am Historical
Foundation*

Pan Am's space-age Worldport with jet planes mid-boarding
Pan Am Historical Foundation

Above: "Seeing quadruple?" asked an employee newsletter article on twin pursers Elaine and Lorraine Vaughn, 1969. Pan Am Clipper, *Vol. 29, No. 14, July 7, 1969. Pan Am Records, Courtesy of Special Collections, University of Miami Libraries*

Above left: New recruits pose around a Pan Am globe at Miami's stewardess school, late 1960s. *Pan Am Records, Courtesy of Special Collections, University of Miami Libraries*

A special issue of the crew newsletter shows off both the new 747 and the new stewardess uniforms, 1969. *Pan Am Records, Courtesy of Special Collections, University of Miami Libraries*

Above: Stewardesses walk away from a Boeing 707, mid-1960s. *Pan Am Historical Foundation*

A stewardess serves dinner in the upstairs lounge of the 747, 1970s. *Pan Am Historical Foundation*

An advertisement falls in line with the era's innuendo, 1970s. *Pan Am Records, Courtesy of Special Collections, University of Miami Libraries*

Top left: Stewardesses on the ground in Saigon between flights, circa 1967 *Pan Am Historical Foundation*

Top right: The first symbol of in-flight service on Vietnam flights: a smiling stewardess greeting the soldiers departing from Saigon, circa 1967. *Pan Am Historical Foundation*

Middle: Troops on the ground in Saigon guard a Pan Am jet, 1966. *Pan Am Historical Foundation*

After a flight from Vietnam to Honolulu, servicemen receive leis from a stewardess, circa 1967. *Pan Am Historical Foundation*

Lynne Totten fills baby bottles
en route to Saigon for Operation
Babylift. *Karen Walker Ryan*

Karen Walker, left, and Tori Werner, right,
assemble and arrange bassinets for the youngest
babies. *Karen Walker Ryan*

The scene on the tarmac upon landing at Tan Son
Nhut *Karen Walker Ryan*

Karen Walker carries an infant
aboard. *Karen Walker Ryan*

President Ford greets the first load of infants at San Francisco International Airport. *National Archives, Gerald R. Ford Library*

Bassinets and cardboard boxes on and below the seats of one of the babylift flights *National Archives, Gerald R. Ford Library*

Get into this world as a PAN AM STEWARDESS

Stewardess recruitment materials advertised less war-torn international travel opportunities, 1970s. *Pan Am Records, Courtesy of Special Collections, University of Miami Libraries*

1962 one of the first plaintiffs smiled from the cover of *Jet* magazine in a Northwest Airlines uniform. "Open Skies for Negro Girls," read a 1963 *Ebony* headline. The Black newspaper the *Chicago Defender* praised American Airlines for promoting its first Black stewardess to supervisor; the Southern Christian Leadership Conference organized a boycott against Delta, whose numbers of Black employees remained low. In 1965, about fifty African-American women worked as stewardesses across all airlines.

By the time the 747 launch approached, nearly one thousand Black stewardesses worked across all airlines. Pan Am would soon employ about one hundred Black women, and though the airline hoped to hire more, recruitment efforts stalled, possibly due to recruiters' biases, the pressure on aspiring stewardesses to conform to white beauty standards, the savings required to float through training and the low-paying first few months of the job, or all of the above. In June 1969, the Pan Am employee newsletter, the *Clipper*, ran a feature profile of twin pursers from Philadelphia that made nothing of their race but highlighted the superb qualifications of the "vivacious twin girls," their identical faces, and their enthusiasm for the job. "You either enjoy dealing with people or you don't. And if you don't, you are not good stewardess material," said Elaine Vaughn. "There are so many places to see, so many people to meet. And we're really anxious to try the 747." The women appreciated the access they had to places and people, to European fashions before they hit the United States, to bargains—one of the twins had seen *Funny Girl* in Portugal for seventy-five cents—and to other similar-minded women. Even as Black stewardesses talked among themselves about the occasional vaguely racist comment at training school, many recognized in their fellow Pan Am stewardesses a genuine interest in people, in other cultures, in thinking outside their own circumstances.

To college senior Hazel Bowie, any airline would do. At seventeen, she had already looked up the minimum age requirement for a stewardess job. The man from the Urban League handed her applications from three airlines that were actively seeking qualified African-American crew: Northwest, TWA, and Pan Am. Hazel's only criterion was that the job get her as far from lakes, cornfields, and snowdrifts as possible.

Hazel had not been able to afford tuition at a historically Black college like Howard or Spelman. When Hazel graduated from high school, her mother wanted her to attend college classes at a school near their St. Paul, Minnesota, home. That way Hazel could save rent money and continue to help around the house and look after her four younger siblings. Besides, Hazel's mother could more easily keep an eye on her if she lived at home. "You have no fear," her mother used to warn her.

Hazel—stylish, quick, and not fearless but close to it—had moved out. Mankato State College, the rapidly growing institution that would soon become the state's second research university, was only eighty miles south but that was far enough to make living at home impractical. She could not stay home and take care of her siblings, work to pay for college, and study on top of it all, she told her mother. Better to live at school and work all the harder at odd jobs.

When Hazel flung her arms around her mother's shoulders and rested her head against her cheek, they looked almost like the same person, years apart. They had the same bright, light brown skin, the same high cheekbones, although Hazel's almond-shaped eyes and thin eyebrows were all her own. Hazel loved her mother, but she wanted to graduate in four years. She could not do it while living at home.

Hazel's answer to the unfamiliar, to challenge, had always been the same. When a Mexican girl at the all-white suburban middle school to which Hazel had been bused from downtown St. Paul invited her over to learn to make tacos, Hazel said yes. High-school jobs addressing letters for administrators and reading to blind students? Yes. Weekend gig at the telephone company singing, "Op-e-*ray*-tor, how may I *help* you?" into the line over and over again? Yes. Strut down a catwalk in the church basement for a fashion-show fundraiser? Yes. Work as a coat-check girl in college, then back to the telephone company in St. Paul? Yes and yes. She learned that she liked being around people; she learned that she did not like working in an office. Hazel always wanted more, always said yes.

In 1968, someone invited her to join an all-night drive from Mankato to Washington, DC, to participate in the Solidarity Day march on June 19 — Juneteenth — and Hazel said yes. Earlier, Dr. Martin Luther King had announced the Poor People's Campaign as a "middle ground between riots on the one hand and timid supplications for justice on the other." Here Hazel's mother drew the line. After Dr. King's murder in April, protests had broken out in Washington, DC, Detroit, Tallahassee, Denver, Oakland, and New York. Some exploded into riots. Thirty-nine Americans were dead, twenty-one thousand had been arrested, and twenty-six hundred were injured. In Washington in April, the violence had begun as a peaceful march but detonated with a rock thrown into a store window, a trash can tossed into the air, lighter fluid sparking a blaze in a tree. The police had shot and killed two Americans, including a fifteen-year-old boy. Nine hundred businesses were ruined, thirteen Americans dead, seventy-six hundred people arrested, and seven hundred residences destroyed. Thirteen thousand troops rolled into the city to impose a strained silence, arresting mostly Black citizens on the streets after a four p.m. curfew. Buildings of brick and stone lay crumbled on the ground. Hazel's mother was not about to allow her own flesh and blood to get anywhere near such violence.

"I'm not asking your permission," Hazel had told her mother. "I'm just letting you know I'm going."

That trip was Hazel's first real time in a state other than Minnesota, where she lived, and Mississippi, where she was born. At the march she listened to Coretta Scott King speaking to a crowd of around a hundred thousand Americans about how racism, poverty, and war worked together to, as she said, "deepen the hatred, heighten the bitterness, increase the frustration, and further alienate the poor in our society." Looking at the crowd around her—people filling the National Mall, wading in the Reflecting Pool, and standing on risers high above—Hazel saw, for the first time on an enormous scale, an inversion of the racial proportions with which she lived. The only other places where Hazel had been among a majority of Black people had been in the offices of the Urban League in downtown St. Paul and on her family's farm in Lena, Mississippi.

Lena had always made Hazel uncomfortable. Her family moved away when she was six, her parents heading north along with millions of other Black Americans. They visited the farm every year, marathon drives made almost without stopping. When Hazel was around eight or so, her mother had rushed, wild-eyed, toward her and her brother as they left a restroom during a rare late-night pause at a gas station. "You know you're not supposed to be in there," her mother had said fearfully. Hazel was confused. Her mother pointed at the sign: WHITES ONLY. Hazel had never seen a sign like that before. "How am I supposed to know that?" she asked. "We don't have that where we live."

"And that's why we live there instead of here," her mother said. "Now get back in the car." As they drove on, she explained to Hazel that this was why she and Hazel's father swapped turns at the wheel rather than stopping at a hotel in a town on the way. This was why they brought food and ate in the car instead of going to a restaurant. Not every establishment along the road would serve the Bowie family, and their physical safety was not guaranteed if they accidentally stopped in the wrong place. In the last edition of the *Negro Motorist Green Book,* which was published as Hazel finished high school in the late sixties, Memphis had two dozen Black-owned cafés, gas stations, and hotels that could be counted on to serve her family. But there were few such establishments outside of cities. The entry on Mississippi listed only three dozen safe stops across the state. And entire towns could pose an ever-spiraling threat to a Black family who stopped there after dark. Hundreds of signs using a particular racial slur warned Black travelers not to let the sun go down on them in whatever town they were passing through, and these so-called sundown towns stretched across Iowa, Missouri, Illinois, and all the states between Minnesota and Mississippi. Over years of family visits up and down the interstate, Hazel watched her mother and father drive, exhausted, over endless stretches of dark highway. Never in her life would Hazel find a way to express what she'd felt as a child in that gas station in the dark somewhere between St. Paul and Lena, looking at her mother's frightened face.

In Mankato, amid the flat farmland pocked by thousands of glassy lakes, Hazel signed up for every class on European history, literature, and art. Windy winters weighted the tree branches with heavy snow and piled the sides of streets with drifts almost as tall as Hazel. She read about the Continent, imagining cobblestoned streets carved through cities built long before the founding of the United States, frescoes in churches painted centuries before anyone had erected a steeple in her state. A Midwest high-school education had steeped her in American history, but Hazel wanted more, further back, farther away.

In her final year of college at Mankato State, Hazel did not care what sort of work got her out of town. But she had not forgotten her earlier dream of becoming a stewardess. She knew a girl in her neighborhood whose older sister worked on Northwest's airplanes. She took the applications, filled in her information, and waited for her interviews.

Her mother made no secret of her nervousness. She thought Hazel could use more fear. She should stay in St. Paul—if not at home, at least safe in her own city. "You got your degree, you've got to stay and do something for the neighborhood," her mother said.

"She's not doing anything for the community until she does something for herself," the people at church told her mother.

"She's always gotten into too much right here in Minnesota," her mother countered. How could Hazel keep herself safe everywhere else?

Hazel did not know. Contrary to what her mother thought, fear did hide somewhere inside her, but Hazel, as long as she was not alone, as long as she was accompanied, would go anywhere. She had never met the women on the covers of *Jet* and *Ebony*, but she knew they existed. She knew she would not be alone.

12

She's So Busy Being Free

KAREN WALKER HAD BEGUN TO RECORD WHAT SHE SAW AND felt in the places she visited when she left the army base in Germany. Please don't throw any letters out, she'd written to her mother from Europe; she wanted to see them when she returned home. She composed letters both for her parents and for herself. She tested voices, described scenes with lyrical turns of phrase and uncommon metaphors. Then she grew self-conscious; her letters were drab, she wrote, her days so full and vibrant in comparison. Still, she tried to capture what she saw.

The way Karen now traveled as a stewardess was a revved-up, businesslike version of how she had traveled on her own. When she had been paying for herself, she moved slowly, camping out, taking jobs, saving up, making friends. Now she moved through grand hotels, or at least hotels catering to the business class of the world—London's Athenaeum, Tokyo's Keio Plaza, the InterContinentals—but she still preferred to eat and wander alone rather than with the other women in her crew. Now Karen wrote in notebooks more than in letters to her parents. She cultivated routines in which she could observe the specificities of places and then jot her impressions down.

Karen hit the ground running in Hong Kong. She was up and out the door fast for her single day in the city; she ate as many dumplings and hot buns as she could, then went for a long walk, burning off the breakfast to make room for more Chinese food at lunch. She nosed into shops and markets along the way. She ate with her notebook on the table at Bernard's French restaurant—escargots, Caesar salad, a glass of wine—then fell into bed at eight to be ready for a middle-of-the-night call time. On Guam, she drove one of the Guamerica Inn's cars to nearby villages to buy the snacks she loved: seaweed, dried octopus, dehydrated fish. In Bangkok, at the Siam InterContinental hotel, with its bright pool and petting zoo, she visited with the gibbon who perched on her shoulder for hours at a time as she read and wrote by the pool.

Alan, Karen's on-again, off-again college boyfriend, was stationed in Maine. They had seen each other in Europe during Karen's time working at the service club and now began to date more seriously. Their plans formed and then shifted; they would live in Maine, she flying out of New York, and continue to date until Alan's discharge. Then a new plan—they would get married and move to Spain when Alan requested a station in Rota, the perfect place for her to refine the Spanish she needed for Europe and South America flights. No, she wrote, she had decided to move back home to California to fly Pacific routes for Pan Am out of Los Angeles. Marriage would wait.

Even amid the thrill of their first, fluctuating plans, Karen sensed an imbalance in their affections. "It's so much better," she had said to her friends once, "to adore than to be adored."

"Oh, no, Karen," her friends replied. "You're so wrong."

Karen disagreed. How boring to be worshipped. In her year teaching in California, Karen had watched her married friends in their suburban houses up to their eyeballs in diapers, their husbands off to work every morning, with no small measure of dread. Now Karen returned to California with plans for a new sort of eventual union with a man whose dynamism had captivated her all these years. His sense of scope—hiking in the mountains, traveling around the world —matched her own.

Karen found a waterfront apartment in Manhattan Beach five miles south of LAX and hung a poster above her bed: YOU ARE YOU, AND I AM I, AND IF BY CHANCE WE FIND EACH OTHER, IT'S BEAUTIFUL. She lived among low-slung homes on a grid along the beach, a place for bodysurfing and volleyball that had easy access to the airport. On the Pacific routes Karen requested, she came to know the varied textures of the cities on the other side of the same expanse of ocean she had dreamily stared across as a teenager.

Karen and Alan got engaged and then, weeks before the wedding, Alan disappeared. He went to Northern California for his bachelor party and never came back. Karen camped out on his parents' couch, crying. Radio silence for days, and then Alan—the boyfriend with whom Karen had spent five years connecting and then splitting apart, Alan of the dark hair, stormy stare, strong jaw, and dimpled chin, Alan who could backpack for days, ski hard, make Karen laugh harder— called it off. He had only just gotten out of the navy and was still figuring out what came next. He was not ready to be married yet, he said.

Invitations were taken down from refrigerators and out of drawers and thrown in trash bins. The invitations, the long white dress, reserving the church—all of it had cost money that Karen's parents could not really afford to spend but that they'd spent anyway for their only daughter's wedding.

From the start of the relationship, Alan had challenged Karen's expectations regarding the kinds of physical pursuits and travel she could undertake. He had admired that about her, the way she jumped toward anything new and exciting—skiing, swimming, skydiving. Now his cold feet inspired her next step. Karen would go on their extended mountain-to-sand honeymoon without him. She had already requested the time off, found the rental apartment in Jackson Hole, and bought the two tickets to Tahiti. The fares were cheap—she traveled for next to nothing and had provided the same benefit to the man she'd thought would be her husband—but the dates were firm.

Karen skied in Jackson and then she flew to Papeete, Tahiti, the capital of French Polynesia, on the flat northern fringe of the green mountainous island veined with valleys that all led to the surrounding sea. As Karen meandered along the piers, she heard boisterous American English wafting from a shoddy replica of Captain James Cook's HMB *Endeavour*, en route, like the original, to Australia. She walked toward the sound.

A few crew members scuttled around the deck, drinking and rigging the masts. "How about it?" one of the men said to Karen. The *Endeavour II* was still short a few crew members.

Karen's decision to jump aboard the *Endeavour II* was less intellectual than adrenal. She did not need Alan to find adventure. She sent a letter to her Pan Am supervisor and told him about this once-in-a-lifetime experience. She would be two weeks late returning to LA—maybe more, definitely not less. She hoped he understood.

The night before the ship left port, the crew ate dinner at an English newspaperman's house. The windows opened onto the sea, and the host had piled a huge table with food: roasted pig, chicken, taro root, coconut, breadfruit, and wine in jugs alongside. Tahitian musicians' ukuleles trilled in the night air and Karen danced until close to daybreak. A few hours later, the crew assembled on deck to set sail, and Karen skimmed out of port on a tall ship.

The first few times she straddled the yards, she felt terror as the roll and pitch of waves sent her closer than was comfortable to the skin of the ocean below. After a while, though, the fear abated. It felt like riding a horse. On quiet mornings, the creaking of the hull and whipping of the sails and endless ocean made Karen feel, in moments, disoriented. She knew where she was but she did not know when she was, she wrote in her journal. The ocean was timeless, solid blue in the distance and so clear right beneath her.

The ship was dilapidated. The head broke two days in; the refrigerator had never worked. But it did not matter. Karen learned to hang off the bow with toilet paper clenched between her teeth and to judge whether a squall would last long enough for her to wash and rinse her hair. Rarely did a sufficient rainstorm blow through. She swam instead. From the water Karen watched the men's bodies arc in great dives from the bow of the ship, the crew's shouts rising and fading as enormous swells lifted her up and tugged her down into their troughs. She had never been so tan, never so comfortable with salt on her skin. The only visible colors were white, blue, and light brown—sail and line; ocean and sky and denim shorts; varnished wood and guitars and tanned limbs.

The days contained tasks—braiding line, managing sails, the collective work of moving a ship through the Pacific Ocean—but evenings were filled with music. Every third person had brought a guitar, a ukulele, a tambourine. "Tom Dooley," "Midnight Special," "Jamaica Farewell," a little "Blowin' in the Wind." Some of the men even had real talent.

Karen dragged her broken heart across the Pacific as if it could be packed in a suitcase—everyone who met her could see its weight. She thought of Alan in the evenings as earth and wind tipped to sunset. She thought of the fun they could have had together and grew sad. Then someone would pull out a guitar, the sky would crowd with stars, and she returned to what she had found on her own.

The boat pulled into port in Suva, Fiji, on one of the country's 330-odd islands spread over a half million square miles of ocean. A guidebook called the town "Maughamesque," with its luxury boats sharing the dock with island schooners loaded with bananas or coconuts. On the streets, women in tailored dresses or saris walked past policemen in long white *sulus*, column-like skirts with zigzagging hems. Few tourists roamed the streets. Karen walked to the post office past stolid British colonial government and church buildings set against the bright colors of hibiscus, jade-green fields for soccer, rugby, and cricket, and low white shops behind columned arcades and swaying palms.

She tore open the letter from Pan Am that waited for her. Karen was out of work. The Pan Am institution would not accommodate someone who could not comply with its regulations. Karen had been a stewardess for only a year. She had little seniority and was not eligible to bargain for more vacation time. A set of fortuitous coincidences converged before the shock of her joblessness set in. Karen met a woman her age in Suva, a teacher. They had been born four days apart; strangers on the street mistook them for sisters. Karen made plans to stay on in Suva with the speed and logistical ease reserved for twenty-somethings in unusual circumstances. A neighbor was vacating a tiny house covered in orchids right near the beach. A teacher at the nearby school was going on maternity leave. Karen would fill in for the teacher and finally have time to write. In a few months, she promised her parents, she could hitch a ride on another boat to Australia, a country with both higher paychecks for teachers and new landscapes. "Some recklessly romantic part of you has always lived in a paradise like this," said the voiceover of Pan Am's promotional *New Horizons* video on Fiji. For Karen, it was true.

The rent on her Manhattan Beach apartment was a hundred and thirty-five dollars a month, and the place had an ocean view; Karen felt certain when she wrote her parents that her landlord could find a new tenant for it immediately.

But during her first few days in Suva, as her letter made its way toward her family in California, the consequences of her decision became clear. She'd wanted space from the unfinished business of her love life at home. Now she would be living on a tiny teaching salary with no savings account and no Pan Am employee benefits, including tickets at a 90 percent discount, and the decision to stay in the South

Pacific would be all but irrevocable. She pictured her father doing exactly as she'd asked: mailing along her teaching credentials, packing up her boxes, asking her landlord to return her security deposit.

Karen waited until the last day her return ticket could be used and went to the airport. She would return to her family, to Manhattan Beach and her apartment. And, she hoped, to her job.

The day she arrived in California, she drove straight to her supervisor's office armed with a manila folder of photos and press clippings covering the passage of the *Endeavour II*. She had not changed from her traveling outfit. Her hair hung past her shoulders, bleached from the sun, her skin as tanned as it would ever be, her body ropy with new muscles.

"See?" she said as she fanned the photos of the *Endeavour II* across his desk. A Pan Am stewardess had been the only woman on the ship's crew.

"I'm so mad at you, I don't want to talk to you today," he said, spinning his desk chair away from her.

Today, Karen thought.

The next day she returned with her folder. She had shaved her legs, put on more professional clothes, pulled her hair back. She said the right things: She would never bail on him again. She wanted her job back. She watched the supervisor as she kept pressing him, and he softened. She would be a model employee, she said.

"Don't ever do that again," he harrumphed. "Ever."

She slipped back into her life easily. The same flights, same apartment, same poster above her bed: YOU ARE YOU, AND I AM I, AND IF BY CHANCE WE FIND EACH OTHER, IT'S BEAUTIFUL. Karen's days at home became what they had been before. Early to bed, early to rise, every possible moment in the sun or water. She played volleyball until the sand stuck to her sweaty skin, then she jumped into the water, jumped back out, and joined another game. Someone was always playing, practicing, at any and all hours of every day. The Manhattan Beach courts hosted the biggest tournament of the professional beach volleyball circuit—fifteen thousand spectators lined the beach and the pier, swinging their legs toward the spray below to watch the games. Like the other women on the beach, Karen spent her days in a bikini. She watched the surf roil around the pier's tall pilings. She hopped on her bike to pick up food or beer. Without Alan, Karen dated the men she met on the beach—volleyball players, surfers.

All around Karen, athletes and airline people milled from beach to home and back again, all with their cultivated distance from the brief-case brigade in the suburbs around Los Angeles.

Karen had once asked her father, a produce broker and former athlete, why he and her mother had settled inland, in Whittier. He'd wanted to drive to work at the markets of East LA with the sun rising in his rearview mirror, he told her, and drive home in the afternoons as it sloped down behind him. She adored her dad for that practicality, the nest of security in which she had been raised. But Karen wanted nothing of the sort for herself.

She returned home not for stability but for its opposite, the easy variability of work and life she made for herself. Suva remained ac-cessible in the South Pacific. Karen would not be hemmed in again. Not that stewardessing was easy. When Karen worked, she worked hard. She spent what felt like entire days on her feet. But she fell back into her round-the-world flights just as easily as she had into life in Manhattan Beach. She flew Europes, up and over the western states on Flight 120 from LAX to London via the polar route, or out and across the Pacific to Hawaii and Hong Kong and down to the now-familiar South Pacific. There was a sense of accomplishment in the repetitive return to places, in the routines established, the familiarity of the vistas from small circular windows.

Since she'd returned to Los Angeles, Karen had occasionally been in touch with Alan. They ran into each other through the college friends neither wanted to give up. Soon they were spending time to-gether and then dating again. Alan still admired Karen's adventurous-ness and beauty. He explained his cold feet: When he got out of the navy, unsure of what he would do for work, no idea of what came next, it seemed to him that everyone's lives had moved on without and past him. Marriage offered a way for him to move forward too. At his bachelor party, with his friends from college, he had seen the cracks in their lives as married men. He did not *have* to get married, he realized.

Karen did not dwell on his explanation. Instead, she recognized the fact that among the men she had met, she had never found anyone quite like him. No one expanded her world the way Alan did; no one else pushed her to the edges of what made her comfortable. She had enjoyed other men but found with none of them the passion, for each other and for life itself, that she'd shared with Alan. The poster above her bed, IF BY CHANCE WE FIND EACH OTHER — now Karen had lived its dictum. She had chosen to come home without him, and they had come back together.

Months of a stewardess's life took place flying tens of thousands of miles above oceans and mountain ranges, making her inaccessible to anyone at home. She spent days and weeks in foreign cities. Only she knew what she did when she was "on the line," as crew terminology went. Any relationship a stewardess took part in held physical separation and something of "the chase" as a structural inevitability. Popular culture simplified this independence — the kind Karen treasured — and winnowed it down to basic sluttishness.

Imagery around stewardess sex appeal, once dominated by coy innuendo, shifted in the early 1970s toward overt implication. Language and visuals changed. The stewardess "authors" of *Coffee, Tea, or Me?* published a best-selling sequel in 1971: *The Coffee, Tea, or Me? Girls' Round-the-World Diary*. It detailed its American protagonists' now international exploits with swarthy foreign men. Ever racier books joined it on the shelf. *The Super-Jet Girls,* published the same year, promised "a mile-high frolic with the playgirls of the air!" *How to Make a Good Airline Stewardess* offered an "expert guide to the luscious stews of every airline" as well as illustrations of stewardesses on thirty-seven airlines, both naked and in uniform. *The Fly Girls* was billed as "the no-holds-barred novel of the stewardesses who swing in the sky—and on the ground!" One stewardess met a Playboy bunny who told her that, during her raciest sexual encounters, she kept thinking that "this was nothing compared with what the stewardesses were up to."

Advertising campaigns had grown yet more lurid, uniforms smaller and tighter. "Hi, I'm Cheryl. Fly me," read a 1971 National Airlines ad, part of an almost ten-million-dollar campaign. In a television spot for National, the camera tracked women from the shoulders up as they walked. In five-second intervals, they detailed their flight routes. "I'm Terry. I've got great connections in Miami and all over the Sunshine State of America. Fly me," said a smiling brunette in frosted lipstick, tipping her chin down and looking up playfully through her eyelashes. Pan Am fell in: "Take the world by the tail" read a mid-1970s advertisement.

National Airlines, which had at one point required its stewardesses to be blond, polled its female employees to determine the sixty most common women's names and labeled its fleet accordingly. On the nose of each plane, bubble letters spelled out *Nancy, Margie,* or *Barbara.* In National ticket offices, customers could purchase FLY ME mugs and T-shirts and Barbie-like stewardess dolls.

United Airlines promised "Extra Care" from beautiful stewardesses. An American Airlines advertisement dared passengers to "Think of Her as Your Mother" as text detailed all the ways in which a smoldering beauty might lavish care and consideration on a passenger: "A cool drink. A good dinner. A soft pillow and a warm blanket."

By the early 1970s, even the more conservative carriers had shifted their uniforms to reflect the changing times, introducing short sleeves, above-the-knee skirts, and knits that clung to the body. Some stewardesses appreciated the change; it was easier to launder jersey knits than wool, easier to move in soft, comfortable fabrics than in starchy suits. And even the raciest uniforms pleased some of the women who donned them. It could feel good to pull on a bold and brief dress like those seen on the bodies of high-fashion runway models since the mid-1960s. "Skirts were up, prudery was down," wrote feminist Alix Kates Shulman. A bare stretch of leg on a woman who chose to show it could signify youth and beauty in service of a woman's own pleasure rather than husband-hunting. "There are lots of girls who don't want to wait," miniskirt designer Mary Quant told a reporter. "Mini-clothes are symbolic of them."

But the airlines pushed it too far. Southwest Airlines stewardesses walked through airports wearing red hot pants and white lace-up go-go boots between flights on which they served "love potions" and "love bites" rather than drinks and snacks. They could slide a pair of black vinyl pants under their black-and-white belted minidresses for what the airline called the "wet look." The new advertising campaigns reflected the speed with which stewardesses' physical beauty and sexual empowerment, in the public mind and marketplace, had made them into vamps.

"We like flirtations when we have the freedom of choice, but do not believe that just because we are Hostesses we must endure the reputation of professional flirts," read a letter that union leadership at Continental submitted to management. Articles detailing the new American uniforms explained that shorter hemlines made bending and reaching in flight difficult. "A girl wants to attract a guy but not that way in public," one stewardess said. And for the new women of color among the crews, who had fought for access to a respectable job, revealing uniforms were yet more fraught.

Whether an unmarried woman wore a miniskirt or slacks, whether she was Black or white, there seemed to be no good answer for the question of what role she played in society. Across the country, hundreds of thousands of women lived on their own now. Amid the rising tide of women filing for divorce and those who were waiting longer to marry, women bought their own furniture for apartments they shared with no one. In Minneapolis, Mary Richards lived alone. In magazines, feature articles on the now established trend betrayed a raised eyebrow through the details reporters used to set the scene of their subjects' singledom: the anemic vegetables in the fridge, the cigarette butts under the couch, the tattered teddy bear on the bed. Other articles debated which women could be called "liberated" and what such liberation meant. Gloria Steinem was "a liberated woman despite beauty, chic and success." Twenty-something women who embarked on international vacations in pairs tested the term. One *New York Times* journalist wrote, "The single working girl from Middle America may not yet be liberated, but she has more mobility and money than her mother ever dreamed possible." Liberated or not, single women sought new labels. "Do not dare call me a swinging single," one woman told a reporter. "I'm an unmarried grown-up." A study of twenty-five hundred singles found women happier than their male counterparts. *Science Digest* marveled that women were, in fact, "stronger than single men in meeting the challenge of their position."

Certain challenges remained real. "No unescorted ladies will be served," read the signs at bars and restaurants across the country. An unmarried woman could not get a credit card in her own name. Prohibitions against birth control for unmarried women would not be dropped until 1972.

And at the same time, here were so many stewardesses—married and unmarried—flying around the world together. Off duty, unescorted in other countries, they drank in bars, collected envelopes filled with Pan Am's money in local currency at the front desks of hotels, and used birth control as they wished. When they were working, their self-presentation, from hemlines to hats—and the way they applied makeup, when they smiled, what they said—served the corporations, the men who ran them, the men they sought as paying customers. The women were more or less willing to go along with such visible constraints to earn so much autonomy.

Some National stewardesses refused to wear their FLY ME pins. At

Halloween, three stewardesses on a New York–to–Miami flight put one of the pins on a cardboard cutout of a witch. If only the airline would insert a *with* between the two words of the slogan, one woman told a reporter. NOW filed a request for a restraining order in Florida's Dade County Circuit Court to render illegal the entire campaign. It was denied.

The campaign continued as the airline defended it to the press. National stressed that "Fly Me" was meant to emphasize the personalized experience a passenger could expect to have on the airline. "The stewardesses become an extension of the airline," the airline's PR representative told *Time*. "We had no preconceived idea of injecting a suggestive leer into the campaign."

Karen and Alan got married, ending the years of distance that had separated them, the on-and-off rhythm of their relationship. They moved briefly to Mill Valley, where Karen's parents did not attend their small and simple wedding. They visited a month later, though — an implicit blessing. Friends would later describe the couple as competitive. When they skied, they went fast, speeding away from each other; when they hiked, it was with vigor. Now Karen hoped that their mutual drive would push their lives forward together. They moved to the mountains above Lake Tahoe. Alan got his commercial pilot's certification and became one of the glut of military pilots applying for the same jobs on the airlines.

The move meant Karen had to drive forty-five minutes to the Reno airport and hitch a ride on a small plane down to Los Angeles. Her employee pass entitled her to a seat in the cockpit if the flight was full. She left a junky Oldsmobile at the airport. It required a jump-start to get going but if she missed a connection on her way, she could get down to Whittier to visit her parents for a night.

She flew regular routes and army charters out of LAX, across the Pacific to Hawaii, and up and over the vast western United States and arctic ice fields on the polar route to London. Returning from London over Greenland and Canada, she traced the scant roads in the verdant forests of the West as the plane trawled southward.

If she lucked into midday over Saskatchewan, the Dakotas, Montana, Wyoming, or Idaho, Karen glimpsed a thin strip of a road, white or gray against the green, and she followed the winding curve out from a town into the thick trees as far as it led. *That's where I want to be,* she thought; not too far outside of a town, a ranch in the mountains, at the very end of a road somewhere.

Maybe there she would find time to write. Karen's aspirations had grown. Really, if she let her mind get carried away, she imagined that Alan would be a photographer—he was wonderful with a camera—and she could write. If she could be anyone else in the world, she would be Frances FitzGerald, she thought sometimes. *Fire in the Lake,* FitzGerald's work of reporting in Vietnam, won that year's Pulitzer Prize and National Book Award. But Karen had no backing from a magazine, no money of her own to live on while she wrote. She dreamed of having the time and energy to compose her notes into something meaningful and then sending it off to a magazine, but she was responsible for the rent on their small A-frame in Squaw Valley while Alan applied for pilot jobs.

When a pilot position for Alan failed to materialize, they moved to Missoula, Montana, so he could go to graduate school for environmental planning. With her regular paycheck, Karen paid the mortgage on a little house in town at the base of range after range of mountains layering into the distance. Karen liked the Montana women. They could kill an elk, chop wood, and hike anything in front of them. They were as far from the suburban California girls she'd grown up with as anyone she had ever known. Here was a place where she and Alan could live a shared life of excitement against a landscape of drama and substance.

Except that Karen and Alan still could not seem to get on the same page about their future. Alan wanted to move to Sun Valley after he finished school; Karen had suggested they look toward Salt Lake City, with its central airport and quality skiing. He thought she wanted him to get a corporate job, that she had forgotten exactly whom she had married; she thought he was sleeping with other women. He might want a divorce, he said.

Karen began to bid longer flights. She went to Bangkok and her gibbon; to Hong Kong and dim sum and escargot. Flights out of Saigon were outnumbering incoming planes as American troops began slowly to come home from Vietnam. Good, Karen thought. She read every issue of *Newsweek*. She knew about My Lai and the *Pentagon Papers*.

The out-and-backs from Saigon to the various R&R destinations, the flights around Guam and Hong Kong, the regularly scheduled and charter flights all started to blend together in Karen's mind. She did not stay long in any single place. To her eye, the soldiers on the planes were all equally tired, equally afraid, equally eager to be done. On one such flight, Karen sat in the jump seat, preparing for takeoff, listening to the purser read the "welcome aboard" message.

She noticed the tone first. The message sounded buoyant, chipper. Karen knew what was happening. The purser was reading, not thinking. She had not registered the specificity of the particular flight whose doors now swung closed. Maybe she had not slept well in their scant hours on the ground or maybe she had spent a late evening under a bar's neon lights.

"And please," she concluded, "have a pleasant day in Saigon or wherever your final destination is."

Next to her, another stewardess stared into the middle distance, stricken.

"Are you fucking kidding me?" shouted one soldier from the rear.

Soon after that, Karen began to stand by the door as the soldiers disembarked onto Vietnamese soil. She hugged a few of the men as they departed. Then she found herself wishing them luck. On one flight she went further. She hugged a man goodbye and whispered, "Come back alive." To the soldier behind him she said, "Don't be a hero."

About a half dozen GIs had walked down the stairs when a lieutenant rushed up to her. "You can't be saying that," he said. He began to yell and his face reddened. An ugly little lieutenant just like the ugly lieutenant in Germany. "You gotta go sit in the cockpit until all of my men are off the plane. Sit in the cockpit," the lieutenant ordered Karen.

The officers were the problem. As if she answered to *him,* she thought, even as she closed the cockpit door behind her.

13

Splendid Capitalist Airplanes

PAN AM'S REVENUES IN 1968 HAD BEEN ALMOST 20 PERCENT less than the year before, and 1969 was worse: $12.7 million in losses in the first six months of the year. As the 747s hit the tarmac, the importance of their success loomed. In January of 1970, Mrs. Nixon had christened the first operational jet with a spray of colored water, but at the ceremony neither she nor CEO Najeeb Halaby could then figure out how to make the gold lever of the hose turn off the flood. In the 1970s, annual losses reached $48 million.

Pan Am had launched a twenty-million-dollar advertising campaign in ninety-seven countries and thirty-two languages. America alone could not fill its 747s, as Juan Trippe had argued to President Johnson, but the wider world could. Pan Am's ability to meet the increased load demands of bigger planes would depend on convincing passengers outside its home country to fly Pan Am rather than a national airline like Air India or KLM.

Neither the United States nor the wider world cooperated. Pan Am had hired hundreds of new stewardesses and its marketing department was drumming up new business, but its new planes had arrived as a mild economic recession began in the United States, as oil prices rose, and as maintenance and labor costs spiked. Under eight-foot-high ceilings, empty seats stretched back in rows. Revenue projections for the early seventies looked dim.

Among the airline's 81,430 miles of routes, new competition crowded the most profitable. Some routes were sheer losses on the corporate balance sheet. Flights to Moscow and Pago Pago and Saigon were undertaken for diplomacy, for the national interest, to demonstrate the sense of showmanship in which training manuals instructed the classes of stewardesses who still left Miami eager to see the world. But the airline was "locked in a shrinking box, with the top, bottom, and sides all closing in at once," Najeeb Halaby had said as he took the reins of the company. Pan Am no longer had a protective relationship with the U.S. government, but it now had increased competition, regulated fares, and ever-rising costs.

Moscow flights had never been cost-effective, but a vague trendiness had built around them in the years since the route began. Visits to the city were, as one journalist wrote, "Not the sort of travel designed to lure tourists primarily interested in surfaces (walls, paintings, anonymous faces, and so on) . . . [but] designed for those concerned with what lies beneath the surface (the people behind the walls, the thoughts and feelings behind the faces)." The *New York Times* published a travel feature on tourism in Moscow laying out an itinerary of sightseeing, opera, and toying with the state security teams—"try James Bond tricks like placing a book a certain way in a suitcase for your own amusement."

In the briefing before Hazel Bowie's first flight to Moscow, the crew supervisor had told her that the Soviet stewardesses she would meet on a flight crewed jointly by Pan Am and Aeroflot were not permitted to talk to the Pan Am employees. The cordiality of the Soviet stewardesses would not extend past professionalism; Hazel should not expect an invitation to anyone's home during her three days on the ground in Moscow. All Aeroflot stewardesses had been recruited from the Komsomol, the youth Communist Party wing, and trained by the KGB,

Hazel learned. For the privilege of foreign travel and foreign money, they were required to stay in groups of three on non-Soviet soil.

Few Pan Am stewardesses had any proficiency in Russian or wanted to fly Moscow routes—so few that the airline offered a monthlong language program in the city in 1971. Some thirty stewardesses signed on. Some took the courses seriously, attending their three hours of daily classes and the group excursions every afternoon, while others skipped out entirely. They preferred attractions in the city streets, taking in bread lines, cathedral spires, and faux-baroque subway stations. They washed pierogi down with vodka at unadorned restaurants. One stewardess bought a samovar at an antique shop and convinced a Marine at the American embassy to keep it until the trip's end, when she could smuggle it out of the country. Another woman had thrown a trench coat over her clothes for a day of sightseeing and had to stare down the drunkard who shouted at her in a crowded street that she was a spy.

On the ground the stewardesses were immediately—and, for many, intensely—aware of surveillance. They observed the woman sitting at the end of each hall at the state tourism agency's national hotel, taking notes. They asked one another if they too had woken up in the middle of the night, bleary, wondering if the flashbulb going off was a dream. They measured the distance between the door and the interior wall of a hotel room and the distance in the hallway between hotel-room doors and discovered three feet of unaccounted-for space, wide enough for a person to sit inside, watching. They told stewardesses new to the route not to criticize the Soviet Union in the hotel rooms or complain about the paltry food or the sandpaper-like towels or the bare bulbs in the ceilings. At first they went out in groups; as time passed and some grew more comfortable, they began to venture out into the city on their own.

After a while, they made up their own "James Bond tricks." One of these was "Shake the KGB." The women would go into the metro, take it one stop, get out of the car, shuffle along the platform under an arched and opulent ceiling, then dash into the next subway car. The men tailing them were rarely easy to shake, but the women had fun in the trying. The old woman at the hotel who noted their movements could be tricked too. After lunch one day, at 1:30 on the dot, half a dozen stewardesses walked out of their rooms and traded places. Five minutes later, they switched rooms again. They did it again five minutes later. One stewardess saw the woman frantically scribbling. She approached her, laughing. *We were joking,* she tried to tell her with words and hand gestures.

On nearly empty flights, stewardesses spoke to American diplomats, elderly women who had not seen their families in years, and, once, Mike Wallace on his way to research a *60 Minutes* segment. The only Westerners the stewardesses saw with frequency were journalists and diplomats. No one knew what, if any, actual danger the Soviet Union posed to a crew of young women on their way to or in Moscow. A nervous stewardess might hand a list of the flight crew's names with a bottle of champagne to a U.S. embassy staffer, "just in case anything happens." Some women stayed in uniform for the duration of their three-day layovers for the protection they felt a Pan Am uniform conferred. Others made sure to toss their company coats on top of their off-duty outfits.

Hazel began to fly soon after her graduation from Mankato State. Though she had applied to work on three airlines, she interviewed only with Pan Am, the first to respond and grant her an interview. She arrived in the morning, and short Hazel considered her odds against tall, gorgeous women of seemingly every nationality. The Pan Am representative told her to return in the afternoon. Though her mother had put up a fight—she had refused to take Hazel to the airport when she left for training in Miami—Hazel knew this was what she wanted. It was not only airlines seeking Black American crews; Hazel saw advertisements for all sorts of companies in new compliance with the EEOC's hiring mandates. As she flew to Miami, completed training, moved to New York, and embarked on her first flights, Hazel knew that she was participating in something larger than her own goals.

At first, every location she flew to dazzled her with its sheer distance, literal and metaphorical, from Minnesota. Caribbean out-and-backs, the occasional flight through South America, a London or a Paris. Unintimidated by the cold and having recently purchased an enormous paperback of *A History of Russia*, she saw Moscow listed as an option and bid the route.

It felt to Hazel, as she walked along the broad avenues of the city on her first trip to the USSR, that the Soviets had never seen anyone quite like her. In the United States, people knew she was a Black American; on a flight in a foreign country or in a customs line somewhere other than New York, she was seen as anything but. With her thin eyebrows and defined cheekbones, dark eyes that drooped slightly down at their outer edges—a dramatic face that Hazel made more dramatic with makeup—she was sometimes taken for a dark Southeast Asian. Other Black American stewardesses reported similar perceptions. In Iran a Black stewardess had to convince a military guard that she was an American, not a dark-skinned Iranian. Women were taken for Caribbean or complimented on their fluent English. Passengers asked where a stewardess was from—"My husband thinks you're from Jamaica, but I bet you're from Trinidad." When the stewardess answered, "Philadelphia," the passengers did not hide their disappointment. Some nonwhite stewardesses felt they were of interest to white American passengers only if they could be compartmentalized as exotic. Some wore their hair in tidy Afros puffed under their derby hats—hair short enough that the hat did not look clownish, long enough to highlight its natural texture—as a gesture of solidarity and a declaration of identity. *Let me make it clear who I am,* one new stewardess thought as she went to the hairdresser in Miami halfway through training.

"Who sat in this seat before me?" a white passenger might ask as

he boarded a plane in Africa or South America. In the early days, as
diversity across airlines began to rise, some stewardesses made sure
that if two women of color worked a single flight, they split cabins
so that any racist passenger would be served by a demurely smiling
nonwhite stewardess. *If you've got a problem, you've still got a problem,* one woman thought. Others noticed that certain coworkers po-
sitioned themselves to room with one another on layovers, leaving a
Black woman in an odd-numbered crew with her own room. As if she
had been dying to have a roommate in a luxury hotel in the first place,
that stewardess thought.

Many Black stewardesses wanted to fly to Africa to experience the
feeling of being in a complete majority. Flying around the world, standing out wherever she was—for her skin, clothes, bearing, or a combination of all three—one stewardess said, "allowed me to be bold, be
beautiful everywhere." Skin color meant different things in different
places. On one of her first trips to Puerto Rico, when Hazel checked
into a San Juan hotel, the clerk—a dark-skinned Black woman—began to speak to Hazel in Spanish, and Hazel felt the collision of both
of their assumptions. Her own skin color made the clerk assume she
was Puerto Rican; to Hazel, the dark-skinned clerk should have been
speaking English.

In Moscow, Hazel noted all different kinds of people drifting
among the mostly white Soviets. People looked Asian or Mediterranean. Small waves of Africans and African-Americans had immigrated
to the USSR in the 1930s and again in the late 1950s, when Cold War
propaganda questioned the United States' claim of world leadership
at the same time that the nation brutally repressed minorities. African
students from Soviet-allied nations had come to Moscow to study in
the late 1950s. Some had stayed. Now, in the early 1970s, Hazel occasionally saw Black Cuban medical students in the city.

Hazel's skin color set her apart, but so did her clothing. While
other Pan Am stewardesses liked to wear their uniforms in Moscow,

Hazel preferred to wear her gabardine coat over her own clothing. So many women walking down the street in the same clothing felt, to her, as if she had enlisted in the military. People looked at her on the streets anyway. She was nearly always the only Black woman around—and certainly the only Black woman who wore a green and yellow leather skirt with cowboy boots, who preferred vibrant dresses, and who did not leave a hotel room in any country without either bloodred or wine-hued lipstick on.

After looking at lacquer boxes one afternoon, oohing and aahing with a crewmate who spoke some Russian, Hazel's friend told her how the women around them had dissected Hazel's appearance, her green cowboy boots, her green eye makeup—green was her favorite color—and her skin color. On a later trip, she and a coworker had been walking on the street one summer night in the ten o'clock dusk, and the coworker joked that the way everyone looked at Hazel, it seemed as if they wanted to kidnap her. Russian eyes ate up every inch of Hazel.

"If you think someone has been in your hotel room, going through your bags, you're right—they have," the other stewardesses told Hazel before her first trip to Moscow. And indeed, her makeup moved around her bathroom counter. She would come back to her room to find her skirts folded in her suitcase differently. As she walked around Moscow and observed the women in their black, gray, and brown clothes, Hazel could not begrudge the housekeepers their curiosity concerning an American's clothing and cosmetics.

And she liked Moscow. Even when there seemed to be nothing to do, Hazel found something. She waited in line with the Soviet women to go into a new cosmetics store on Red Square, a thick snake of people stretching along three blocks. She saw the sights, including St. Basil's Cathedral with its elegant frescoes, ornate ironwork, spinning tops, and gold domes glinting in the summer sun or faintly glowing in a dull winter twilight. In the rest of the city, men with long coats and straight backs waved cars along avenues slick with rain or snow. Extravagant old buildings stood alongside newer, unadorned blocks of flats so wide you had to stand in front of them and swivel your head left to right a full 180 degrees to take them in fully.

That afternoon, outside the new cosmetics store, women waiting in line on the street around Hazel mirrored their city. They wore dull clothing—*every shade of blah,* Hazel thought—and pulled scarves over their faces in the winter; Hazel had heard that the KGB could read lips. But she saw that the women wore immaculate haircuts and carefully composed makeup. Soviet women were portrayed in the West as dowdy, stolid as they worked beside men. A decade earlier, an American Airlines stewardess had won a trip around the world, including an unusual stop in the USSR, which then very rarely offered Americans visas. She had written a series of articles for the *Chicago Daily Tribune:* "American Girl Introduces Russian Girl to Lipstick." In 1959, Yves Saint Laurent had premiered Dior's "New Look" in Moscow; Western photographers had followed the willowy French models in bright reds and greens through the gracious central greenhouse arcade of GUM, the famous department store on Red Square. Their cameras snapped the models' wide circular hats and defined red lips meant as a contrast to the drab kerchiefs of Russian women, who looked on with curiosity, confusion, and perhaps disdain or pity for such objectification. Hazel observed more complexity in how Soviet women presented themselves. She always trusted her own experiences over what other people said she should expect. Moscow was no different.

She requested more Soviet trips. There was no place like Moscow. On one flight, a passenger invited her to see the Bolshoi Ballet. The experience was impressive in every way, from the Grecian columns of the famed Bolshoi Theater facing the park—across the flat greenery of Theater Square, the Pan Am sign glowed in the bay window of the airline's office at the grand Hotel Metropol—to the extraordinary dancers on the stage. It was music she would never play in her own house, but the dancing was superb, the women of the corps spinning across the stage in precise unison behind the prima ballerina.

On another flight, Hazel served martinis to two Americans on their way to scout for circus acts. "Come along," they said. "We'll give you tickets."

Hazel walked into a big, empty barn of a building, watching the men on high wires, the tigers roaring, bears juggling, and animated clowns. In 1919 Lenin had nationalized the circus; it was, in every way, the people's entertainment. Its acrobats acted out Russian folk legends and parables with their feats of daring and grace. Tiger trainers used batons, not bullwhips. By the second half of the century, acrobatic training was so rigorous that a woman tossed across open air in a trapeze performance would have had her choice between performing in the Bolshoi or the circus.

Moscow dwarfed the human scale with the width of its avenues, the massive columns on the façades of the important buildings, the metal sculptures of important men standing twice as tall as their natural height. Moscow was a city of bronze busts: Vladimir Lenin, writer Alexander Pushkin, and Iron Feliks, the founder of the Soviet secret police. On a street corner one day, Hazel found herself standing in front of a bust of Pushkin. She examined Pushkin's expressive mouth and wild hair. Hazel thought, *It can't be.* But what Hazel intuited was true. "His family came from Africa way back," another stewardess, a Russian speaker, told Hazel. Even in Moscow, Hazel thought, she found Black people.

Americans had begun to travel to the Soviet Union by now, but few were as beguiled by Moscow as Hazel. Celebrated war correspondent Martha Gellhorn visited Moscow the same year as Hazel's first trip. Also the same year—1972—President Nixon and the First Lady visited the USSR and China. The presidential trip was a once-unbelievable reversal; American troops remained in Vietnam, fighting by proxy with these same world powers.

After six days, Gellhorn could not wait to leave. Boiling hot, hungry, bored, dry—she had found so much less chilled vodka than she hoped—Gellhorn had been uncomfortably intimidated by the police state, an unusual emotion for a war correspondent visiting a city at peace. "When the flight was called, I was first aboard the British Airways plane. A cool correctly smiling English stewardess stood by the door. I said, 'I'm so glad to see you, you'll never know how glad I am to see you,'" she wrote. Also: "I overcame a desire to kiss the carpet which was technically British soil and sank back into air conditioning and iced drinks, served with a smile, and read avidly the little booklet that lists all the junky things you can buy on our splendid capitalist airplanes."

Hazel bought lacquer boxes in Moscow to bring home and scarves for herself and for her mother. At GUM, the floors were so old she thought she saw puffs of dust rising from the floorboards where she stepped and motes floating through the four-story arcade. She noted the filigreed iron railings on the second floor and the well-heeled women lining up at glass counters. They asked to touch hats and books, lipsticks and scarves—everything was kept behind the counter; there was no unmediated access to these precious goods. The women walked out with packages wrapped in paper and crisscrossed with twine. Gellhorn had purchased thick and ugly upholstery fabric at GUM to fill her suitcase going home; she'd packed little more than gifts on her way in and feared the implications of an empty suitcase to the KGB on her way out.

Hazel learned to bring her own food on Moscow flights so that she would not have to rely on the available chicken, borscht, and canned vegetables at restaurants. Even hotel restaurants served little. The Metropol's restaurant was "a Russian peasant's dream of capitalist splendors—immense candelabra, oversized lights, heavy furniture," one correspondent had written in the 1930s. But its menu was an ideal that could not be reached under current circumstances. The Pan Am Moscow station chief's wife, who waited in line with Soviet housewives for limited quantities of meat, served pointedly small portions to the foreign businessmen and their wives who came to her dinner parties. Everything was a statement.

But even amid the scarcity, Hazel was engaged by novelty. Where else could she go to a restaurant and sit down to a menu replete with delicacies only to be told that none were available? Though she wanted to ask what they *did* have for her to eat rather than choosing from a fictional menu, she learned that waitstaff disliked skipping the ritual of menu consultation. Hazel ordered item by item, pantomiming desire for something she knew she would not receive. In New York she packed hard-boiled eggs, cold chicken, a can or two of tuna fish, maybe mayonnaise, a gallon of water.

To Hazel, the value of Moscow was its total difference from Rome or New York or Minnesota. Moscow was a place where nothing on the menu was actually available. A place where malls looked like greenhouses, where women lined up for lipstick. A place where fun and food were subversive statements—nowhere else did Hazel see this so openly.

The Aeroflot stewardesses gave Hazel recipe cards. If she wanted to learn to make piroshki or goulash in her New York apartment, she could follow their directions. After years of flying Moscows, Hazel would regret that she had never seen how any Russian lived. The Aeroflot stewardesses were, as advertised, never intimate. But her initial briefing had been incorrect—they did not appear fundamentally limited by the rules they faced. In the recipe cards, Hazel recognized an attempt at what connection was open to them.

14

De Facto Feminist

THE UPSTAIRS LOUNGE WAS LYNNE TOTTEN'S FAVORITE AS-
signment on a 747. Upstairs, the cabin was shaped like a cathedral, despite its diminutive size. Boeing's designers had envisioned tall
banks of windows each topped by a chevron that pointed up to the
ceiling. Windows, one after another, visible behind the low backs of
dining chairs spaced around wide tables, led passengers' eyes to drift
up to ceiling lights. Higher still, the sky—atmosphere, stars, the moon.
A warm, social space pressed tight against infinity.

Pan Am intended the upstairs lounge not to reach capacity, though
it usually did—across airlines, the 747's bar lounge became the most
exclusive club of the early 1970s. On one end of the lounge, at the
top of the spiral staircase that led back downstairs, perched a galley
that could serve fourteen diners. A screen, printed with an image of a
square-rigger's sails and lines, could be pulled out to block the kitchen
from diners' view. On the other end of the room, set against shiny
back panels, a clock surrounded by a sunburst of spokes showed the
time in a zone that was inevitably incorrect in the abstract time of the
sky. Time coalesced only at departure and arrival. Except for the clock
and seat belts around each molded plastic lounge chair, passengers
could imagine they were in a stylish if cramped restaurant down on

Earth. And yet this space, designed for coming together en route to a destination, also felt rich with the awareness of its impermanence. Passengers filled it quickly, with the well-traveled chatting about bests and worsts: hotels, car-rental services, airports. Stewardesses loved to work the lounge.

As Lynne's seniority grew, she requested the upstairs first-class lounge for the opportunities it offered her to know the passengers. Lynne flew into and out of countries but was rarely on the ground for long. She landed and consumed views and food, experiencing what she thought of as the *National Geographic* version of a place. She wanted to know about people—how they lived, who they were, something beyond what a taxi driver with passable English could tell her. Passengers offered Lynne the best shot at constructing a scaffolding of knowledge around which her experiences on the ground could grow. In the lounge, numbers and disposition were in her favor—a dinner party's worth of passengers who wanted to be social.

Somewhere between New Delhi and Tokyo, Lynne learned about the cultural and religious differences between northern and southern Indians from an Indian neurologist, who also explained the way customs officers in New Delhi took their time with the Pan Am stewardesses. Indian civil servants, he explained, expected payment for their services. Later Lynne met the University of Chicago scientists who'd discovered REM sleep. Charles Lindbergh flew one of her flights. (She was not too proud to ask for his autograph on Pan Am stationery. It would hang on her wall in each of the countries in which she eventually lived.) Every plane was a vessel filled with people and their stories. In Lynne's loftiest dreams, in which she was older and gutsier, she circulated a survey to all three-hundred-odd passengers on a 747: What country are you from? Where are you going and why?

Sometimes the passengers had questions for her too. They asked where she was from, how she liked her job. One night, somewhere in the air, Lynne sat on the staircase reading *Scientific American*. The cabin was quiet and dark, and from the lounge above, a column of

light shone on her magazine. One passenger sat awake in the seat clos-
est to Lynne and leaned toward her.

"Wouldn't *Vogue* be a better magazine for you to read?" he asked,
smiling.

Lynne smiled back at him. No, she said. She rarely read any magazines outside of her subscription to *Scientific American,* the same way
she never read fiction. She preferred information she could use to interpret her surroundings. In college she had studied biology, she told the
man. She had enjoyed her studies enough that she still kept her *Scientific American* subscription—she found solace in learning more about
the world's order. Even so, she often wished she studied cross-cultural
communications or anthropology instead of science.

The man looked confused. "I don't mean to be rude, but all of this
comes as a surprise," he told Lynne. "Surely you must be an exception
to the rule [for stewardesses]?"

Lynne pointed to where a few other stewardesses were visible. She
told him what she knew about each woman: her language qualification, where she had gone to school, what she had studied. She could
have cited a stat—throughout the 1960s, 10 percent of Pan Am stewardesses had attended graduate school at a time when only 6 to 8
percent of American women had graduated from college. The respect
she had for each woman was genuine. Lynne now felt that those four
years ago in the Pan Am Building, when she had considered herself so
different from the others who wanted to be stewardesses, she had been
wrong.

On arrival, the passenger stopped at the door to speak to Lynne.
Other passengers streamed by them, squeezing past the man as he
stood. "You know," he said, "my daughter wants to be a stewardess.
I told her no way, but maybe I was wrong. You're not empty-headed.
Maybe I was wrong."

———

A cohort of largely male writers and PR executives had defined the wider perception of stewardessing with Braniff's "Air Strip" and National's "Fly Me" campaigns, with *The Super-Jet Girls* and the various iterations of *Coffee, Tea, or Me?* But around the increased attention of lawsuits and EEOC rulings of the early 1970s, stewardesses began to reclaim their images.

The National Organization for Women urged letter-writing campaigns against National Airlines when its brazen advertising campaign debuted, but the women went further. One demonstration gathered enough support to block Fifth Avenue foot traffic outside the ad agency that had created the "Fly Me" campaign. A former Elvis songwriter composed a song for the occasion. It noted that women didn't have propellers or wings or any of the mechanical objects necessary for flight — "I'm only a woman, and as you can see / I can sure be walked on but you can't fly me," the writer sang.

By the end of 1972, two groups of stewardess activists had formed. Both Stewardesses for Women's Rights and the Stewardess Anti-Defamation Defense League aimed to organize the latent support for their goals among the wider ranks of flight crews. At a press conference, two women from each group told reporters that they were more afraid of being written up for talking back to a drunk passenger than they were of a hijacking.

The week before, two Iranian passengers were arraigned in Brooklyn's federal court for "assaulting, intimidating and threatening" a stewardess. The men faced fines of up to ten thousand dollars and up to twenty years in prison. And, the women pointed out, thousands of less extreme examples of harassment kept the average stewardess distracted during flight time. "The airline hostess who tells the departing passenger, 'It was nice to have you aboard, sir,' may be, behind her smile, a closet feminist on the verge of adding: 'And you acted like a male chauvinist pig,'" according to one article.

When stewardesses spoke out, they often discussed, not the acts of chauvinism, but its practical consequences. The focus on their looks and adherence to wardrobe requirements, the women said, pulled their attention away from the true stakes of their job. That they had little leverage within the airlines endangered everyone's safety. A stewardess with her eyes peeled for grabby hands might not notice the shifty gaze of a potential hijacker in row 34. She might not register the blinking light on the wing that could tip a pilot off to malfunctioning equipment. If she had no recourse to help, no credible consequence with which to threaten a drunk or aggressive passenger who monopolized her attention, her flight crew would number one fewer stewardess as she focused on keeping the passenger safely contained. "I don't think of myself as a sex symbol or a servant," one stewardess told a reporter. "I think of myself as someone who knows how to open the door of a 747 in the dark, upside down and in the water."

Three months later, seventy-five stewardesses came from ten cities to attend a two-day Stewardesses for Women's Rights conference in New York. The group created a logo and hosted talks by Gloria Steinem—who on her frequent flights had recognized in the flight crews a "revolution waiting to happen"—as well as a feminist labor attorney. Their numbers grew to one thousand. The women began to publish a newsletter. Yet membership would never rise over 3 percent of the labor force. Far more stewardesses spent their attention on the unions, which focused specifically on collective bargaining for fair wages and labor practices.

Future Stewardesses for Women's Rights conferences would feature feminist celebrities Betty Friedan, Erica Jong, and Alix Kates Shulman. Steinem would speak at multiple conferences. But other feminists patronized or behaved with open hostility toward a group of women they saw as embracing the traditional trappings of femininity. One Stewardesses for Women's Rights representative reported climbing the dais at a women's movement event to a roiling hiss from audience members.

Two issues of *Ms.* magazine reflected the duality with which feminists perceived stewardesses—were they glorified Playboy bunnies or feminist allies? In one issue, Kate Millett mocked a woman by calling her, insultingly, "sugar cute—a 'stewardess' type." In another, months later, a feature applauded Stewardesses for Women's Rights' efforts.

Feminist activism felt less urgent to most stewardesses than collecting a paycheck. The term *feminist* did not feel like a fit for some women whose interests and inclinations defied easy classification, women who participated in jet-set parties but also sought better pension plans, women whose volunteer endeavors included hosting a charity craft sale to benefit a local orphanage and leading a Boy Scout troop for girls in Phoenix. To certain women's rights activists, the stewardesses were sellouts for their adherence to rules dictated by men. To sexists, they were loose, easy women.

All longtime stewardesses were de facto feminists, said the self-identified among them. They wandered the world as independent women, cashing their checks, participating in union bargaining. A water molecule did not need to know it sat atop a cresting wave. "I've always thought it was ironic that we have this docile image," one of the founders of Stewardesses for Women's Rights told *Ms.* "Maybe in the past that's been true, but most of the women I know began to fly because they were just too independent and curious about the world to sit around in a nine-to-five job getting cramps in their shoulders."

Lynne still wrote her parents two letters every week. Her letters grew longer as she struggled to explain where she went, what each place meant to her, and all the things she learned. Her parents had traveled, too, using Lynne's employee benefits. But for Lynne, the impact of her travel, her work, was still hard for her to express, especially when she sat tired in a hotel room.

In Beirut, where the hotel's balconies looked out on the waterfront's scythe-like curve around the bay, she found herself in a market closed for Ramadan. She had already visited Byblos; the taxi driver suggested a day trip to the mountains, and soon Lynne stood amid pine trees with a light whisking of late-spring snow on them. She never saw snow anymore, Lynne realized as she stood looking down toward the city on the sea.

From New Delhi, she went with two other stewardesses to Agra to see the Taj Mahal. The car swerved among carts and trucks and daredevil cars, among buffalos and cows and donkeys and dogs. She and the two women laughed about fearing for their lives. At a roadside stop, she watched a snake charmer hypnotize a cobra with a mongoose. When they arrived, the Taj Mahal struck an odd contrast with the fascination of the journey. "Nothing is ever as great as the anticipation itself," she wrote her parents later.

These days, geopolitical conflicts decided by global powers not infrequently shifted Lynne's daily plans. Lynne did not bid Vietnam flights, but a crew could be pulled off a route to pick up soldiers with no notice. Flying the load of American soldiers into Vietnam had been her worst flight, but the speed with which flights kept her moving— the exhausting pace of it—had taken her away from the experience. She thought in the interim about how she could be of use. She could offer an individual soldier dignity despite her opposition to the war. War flights, rather than representing all that was wrong with her job, reflected her work's vast opportunities for understanding and empathy.

In the first days of 1972, flights to New Delhi were canceled due to Indo-Pakistani conflicts over Bangladeshi independence. Lynne was in the air on New Year's Eve as a result, which did not bother her, she wrote to her parents, because she would have missed her new boyfriend at home in Manhattan Beach wherever she found herself in the world.

Lynne had met Alex at a small party not far from where she lived. She'd arrived wearing what she considered appropriate cocktail-party clothes: a skirt, a blouse, and knee-high boots from Tokyo. When she walked into the room she saw that the other dozen or so people wore flip-flops, shorts, and T-shirts. Where had Lynne come from, Alex asked as he shambled toward Lynne, dressed like that?

"I can't help it if you don't have any class," Lynne countered with a glance toward his beach shorts.

Eight years older than Lynne, English, and a structural engineer, Alex had a dry demeanor and a crooked smile. He'd been born in Yorkshire shortly after the German attack on the British coast. After five years as an aerospace engineer for Boeing in Seattle, first working on the 747 and then planning the company's supersonic transport project, he was laid off amid budget cuts, and he'd moved to Los Angeles to take a break as a beach bum. He knew enough about airplanes and the economy of Southern California to understand that he would find another job soon. California, in Alex's mind, represented sparkling lights on his horizon. Now he had time to enjoy its pleasures. Life was fun, and petite Lynne, with her long hair down to the middle of her back, was sexy. *Let's ridicule this female and see what she's got,* Alex thought.

Lynne and Alex shared a love of witty conversation, dogs, and the vernacular of travel: European geography, the cities around the world in which they had both spent time; airports, airplanes, and, once Alex began to work again, jobs having to do with them. After months of walking between their two apartments, Lynne moved out of the bungalow she shared with Betsy and two other stewardesses and into another Manhattan Beach apartment with Alex. After a year, they got married in Las Vegas with twenty friends and family. There was no honeymoon; neither one could press pause on work.

Between marriage and the now routine work of flying, Lynne noticed her perspective shifting. Each of the American soldiers she had flown into or out of Vietnam, the businessmen on their way to Hong Kong or London—perhaps they had wives or lovers too. Certainly they had mothers, maybe daughters. Women on her planes wore saris or suits, they were homemakers and feminists; they were refugees from nations in tumult or the world's wealthy. But they were all women, and

Lynne felt a certain bond. And they were on a plane, where all people shared the same vulnerabilities. On the ground Lynne began to look for commonalities too.

Though Lynne and Betsy drifted apart—they no longer traveled together as their priorities changed—among her crews, Lynne felt a pronounced sense of belonging. In college, she had worked amid lab equipment *despite* her gender. Here, on a plane, Lynne had been chosen *because* she was a woman.

When Lynne was home, Alex planned dinners and parties, eager to introduce friends to his beautiful, bright new wife. He'd pick Lynne up at the airport, and, after she'd quickly changed out of her uniform, they usually met his friends for Mexican food in El Segundo. The next night the same friends, Englishmen who also worked in aerospace and their wives, would come for dinner.

Lynne returned from trips tired, wishing only to relax, to sit and look at the ocean. Instead, she walked to the grocery store to fill their empty refrigerator while Alex was at work. The grocery bags cut into her hands as she walked back home across Manhattan Beach. She cooked a casual dinner and dozed off in a beanbag chair as guests ate around their coffee table.

In transit, Lynne had obligations to her airline, her passengers, and herself. Among the crew of women performing their tasks together, she relaxed into a well-defined role. During layovers, no domestic duties encroached. At a hotel, she rested among unknown faces. And the foreign cities whose streets she had traversed before brought Lynne back to herself. These lightly known geographies—familiar to her but still a bit of a jolt, refreshingly different from the routine scenery and responsibilities of home—reminded Lynne of her own priorities and yearnings.

On her short Bangkok layovers, average humidity in the city hovered around 80 percent throughout the year. At first Lynne had explored the city—taken a long-tail-boat ride along the river, visited temples, eaten at restaurants. But the undercurrent of sexual tourism in Bangkok—supply had risen to meet the soldiers' R&R demands —repelled her. Now she more often stayed at the hotel, catching up on sleep.

Thai locals did not visit the Siam InterContinental. They saw its design with swooping eaves as a nod to the shape of a royal hat, disrespectful to their king. The fact that woven into the carpets upon which foreign feet walked were images of sacred temples was equally offensive. The hotel, seen from a certain angle, was a conference-size insult.

One day, wanting more than cloistered rest, Lynne went with two other stewardesses to a building deep in the city and followed the women into a fortune-teller's room. One by one, each woman held her hand out to him. Nothing the man said about Lynne struck her as memorable or unique; platitudes, encouragements, a directive or two that she would soon forget. It was what happened next that she remembered. The third and last woman held her hand out to him and the man blanched.

He could not read her hand, he told her.

"Why not?" all the women asked in chorus.

"I can't read her," he said, shaking his head. He collected his payment and shooed them out.

The women returned to the Siam InterContinental. The pool glittered blue. They went to dinner. Lynne slept, a luxurious, brief sleep in a crisp hotel bed, before her two a.m. call time.

The woman whose fortune could not be read was not on Lynne's flight to Tokyo. In the middle of the night she had been called to fill in for a stewardess who had fallen ill. She'd deadheaded to Hong Kong and stepped onto Flight 812 to Los Angeles via Bali, Australia, Fiji, and, eventually, Hawaii.

When Lynne landed in Tokyo, the news came: Flight 812 had crashed into a mountainside thirty-seven miles from the Bali airport.

15

A Matter of Serious
and Continuing Concern

WHEREVER SOLDIERS WERE STATIONED ACROSS VIETNAM, they left their children when they went home. The children's mothers were women who had worked as cooks, laundresses, or janitors on military bases, or they were the temporary wives of officers and GIs, or they were prostitutes. Many of the women had other children with Vietnamese husbands who had left or disappeared during the years of war. Most of the children were cared for by their families, but some—those with mothers who had died, or whose servicemen fathers had left, or whose families had simply grown too large to manage—began to fill the country's orphanages.

Public awareness of the orphans' plight grew in inverse proportion to the popularity of the war as more soldiers left than entered Vietnam. American commentators debated the thorny ethics of international adoption, a solution for the "relatively few who are truly orphaned." Estimates of their numbers varied wildly. Between three and four hundred orphans, the U.S. government said, spread across a hundred-odd orphanages. The South Vietnamese Ministry of Social Welfare estimated there were ten to fifteen thousand children fathered by American servicemen, but one American expert put the figure at two hundred thousand, using the number of bars near military bases and averaging how many bar girls, prostitutes, and "temporary wives" were in each.

By the early 1970s, the stewardesses who had flown R&Rs had listened to gunfire whistling past a plane's door, examined bullet holes in the fuselage, and watched coffins carried across the tarmac and hoisted into the cargo hold below them. Some had hiked their skirts up their thighs and done a cancan to draw out a laugh from a group of especially exhausted men. When diverted flights had landed stewardesses overnight in a barracks in Da Nang or a brothel in Singapore, the women had watched the GIs eat breakfast with the previous night's company. They had rejoiced with relieved and scarred men on homeward flights, keenly aware that not everyone was coming home. But nothing made these flights into anything that could be celebrated. The soldiers slowly retreating from South Vietnam received little fanfare at home. Sixty percent of Americans polled called the war a mistake. More than half called the war "morally wrong."

Every Tuesday and Thursday, Pan Am's commercial flights still touched down at Tan Son Nhut airfield, taking military contractors, nonprofit workers, and private citizens to and from South Vietnam. Flight 841 originated in San Francisco and, after stops in Honolulu, Guam, and Manila, landed in Saigon. Flight 842 traced an identical route back across the islands.

Increasingly, orphanage and adoption agency staff took seats on Flights 841 and 842. In 1971 the U.S. embassy urged the State Department to more seriously consider the plight of thousands of orphaned or abandoned children fathered by Americans, children who presented "a matter of serious and continuing concern." Illegal but "lucrative" adoption, the embassy said, was growing more common. Fair-skinned children sold on the black market while the "racially mixed" children filled orphanages. The U.S. government called the situation faced by these children "unfortunate" but officially of no relevance to the administration.

The actions of ordinary citizens across all levels of society refuted the U.S. government's claim that it bore no responsibility. Americans who still lived in Vietnam as government or aid workers and their teenage children volunteered with orphanages or worked at schools for orphans. Actor Dick Hughes ran children's homes in Vietnam. Across various airlines, stewardesses, who were anything but naive about the stresses of war and the attitudes and experiences of the GIs fighting, volunteered to use their employee travel passes and time off to accompany some of the legally adopted, unrecognized children of American GIs to new families around the world.

A few hundred orphans made their way across the Pacific to families in the United States in the very early 1970s, and the number began to grow as the decade progressed. A military attaché convinced a businessman to carry a seven-month-old baby on his lap from Da Nang to Saigon. An orphanage director found herself in charge of eight babies on a Pan Am plane from Saigon to New York; she walked in constant loops from seats scattered around the cabin to lavatories to change the squalling infants. At the San Francisco layover, two of the babies went to new families, and the airline provided a stewardess to help with the six remaining babies on the last leg of the trip. An Air France stewardess shepherded a two-and-a-half-year-old to John F. Kennedy Airport. The child would suffer diarrhea until she adjusted to a new diet, the woman who had accompanied the girl from Saigon told the new mother amid tears and kisses.

One Pan Am stewardess watched as the chaperone for a set of twin toddlers tried to comfort them. The traumatized children's miniature faces were red, their cheeks lined with stale tears, their shirts covered in streams of spit-up. After a quick word, the stewardess brought each one into the bathroom, wiped off the child's cheeks and neck, and changed her into a clean dress. Their new parents—a military couple on Guam, the chaperone told her—should meet their children for the first time looking their very best, the stewardess thought.

On one withdrawal flight, a stewardess told a soldier he had to put the boot box he held on his lap under his seat. "Nope," the man said. She repeated her request.

"Not gonna happen, missy," he said. His rudeness surprised her.

An older officer tapped her on the shoulder. "Just trust me, it's okay," he said. She strapped into the jump seat. When the plane climbed into the air she heard the hooting and shouting of soldiers on their way home, and also a piercing, thin wail. When it was safe she walked back to the rows where the men sat.

"You have to tell me what's going on, right now," she said, mustering as much authority as she could.

"You promise we're not going back?" the soldier said.

"We're not going back," she confirmed.

He lifted the lid of the box. The babies were so tiny, too tiny, born weeks too soon. Their mother had given birth in a field and died nearly immediately, he said. The soldier had brought them to a nurse, who'd said they would die. But they had not died.

I didn't know that preemies were coated in downy fur, the stewardess thought as she looked at the twin babies in the boot box on the soldier's lap.

16

An Extension of the Airline

TORI HAD BEEN RIGHT TO WONDER WHAT HER FIANCÉ'S SUS-
picion of her behavior suggested about his own. He had been
messing around on his layovers. Tori, twenty-four years old, betrayed,
and living in California alone, was devastated. She moved out of her
shared rental and into her own place, a furnished apartment with
avocado-green kitchen appliances and gold shag carpeting in a building alongside the Hollywood Park racetrack, where actors and studio
executives examined the *Racing Form* and picked their horses. She had
sacrificed her seniority with Pan Am for the move to Los Angeles, but
Tori was moving forward.

She had never owned a car. Her ex-fiancé set up driving lessons
for her; she took the lessons and bought a used car with her saved
money. She became friendly and then friends with the people in her
half-finished apartment complex, which was so new that not all the
apartments were occupied. There was a retired United Press International photographer and his wife, a former Eastern stewardess, and the
itinerant racetrack crowd that followed one race to the next. She met
a new collection of Pan Am stewardesses, the West Coast women. She
became close with some of the Europeans among them, a Swede and a
Brit who lived together in Marina del Rey.

A shadow, a note of social consciousness and individualism, had emerged within the California sunshine sound. The Mamas and the Papas had broken up. The Beach Boys sued Capitol Records and left their anticipated *Smile* album unreleased. Men were still dying in Vietnam. The Manson murders were a horrific recent memory. Complexities entering the soundscape reflected yet wider social unrest: the Watts rebellion of 1965 had sparked community organization and a Black arts renaissance in the city. Civil rights movements unfurled alongside anti-war marches brutally quelled by the LAPD. Chicano leaders fought for fair wages and full citizenship. Arrests at an LGBT club sparked a five-hundred-person protest and the country's first gay pride parade.

Even amid this roil, to Tori, the sunny attitude of California—the sheer genuineness of the Beach Boys sound—still seemed a part of nearly everyone she met. Compared to New Yorkers or the Oslo Norwegians, Californians' interactions overflowed with smiles and pleasantries. *Have a nice day! How can I help you?* Soon enough Tori began to smile back.

In New York everyone drank cocktails—brandy Alexanders, grasshoppers, rusty nails, black Russians, white Russians—but California was all about wine. Sometimes in the evenings when Tori flew home, a friend would pick her up at the airport and take her straight to a party at one of the singles-only apartment buildings up in Torrance. There were weekly dances, cocktail parties, dinners. One 248-unit complex housed five hundred "stewardesses, doctors, teachers, engineers, secretaries and salesmen," all single. The complex hosted more serious events, too, nightly discussion groups on Vietnam, drug addiction, or civil rights. Tori never said no to the parties.

There was always a party, always somewhere to go, someone to go with. A handful of other European stewardesses had transferred to Los Angeles from New York. When they all got together, they never stopped laughing. Tori competed with them to tell the best joke, to generate the loudest guffaws.

Tori and the friends she made flying hosted a Santa Lucia party; the Swede made sixty gallons of glogg, mulled wine that went down like water. They planned eight-course progressive dinners, walking from apartment to apartment, rotating around the pool of a U-shaped complex with drinks in hand as courses went on. Not once did they make it to dessert. They could go for a month of between-flight downtime trying to get to the bank before it closed at three p.m. but sleeping past closing every day.

Some of the other stewardesses improvised games to play when they bid flights across the Pacific together too. Crews swapped out in Tokyo while passengers — businessmen in first class, in particular — often continued on to Hong Kong. Two stewardesses glanced at the flight manifests to check the final destinations of the men in first class and then competed to see who could entice the most attractive men heading for Hong Kong to get off the plane in Tokyo for a night on the town with the women in the crew. They'd often get one or two to defer other plans, but on one flight, five men walked away from whatever they were supposed to do the next day to join them. Where the men were from, where they would return home to, did not matter. The game wasn't about love or even always about sex; it was about adventure and desire and power. And when it *was* about sex, there was no shame in that. The pilots had lovers in various ports, reasoned one stewardess; why shouldn't she? Men made plans for nights out with her at intervals of every few thousand miles. She snuck out of a man's room in the middle of the night only one time, and she regretted it nearly immediately. That had been unkind and cowardly.

Tori was the new girl again, vaulting into established friendships and established routines. She found herself choosing among the routes that more senior stewardesses disdained, spending Hawaiian layovers in urban Honolulu's lively streetscapes instead of desirable Hilo with its incandescent shimmer of Rainbow Falls slicing through the jungle. She crewed on MAC-V charter flights around Vietnam, to and through Guam. She too was issued her Geneva Conventions identification card.

Fool me twice, Tori had thought years earlier in Johannesburg when she saw the bullet holes in the tail of her plane and decided to play it a little bit safer. Taking the soldiers home was a different sort of war flight. They slept with what looked like gratitude on their faces on the plane they called the "Freedom Bird." They played hearts in the galley. Tori felt that she was participating in a global effort to defend a small, oceanfront country from the ravages of Communism. She loved these flights.

Tori made more money than her parents now, between her base pay, overtime, and per diems. She provided a trip to Bangkok for her mother, and she paid the rent on the first apartment in which she lived alone. These things counted as success, but on top of that, Tori was bringing men back home to a country she thought they had bravely protected.

Flight crews and soldiers alike rotated through Guam. The island's strategic position in the Western Pacific had rendered it central to American military operations since the turn of the century, when the island was annexed in the Spanish-American War. The colony was crucial to Pan Am's expansion across the Pacific Ocean too. Military facilities spread across a third of the island: the air force base on the northern peninsula, a naval harbor complex to the west, a weapons magazine in the center. In the 1930s, Guam had been a key stopover in the Pacific for commercial aircraft. Now the airlines wanted to market it as a vacation spot of its own. In 1965, only five thousand tourists had come through, but those numbers soon started to rise. Construction began on the island's first luxury hotel as various airlines, including Pan Am, ran charter flights from Tokyo.

Across the low, lean island—thirty-some miles end to end, five to nine miles wide—orange frangipani and fuchsia hibiscus bloomed, and the ocean was visible from nearly any vantage point. Palm trees stood stark along the water. Guam offered a "forever summer latitude," where a "completely informal summer wardrobe" was always appropriate and the villages of the once Spanish colony hosted "tremendous fiestas," the *New Horizons* guidebook said. Little of the island's original architecture or even the stone buildings of the Spanish colonial era remained; two typhoons had sliced across the island in the early 1960s and taken nearly all infrastructure with them. American aid had installed prefabricated concrete homes and schools—small, brightly colored structures with wide, flat overhanging roofs. In the middle of the island sat the naval hospital with its white-suited nurses; the international airport; the military stores to which the stewardesses' Geneva Conventions cards gave them access. Some of the stewardesses liked to visit with the burn victims in the naval hospital, but they didn't stay long because the combination of jet lag and wounded men could make them too emotional to be useful.

To Tori, the island felt like what the Hawaiian Islands might have resembled before the Californians began to vacation there. On nearly every MAC-V charter she flew, she passed through Guam, the U.S. military's operational base for Vietnam. She always stayed at the dumpy Guamerica Inn, where an automat kept tired-looking sandwiches behind glass. She often ate at the officers' club, Top o' the Mar. On Tuesday nights the restaurant set up a Mongolian barbecue buffet in metal chafing tins on its outside patio. Straight-shouldered officers sat alongside the crew tables filled with stewardesses in their lightest off-duty skirts, pilots, and flight engineers. The former military fliers leaned over to ask questions about equipment, units, assignments. Together, crews and officers ordered rounds of drinks, played games of liar's dice, danced in the warm night air, and ordered more drinks. Tori insisted, although no longer with the authority that she had held as a purser, that the women who came together had to leave together. If flights got in too late for Top o' the Mar, the crew party happened in a hotel room. In the morning, the pilots and stewardesses would go to the orange A&W root beer stand and eat hamburgers to sober up.

During the day, Tori took a car to the PX with the other women.

"You're European," the other stewardesses said, "you know how to drive a stick shift," so even though Tori had never driven a car in Norway, she said yes. She frog-jumped the car to the guard post, where a young soldier offered to drive them the rest of the way to the store. Every time in Guam, Tori picked up a bottle of liquor at the PX for her new bar in her new apartment. The furnished apartment near the racetrack had been a short-term solution; she'd moved into a place of her own an hour south of LAX in Newport Beach. She found a shop that specialized in Scandinavian modern and bought a low hutch, two bar stools with leather seats, and a square coffee table with a panel that folded up to reveal a bar inside. In the living room she displayed the temple candle block she'd brought back from Tokyo and a samovar from a Tehran bazaar. She began to make a home.

Guidebooks recommended the shops in Guam's small "capital 'city,'" Agana, for silks and jewelry, but Tori only brought back the gallon of liquor allowed duty-free. More often she spent time relaxing or exploring the interior of the island. In the jungles and on more remote beaches, she often found World War II debris. Rumor had it that a handful of Japanese fighters, holdovers from when the Japanese occupied the island for three years, hid in the caves in the center of the island.

On Guam, the stewardesses worked alongside the soldiers now exposed, amid the other enormous revelations of the *Pentagon Papers*, as being cynically manipulated by a government that never hoped to win the war it fought. On the military airfield, the runways stretched to accommodate the increased length a B-52 bomber required. When flights left from Guam, stewardesses stood behind pilots in the cockpit counting the B-52s on the airfield below sent in secret in 1969 and 1970 to bomb targets across Vietnam and neutral Cambodia. Once, a stewardess had watched an airman checking in to a beachfront hotel, his elbow juddering so hard that he could not write his signature. He stood at the desk even after she claimed a key and walked away, unable to sign his name. At the Guamerica Inn, rumor spread that one of the Pan Am stewardesses had gotten into it with one of the airmen who stayed at the nicer hotels where the women used to stay. "Baby killer," she had called him.

Tori had heard about protesters who name-called and spit on soldiers. Garbage cans at LAX were reportedly filled with uniforms peeled off by soldiers who did not want to be seen walking through city streets in army attire. The stories proliferated rapidly across the media, though no photographer ever captured the spitting, the garbage cans. For some men, one scholar later argued, spitting was a metaphor for the betrayal of an ungrateful nation.

But some disdain and abandonment were real. At anti-war protests women lofted handmade signs reading, GIRLS SAY YES TO BOYS WHO SAY NO to the draft. Women had left home for jobs, moved into their own apartments, and led protest movements. A nation of Penelopes did not wait for Odysseuses. Joan Baez and Jane Fonda visited Hanoi. Fonda had traded her Barbarella sex appeal for activism. She cut her long blond hair short and let her natural brown grow in, wore turtlenecks and loose long-sleeved shirts. She was the sex kitten turned anti-war protester.

Vietnam Veterans Against the War worked toward an understanding of post-traumatic stress disorder that illuminated the contradictory sensations of guilt, persecution, and betrayal. The horror of sanctioned acts of mass murder washed over men who had not committed the crimes. "The country doesn't know it yet, but it has created a monster," VVAW member John Kerry said before the Senate. "A monster in the form of millions of men who have been taught to deal and to trade in violence, and who are given the chance to die for the biggest nothing in history; men who have returned with a sense of anger and a sense of betrayal which no one has yet grasped."

After two years of military flights, Tori called the soldiers "my boys." The idea of a protester spitting on them appalled her. *War is hell,* she thought. The men on her flights would never have committed the war crimes to which Kerry testified, she thought—raping women, razing entire villages, shooting at civilians, cutting off ears, limbs, heads. Her boys were respectful, grateful, honorable. Tori's Geneva Conventions card named her a second lieutenant in the U.S. Armed Forces and she felt great pride in that fact. As soon as she got her car, Tori smoothed a sticker across its bumper: SUPPORT OUR TROOPS. She set up a small monthly donation that went straight from her paycheck to the Veterans' Association. She felt mad, really mad, that any American would disrespect her boys.

The soldiers had always climbed onto planes directly from the field; the contrast with the stewardesses' prim uniforms would make you laugh if it didn't make you cry. Red clay cracking off their boots, a scent of mildew, the men so collectively dirty that it was only against white—bandages, airplane walls—that you understood how truly filthy they were.

In the early 1970s, about one in five soldiers stepped onto a plane high. Different airlines and different crews dealt variously with the drugs that soldiers tried to carry with them. On some flights, stewardesses read an announcement over the PA system dictated by the airline: "We'll be coming through the cabin to collect any illicit substances you may have." Then they walked down the aisle with laundry bags. A stewardess would try to strike the right note between authoritarian and approachable girl next door. A stewardess friend of Tori's once collected two full laundry bags of vials and sachets. Another stewardess told the men to throw their drugs into the aisle all at once; she watched tiny baggies flying from behind the seats, arcing toward the center of the plane. Soon the army began to bring dogs to the South Vietnamese airports to sniff luggage and fatigues. In airport waiting rooms, trash cans filled with heroin and marijuana.

"Let me see those baby blues," a stewardess might coo at the bottom of a set of stairs to a GI with especially glazed eyes or twitchy limbs. Marijuana did not matter much, but in a worst-case scenario, a soldier could go into heroin withdrawal on a long flight home, shuddering and sweating. He might hit a woman who gently tapped his shoulder for meal service. Or, manic, he might run down an aisle until a flight engineer tackled him to the ground and a sergeant cuffed him to a seat.

For Tori, in her first months in Los Angeles, the war flights had offered an easy way to compensate for her sudden lack of seniority. Then, once she had checked out as purser again, they had given her a way to do something for both the country she called home and the international treaties that defended small countries on the sea. In the soldiers' gratitude, she had recognized a need. She loved taking care of them. Youth was its own class of personhood, she thought, across all nationalities and professions. She had moved out of that youth and into an adult life in Los Angeles — she owned furniture now — but she was close enough to respond to it.

Siv, a Swedish friend of Tori's, cut out *Playboy* centerfolds and taped them across the bathroom mirrors, curved and splayed limbs diving across reflections of the men's dirty faces as they scrubbed clean. Siv laughed as the purser on one of her flights served a rubber chicken to the highest-ranking officer on board. They did anything to get the men to smile. Her crews lofted a hand-lettered banner in the rear galley: KISSES $1. When the men presented their cheeks and waved their dollar bills, Siv kissed them and then pushed the money back at them. "This is for your service," she said.

On one especially loud flight, Tori stood in the front of the plane and shouted for the men to shut up. "Everybody stay in your seats," she said, clapping her hands. "If you all behave, coffee service will be performed topless."

The volume dialed immediately down. Tori and the other women smiled as they served dinner. They stretched their arms over the men in aisle seats. They winked and laughed at the mute and expectant men.

When dinner service had finished, the women retreated to the galley.

The men craned their necks.

Tori and her crew waited in the galley, grinning, as the coffee cart began to rattle. The hoots and then boos rose from the fuselage. This flight had an extra flight engineer; he and the second pilot were now serving coffee shirtless. The men had strapped aprons over their bare skin, pulling the strings tight around their thick male waists.

In the winter of 1973, the last of the soldiers came home from Vietnam. Five hundred ninety-one freed prisoners of war hobbled off planes at Clark Air Base in the Philippines in waves of about forty men. They met teenagers they had left as children or kindergarteners they had never before seen. "I walked out in the sunlight and the first thing I saw was a girl in a miniskirt," one POW recalled years later. "She was a reporter for one of the news organizations. I'd never seen a real live miniskirt."

At the end of March, the only American soldiers left in Vietnam were the Marines guarding the U.S. embassy in Saigon, though American influence would remain. The Defense Attaché Office replaced the Military Assistance Command–Vietnam offices to run twenty-three thousand contractors as of January 1973. Whether its operations would adhere to the Paris Peace Accords remained to be seen. "Peace with honor," President Nixon had called the cease-fire agreement, but newspapers decried what looked like a stalemate. On paper, the political situation appeared no better than it had in 1966, fifty-eight thousand American and at least one and a half million Vietnamese lives ago, though those estimates would grow. South Vietnam's defense of its independence was now in the hands of its own politicians and its own army.

Although the war had devastated the Vietnamese countryside, its infrastructure reconfigured nearby cities and countries. American military and business contracts had spiked tourism and Japanese economic interests in Thailand. In Bangkok, fresh unrest threatened to upend the fast clip of its recent economic growth. A widespread uprising, spurred by inflation, a rice shortage, and government corruption, resulted in the overthrow of the country's military dictatorship; now a new constitution was being written, and elections were coming. Around the pools and at the bars of Bangkok's hotels, American, European, and Asian pilots, businessmen, aid workers, and stewardesses still converged. Outside hotel gates, the country struggled to redraw its relationship with the West. Among the grievances of the previous year's uprising had been the influence of American priorities in Thai development and politics. Around the globe, across industries, where that involvement began and ended was unclear.

When anti-war activists turned their attention to American corporations reaping possible profits from the Vietnam War—IBM, General Motors, Chase Manhattan, Bank of America—Pan Am's links with covert government operatives came under scrutiny. "Does Pan American have any financial ties to Air America? Do you know of any connection between Air America and the CIA? Does Pan American Airlines have any CIA agents on its payroll in South Vietnam or Laos? If so, do you think this is a proper role for an American public company to have?" read a letter submitted by Business Executives Move for Vietnam Peace to CEO Najeeb Halaby in 1970. "All Pan Am employees everywhere are on Pan Am payrolls and, to the best of my knowledge, none of them are CIA representatives," Halaby answered. He did not know of a connection between Air America and the CIA.

Most stewardesses knew that not everything was as it appeared in the international airline business, but they had little hard proof to confirm rumors of government involvement. They assumed, though, that some among them worked with the CIA. Rumor had it that stewardesses collaborated with CIA agents, conveying documents and reporting on passengers. In other countries, stewardesses were trained to divert the attention of official passengers in the airspace over sensitive ground facilities. A story circulated that one redheaded Pan Am stewardess was a CIA agent herself.

Halaby's answer to Business Executives Move for Vietnam Peace could only be taken as willfully ignorant. Air America's cover, at least, had long since been blown. News articles openly referred to it as "a pseudo-private airline run by the C.I.A." and "the servant of the United States Central Intelligence Agency." Tori knew that Air America was the CIA's arm in Southeast Asia. Around the Siam InterContinental's pool, she talked to the Air America pilot with the gorgeous young son who lived at the hotel. The stewardesses always volunteered to babysit. The pilot told Tori about an acquaintance in Hong Kong. He sometimes asked her to go and find so-and-so; the man would buy her a drink, and she should tell him—and the pilot would give her a casual message, something about his arrival time on Wednesday after he flew to Cambodia or about the cancellation of an eleven o'clock shuttle. Tori felt the illicit nature and potential danger of these interactions but she did it anyway. The responsibility of one airline crew member to another was irrefutable, while the risks were abstract.

For the entire decade during which Tori had been flying, Alison Palmer had been trying to achieve her promotion within the U.S. Foreign Service. The outside examiner had found in Palmer's favor in 1972. Still, years later, Palmer said, "I take it as a given fact that I will never receive another promotion." The Women's Action Organization had grown out of a small working group into a dues-paying organization of six hundred members from the State Department, the Agency for International Development, and the U.S. Information Agency. A few gains had been made—the requirement to retire upon marriage had been dropped, and female officers were now allowed to bring dependents abroad. The Foreign Service exam was open to the wives of career diplomats, and fifty women had taken and passed it. Yet still it was "a rank-ridden establishment—and rank in this building is white and male—even the parking garage is a white, male world," one State Department woman who asked to remain anonymous told a reporter.

The sense of glamour, intrigue, and duty remained among the increasingly diverse ranks of Pan Am stewardesses even as the company struggled financially. Losses continued to accumulate as the company shed employees and routes. Published maps changed as the airline began to trim. All money-losing flights—one-fourth of the airline's total routes—were soon discarded. Layoffs cut personnel in increments, by nearly 10 percent from 1969 to 1972, 20 percent by 1974, one-third by 1975. Ever more experienced flight crews were composed of women, like Tori, with growing seniority. Airline crews existed apart from normal society, pushed and pulled along with the currents of business and statesmanship. For that matter they existed apart from time itself, together in a cycle of light and dark that did not adhere to the twenty-four hours of an earthly day.

Each airline engendered different work cultures, unique variations on the sense of distance from civilians. Pan Am, with its conservative uniforms, its language requirements, its rigid rules, and its chartered press corps plane that followed the U.S. president around the world, attracted an earnest sort of stewardess. On World Airways, which appeared to operate almost as an unruly branch of the U.S. military, the stewardesses stayed in crew hotels just outside Clark Air Base in the Philippines. They could reasonably have watched the returning POWs running across the tarmac toward their children. They lived in Vietnam for months at a time to crew planes leased to Air Vietnam. Braniff stewardesses too flew soldiers in and out of combat, but they did it wearing three-inch heels and Pucci dresses. "Living the way I wanted to die," said one woman.

On Pan Am and other international airlines, crews held deep convictions that *their* airline afforded them the ability to rise, that *their* airline was different. Only on their airline would they fly generals and refugees with such intimacy and attention, many thought, even as military charter contracts across various airlines perhaps contradicted the instinct. Still, only on their airline would a pilot wrangle a car in the Philippines to pick you up at three in the morning in the middle of nowhere and expect nothing in return. Only among their coworkers could they find the women who would bend toward one another over a surreptitious cigarette and strategize to avoid passenger panic on a plane with malfunctioning flaps. Their crews were the best.

Like a family tree with branches for individual clans, airline crews perceived themselves as distinct from yet connected to the wider milieu. A crew—of a boat or an airplane, a spaceship or a train, all vehicles for movement—stood apart from the land-bound population. The word itself derived from an Old French word meaning "augmentation, increase." Growth in numbers. And the things that a crew saw and did in numbers, together in motion, sealed its separation from the general public.

PART III

WOMEN'S WORK

17

Everything Flyable

FIGHTING IN 1974 WAS THE HEAVIEST OF ANY YEAR OF THE war despite Secretary of State Henry Kissinger assuring Congress that the Paris cease-fire had put a stop to major combat. American soldiers no longer fought alongside the South Vietnamese, but munitions and men continued to support their army; over eight hundred million dollars was budgeted for 1974 and the Pentagon asked Congress for $1.45 billion for 1975.

The rush of refugees toward Saigon had begun in mid-March of 1975 when the North Vietnamese army prepared their drive south. In the face of this advancing threat, the president withdrew South Vietnamese troops from the highlands that pressed close to the border with North Vietnam; villagers across the region saw in the withdrawal the shape of a looming final defeat. Rumors spread that half of the country was to be immediately handed over to the North Vietnamese. Thousands of vehicles crowded the highway to Da Nang, hundreds of thousands of soldiers and civilians snaking along a ten-day march remembered as the "Convoy of Tears." Only one of every four people who joined the column made it to Da Nang.

As the ground situation appeared increasingly dire, embassy staff remaining in Vietnam, along with USAID workers, contractors, journalists, CIA operatives, and NGO representatives, began to send lists of Vietnamese employees and informants to the U.S. embassy for evacuation. Pan Am, Citibank, Time, IBM, and more each had dozens of employees, many with dependents they wished to evacuate. Half of Saigon, it seemed to some onlookers, filled the lists. As to how they would all depart, commercial airliner, military airlift, sealift by cargo ships in Saigon's port, and helicopters were all considered. But which airline would do what was unclear.

Children now flowed toward Saigon as stories of Communist brutality, especially toward the biracial children of American soldiers, spread among Vietnamese mothers. The violence reported as South Vietnamese troops and civilians fled toward Da Nang from the highlands—Communists and mountain tribes firing on the caravans of refugees, blood flowing "in tiny streams," children and elderly who "fell everywhere," wrote one Vietnamese journalist in a widely read newspaper—increased the mothers' fear. Rumor had it that the incoming soldiers would kill all children fathered by American GIs. They would slit a child's belly and eat the liver. Terrified mothers left sobbing children in orphanages in Da Nang and Saigon; workers reported babies dropped over exterior courtyard fences of the French-style villas where orphanages operated. Older children appeared clutching notes of identification. These joined the children who had formally been given up for adoption and those whose parents had, they'd thought, left them for temporary safekeeping.

In the last days of March, orphanage workers rushed to process the necessary visas and competed for space on flights. But even as the South Vietnamese military retreated, U.S. ambassador Graham Martin would not process visas at an expedited pace. To do so even for children with waiting adoptive parents, he feared, would confirm suspicions of an imminent large-scale evacuation of Americans. It could engulf Saigon in panic. A combination of forces—the reluctance to move forward with visas, internal opposition to the orphans' removal from the country, lack of funds, and diminishing space on airplanes —threatened to ground them all.

Pan Am continued flying its regular biweekly flights amid the chaos. Lufthansa and Air France kept their planes flying into Saigon too. As March moved toward April, Pan Am's passenger lists stretched to a thousand reservations. But each Tuesday and Thursday, only about two hundred passengers had successfully collected the paperwork, passports, and money required to purchase tickets. Names on passports did not match names on manifests. Most people who noticed this reported it to no one, given the increasing panic of South Vietnamese citizens jamming the airport, hoping to flee the country before the North Vietnamese fighters arrived and with them a Communist government that, many believed, would massacre all who had collaborated with the occupying Americans.

Flights departed hectically. A Lufthansa DC-10 took off with German nationals after the men bade sobbing Vietnamese women goodbye. One goodbye was especially dramatic: the Pan Am station manager watched one crying Vietnamese woman claw the face of a young American man who had not acquired a visa or ticket for her or their child. His face bloomed with red streaks as she dragged her nails from his eye to his chin. A chartered Pan Am 707 took off after curfew with employees of American banks and their wives and children. A South Vietnamese air force major and three fellow officers commandeered a plane to fly fifty-two passengers to Singapore. One flight with ninety-eight orphans ranging in age from one to fourteen were strapped into all possible areas of a DC-3 manufactured in 1942 with a commercial capacity of twenty-eight passengers and flown from the central highland town of Da Lat to Saigon. "Everything flyable in Vietnam is being used to ferry refugees," a news article reported. An East German would have an easier time leaving the Communist bloc than a South Vietnamese had leaving Saigon, one expert said.

———

Ed Daly, CEO of World Airways, made himself a protagonist of the retreat from the highlands to Saigon. Under embassy contract, the airline had flown Americans and refugees from Da Nang to Saigon amid the crush from the highlands. But at the end of March 1975, as the ground situation there grew more dangerous, the embassy canceled World Airways' charters. Daly only grew more determined to contravene Ambassador Martin's insistence on doing less rather than more. When Daly asked Martin what security at Tan Son Nhut would do if his planes took off for Da Nang without clearance, Martin replied, "I imagine they'll shoot you down." When Daly asked what Martin would do, the ambassador said, "Applaud."

Daly ordered a plane to Da Nang to evacuate women and children anyway. On March 28, an air traffic controller at takeoff at Tan Son Nhut told Daly's pilot to taxi straight to the hangar, but Daly had instructed him to "experience radio failure." The plane lifted into the air. The two pilots, three stewardesses, CBS news crew, and UPI reporter on board had barely touched down in Da Nang when one stewardess, Jan Wollett, saw thousands of people running toward the plane, motorcycles and bicycles, trucks and jeeps and personnel carriers rushing faster yet. The plane did not stop moving. Jan stood at the cockpit door and watched as a man jumped off a truck, raised a pistol, and began to shoot. She had the unnerving feeling that she had stepped straight into a Western. The doors of the plane were opened and the stairs lowered. Even as the plane continued to taxi slowly, it began to take on passengers. Jan stood at the door watching the roiling crowd mass around the moving vehicle. Screaming people clawed at others as they ran next to the plane, pushing them aside. At the back of the plane, Jan saw one of the other stewardesses on the stairs reaching over the railing, pulling people up, and she moved to help. Below her on the stairs, Daly waved his pistol in the air. A family of five—mother, father, infant, two children—ran alongside the stairs, and Jan reached for them. Shots rang out; the five crumpled to the asphalt—whether they had tripped or been shot was unclear—and another man rushed past them, up the stairs, and into the plane. A woman pulled on Jan's arm. Jan grabbed the woman's hand but before she could yank her up, a man began trying to climb over her. Daly hit him with the butt of his gun and Jan saw a spray of blood. *Good,* she thought, and she turned back to the cabin to seat the people on board. They were mostly men in South Vietnamese military uniforms. "Take off, take off," one man was screaming.

"Where are the women and children?" Jan shouted at no one. A grenade flashed under one wing and shook the plane as it took off at the end of the tarmac. Bullets had damaged the gas lines and the plane lost fuel by the second, but it lifted. Human bodies dropped from the wheel well as the plane climbed.

In the newsreel of the scene broadcast by the *CBS Evening News* the next night, the newsman's voice was stiff with disdain. "As calm fell on the smug men who had managed to fight off their friends and relatives to get on, the hardworking cabin crew took a count," the newscaster read. "Two hundred and sixty-eight people were on board, among them five women and two or three small children. The rest were some of the men whom President Thieu said would [stay behind to] defend Da Nang."

The stewardesses had looked across the seats at the faces. As Jan walked the aisle, she saw a man whose intestines spilled from his body. She tied a towel around his waist. She bandaged another man's head with a shirt. As the stewardesses passed around cool towels—really, they were rough-edged squares of galley curtains they had dunked in melted ice—the men handed over bullets, guns. One strapped a bandolier around Jan's chest; another hung a pistol off her fingers; yet another placed a grenade atop the pile of ammunition she carried. She walked to the cockpit. "No smoking," the Vietnamese CBS sound engineer said over the PA system.

The plane crept through the air at ten thousand feet—no higher, since the main cabin would not sustain pressure. The air was hot and fetid. Daly offered Jan a Coke, and she held it to her lips only to feel the warm liquid running down her chin and onto her uniform. She passed it back. She realized that the gas line had held only when she looked out the windows and saw buildings racing alongside. At dinner later Jan drank and drank the beers Daly gave her and she never felt drunk. At the hotel, every time she closed her eyes to sleep, she saw splayed and broken bodies.

In a way, the 747 had been destined for wide-scale evacuation. Among Juan Trippe's arguments for investing in the enormous airplane during a time of financial austerity almost a decade earlier—before the full scope of the war in Vietnam had revealed itself—had been its airlift capability in the event of a national emergency. Trippe no longer helmed Pan Am but the airplane he had pushed to market now permeated the American airline industry.

But it was a different swashbuckling airline CEO who once again dived into the chaos of international disaster to shape its outcome, and he did it with a different airplane than the one Trippe had had in mind. After flying a first, small load of orphans out of Vietnam soon after his failed refugee flight, Ed Daly told reporters that he would pay to fly nearly one thousand infants to the United States on a DC-8 and another four to five hundred to Australia on a 727. "Let 'em stop us," he said. But Ambassador Martin had tired of Daly's swagger. Rather than allow World to fly the children out, the U.S. government matched Daly's offer of a pro bono flight for the orphanage's charges. A load of military and medical supplies for the remaining South Vietnamese army had arrived on April 1. The U.S. Air Force C-5A Galaxy cargo plane, the biggest transport plane in the world, would bring munitions to the South Vietnamese army and return to the United States with children. The South Vietnamese government understood that foster parents in foreign countries were waiting to receive fourteen hundred orphans. The deputy prime minister wrote, "Their immigration, plus the fact of million people leaving the sections occupied by the Communists, will provide a good propaganda for Vietnam, especially including the TV and newspaper of America exploiting deeply this event."

On April 3, President Gerald Ford announced an orphan airlift, code-named Operation Babylift. "I can't guarantee that every single South Vietnamese war orphan will get here but I can assure you that we intend to do everything possible in that humanitarian effort," he said in a news conference from San Diego. The Red Cross offices in San Francisco reported switchboards alight with phone calls from prospective adoptive parents. "It is the President's obvious intent to spare no expense or trouble where the welfare of these helpless victims of war are concerned, and the nation will applaud him for it," read one newspaper editorial. The front pages of newspapers carried stories about the late-night arrival of the first group of fifty-seven orphans, and a toll-free hotline that USAID had set up in Washington received twenty-seven hundred phone calls.

On April 4, Karen, Lynne, and Tori flew on a regular flight path in two broad arcs from New Delhi to Bangkok and then up and around Vietnamese airspace to Hong Kong. This was the first time all three of the women had flown together. Their minds flitted among the usual concerns, their actions now the muscle memory of repetitive flight. Karen, on her jump seat between meal services, read whichever book she had tucked into her bag and considered how she would spend this brief layover in one of her favorite cities. Lynne, serving in the upstairs lounge, studied the passengers. Tori, one of the two pursers on the plane and among the most senior of the crew, kept control with her definitive gaze.

The three stewardesses did not know that on the ground below them, two hundred forty-three children waited in a convoy of half a dozen buses on the hot tarmac at Tan Son Nhut. None had an official exit visa. A senior official eventually allowed them to board the U.S. Air Force C-5A.

Orphanage workers, escorts, and an air force colonel carried the smallest infants, some of whom were blind or injured, through the enormous hold and up a slim ladder to the flight deck of the cargo plane. The press snapped photos of babies and children placed on the plane where ammunition had just been unloaded. Upstairs, a first lieutenant strapped them in two to a seat. Downstairs, the older kids lay on blankets, strapped down using the same restraints that had secured arms and ammunition westward across the Pacific. Most of the escorts —many dozens of them—were embassy and female Defense Attaché Office and Defense Intelligence Agency staff, about to be quietly ferried out of the country. With the escorts crouched in the aisle, gripping armrests, the plane took off.

Approximately twelve minutes later, the C-5A crashed into a rice paddy. Concrete dikes split the fuselage into chunks. The bottom half of the plane sheared off with the impact. The older children, the orphanage staff, and many of the Americans, nearly all contained in this lower level, were killed.

Amid the flames and smoke of the burning plane, survivors ran across the field, turning over the bodies of children in hopes that they would not drown in the shallow water. Helicopters soon thrummed overhead to take survivors back to Tan Son Nhut. About sixty children were recovered, though it remained unclear who, exactly, they were. The passenger lists were inconsistent. Numbers compiled later would indicate that seventy-eight children and between forty and sixty adults had died in the crash.

In Saigon, the event was seen as possible sabotage. On the day of the crash, the South Vietnamese Interior Ministry announced it had uncovered a plot to overthrow the president. It was the second such announcement that week. The citywide curfew was set back an hour, to nine p.m. Anyone resisting arrest, a loudspeaker blared through the streets, would be shot on sight.

Karen, Lynne, and Tori did not know it yet, but their 747 would soon become part of this sequence of events. A businessman-philanthropist had mortgaged his Connecticut home to write a check that would allow a U.S.-based adoption agency to charter a Pan Am flight. Another agency leveraged its own funds to hire a second plane. Both airplanes would be diverted from regular flight routes in the region — including the one from Hong Kong on which the three women now went about their standard business — to fly to Saigon and then to the United States with the evacuated children.

The Pan Am Saigon station chief was instructed to allow no Vietnamese airport staff to board either plane on arrival; in these first hours after the crash, all were seen as possible saboteurs. He was also to keep whichever jet arrived second waiting in the air. Two 747s on the Tan Son Nhut tarmac presented too much of a target. The airline wanted potential loss of crew and equipment mitigated. Once one plane was wheels up, the other would swoop down to land.

18

War Comes Aboard

THE GREAT RETREAT" READ THE WORDS ON THE MAGAZINE'S cover, white against the mud and grass of the photo. As Karen walked toward the rear of the plane, she saw the March 31 issue of *Newsweek* held in front of more than one passenger's face.

The cover photo showed a Vietnamese woman standing against a barren field holding a baby girl in her arms. The woman wore a conical straw hat that cast half of her face in shadow. She held her mouth tight at its corners. Her eyes weren't visible as she looked down at the child. The child wore a red shirt and no pants. Her head, arms, and legs hung limp. Mud smeared her round forehead and stomach, and dried blood spread over her plump legs. Her eyes looked out of the frame. She could have been alive; she could have been dead.

Karen had met the Norwegian purser Tori before, but none of the other women in this crew traveling from New Delhi to Hong Kong looked familiar. She enjoyed Lynne's quiet, dry wit. In the galley, the women talked about Hong Kong—their favorite places, whether they would eat Chinese or French food. Karen felt a snap of guilt, thinking about food as the copies of *Newsweek* and the path of the airplane reminded passengers of the suffering below. Karen heard the pilot announce that the plane would go around Vietnamese and Cambodian airspace.

In Hong Kong, the stewardesses smiled at the passengers as they departed. Once everyone had left, they boarded the crew bus outside the airport and settled in for the short drive to the hotel. The stewardesses had still not settled on whether to have French or Chinese food when a man boarded the bus and began to read a telegram.

"'Scheduled pattern canceled,'" the man said. Tori, Karen, and Lynne listened. "'Depart April fifth for Saigon to pick up orphan charter. Two hundred ninety-five infants. One hundred children between two and twelve years. Sixty escorts—five doctors—ten nurses. Place infants two per bassinet under middle seats. Use only zones C to D to ensure constant surveillance.'"

The man made no mention of the previous day's crash. The flight scheduled to continue north to Tokyo would head south again. A midroute diversion was not so unusual, but this passenger load was. Tori, Karen, and Lynne knew that flying into Saigon rendered a crew's participation voluntary—they could not be forced to fly into a war zone—though none of them considered declining the assignment.

Tori stood at the front of the bus. Karen admired the way she took charge. "This is gonna be some work," Tori said. "We're going to have to be at our best. We're going to have to be organized."

The bus ride to the hotel was fifteen minutes or so, stop-and-go through downtown Hong Kong. Karen added the numbers in her head. The most children she had ever seen in one place was around a hundred and fifty, an elementary-school gymnasium's worth of kids. And many of these passengers were infants. Karen could not envision what nearly four hundred infants and children on an airplane would look, feel, or sound like.

As the bus knocked down the city streets, Lynne looked out the window at familiar Hong Kong passing by: laundry above, shop doors open, women in skirt suits carrying structured purses or groceries slung over shoulders. Lynne's husband, Alex, had just applied for a job here, a logistics engineering position at the airport. He had not officially been hired yet, but they were confident enough that they had begun to dismantle their Manhattan Beach life.

At the hotel the women took the elevator to their rooms. The usual clientele milled through the lobby—the stockbrokers and merchants in the city for business, the tourists exploring Hong Kong before venturing farther into Asia.

As Tori, Lynne, and Karen were entering their hotel rooms, Ingrid Templeton, one of the stewardesses on a different Pan Am flight into Hong Kong, was sitting in her hotel room watching the news reports on the C-5A crash into the rice paddy just outside of Tan Son Nhut. The plane had torn deep ruts into the field. Now filled with water, they reflected silvery sky. Across the field, mangled chunks of plane still smoked.

Ingrid heard a knock at the door and opened it to a bellhop with a telegram. Schedule pattern canceled; she would go to Saigon with an orphan charter.

Ingrid was three months pregnant; she had planned to tell her supervisor the next month, when she could not hide the bulge so easily. Although the new union had brought maternity and weight complaints against twenty airlines, the restrictions against pregnancy were still in place, and Ingrid would have to stop flying when she told her supervisor she was pregnant. She wanted to collect a paycheck for as long as she possibly could.

In her hotel room Tori's phone began to ring. She had turned on her television too.

"I don't want to go," a voice on the phone said.

"It's your choice, of course," Tori said. "None of us is required to fly into a war zone."

Tori placed the phone back in its receiver. Minutes later, it rang again.

"I'm not going," another woman said. More women from her crew dropping out.

Ingrid, in her hotel room, considered her options. She was thirty years old, pregnant, loved the work she had been doing for nine years. From San Francisco she had flown servicemen in and out of Vietnam. She had waited out mortar fire at Tan Son Nhut, taken a helicopter ride over Da Nang. She could handle this new assignment, she thought.

Outside the hotel, Kowloon had quieted. Across the street, the neon Rolex sign, with its swooping Chinese characters, had shut off. People were still walking along the road, their shoulders crooked with the weight of shopping bags, but the commuters passing through had gone home, and the buses had returned to the depot.

Tori's crew was down to nine other women, then eight. Still fine by FAA rules, she thought before she got into bed, considering the angles. The role of purser, ideally, meant conducting a practiced orchestra. In an emergency the role grew more complicated. The safety of a plane full of people would come down to her. It was the price of leadership.

Lynne sat hunched at the desk in her room, writing to her parents on a blue onionskin aerogram provided by the hotel. "This is a very historic moment and I wanted you both to share it," she wrote. "As with most things, I'm not too sure [if] I'm very excited or afraid at this moment . . . I'll probably want to adopt all 390 kids when I see them."

In her hotel room, Karen flopped across the bed. She thought of calling her parents but the expense didn't make sense. She had no one else to call. A friend had told her she would have a difficult year after she divorced Alan. She had left him for good after Valentine's Day, when she'd opened their trash bin upon returning from a trip and seen the detritus of a romantic date with someone who was not her. Now Karen lay on the bed in the Hong Kong Hyatt, grieving the failure of her marriage, about to fly into a war zone. *Isn't my life just grand,* she thought, aware of her self-indulgence, feeling sad all the same. It was easier to pity herself than give in to the fear.

Tori tried to sleep. She had seen the news as she walked through the lobby. A U.S. Air Force C-5A had crashed; her plane could crash. But of the over three hundred passengers on board, more than one hundred seventy had survived. *If we are prepared we will have our best chance,* she thought. She reminded herself again that the preparation of her crew came down to her.

The women who gathered the next morning had earned their seniority. Five of the women from the original crew had chosen to fly to Saigon. Two more women, Joanie Carnell and Paula Helfrich, had flown in from Tokyo and Honolulu, respectively. Joanie had flown for fourteen years, Tori and Ingrid nine, Karen and Lynne six each. Paula had five years of flying and a well-earned reputation for thrill-seeking. Against all safety regulations she liked to strap herself to the tarmac in Honolulu at the outer limits of the landing strip and watch, screaming, as a 747 bore down toward the ground above her. Joanie, in contrast, had a dry personality, was English, and had been among the first women assigned to Pan Am's San Francisco base a decade and a half earlier. She had flown countless R&Rs and sat out two typhoons on Guam. Neither Paula nor Joanie was the anxious type.

The cool recirculated air wafted through the permanent sunshine of thirty-five thousand feet as the 747 flew Tori and her crew over the China Sea to Saigon. There were no passengers in the seats to warm the recycled air, but the vivid yellow and orange upholstery gave the impression, if not the reality, of heat. The carpet underfoot stretched down the plane's two aisles that looked to Karen to be the length of football fields. In nodes of two or three, the women worked with a dozen or so civilian volunteers from Hong Kong. The women assembled cardboard bassinets and slid blue plastic Pan Am carrying cases around each one. Some bassinets would be placed lengthwise, one to a seat and stretching the length of a man's thigh, with a seat belt threaded through the handles. Others sat in piles atop seats in the rear of the plane where older children could sit in their own seats, interspersed with the infants. In the galley, row upon row of empty bottles refracted the light until Lynne mixed the powdered milk at half strength—the babies' stomachs were not accustomed to milk—and filled them partway. Karen ferried bags of diapers and donated clothes to closets and stacked them up for the easiest possible access.

As Lynne stood in the galley, Austin Lee—the Hong Kong station's head of public relations, who had volunteered to help on the flight—told her about the crash of the C-5A. She had not known. The children they would pick up were not only orphans, as the airline's message had said; some were also survivors of the crash.

Quiet talk about the crash spread through the empty plane like ink through water.

The plane could have gone down for any number of reasons, Karen thought. Ingrid listened to what she thought was someone saying a prayer over the PA system. Joanie reached for more diapers. Austin Lee's camera caught Paula mid-laugh, her head thrown back.

The pilots dipped the plane low as it approached Saigon. Tori knew the captain had been told to keep the tail number for this refugee flight clearly visible to the North Vietnamese troops surrounding the city. Karen leaned toward a window and snapped a photo of the flat land to the east of Saigon with gray rivers twisting back and forth, a dozen tiny white puffs of cloud between plane and ground.

People on the plane strapped themselves into seats near wherever they had been working.

The plane landed on the tarmac and rolled to a stop. Tori pushed open the door and proceeded down the stairs. Lynne looked out as jeeps and buses began to drive toward the plane. The 747 stayed far out on the tarmac—as far from the terminal as possible, it looked to her. Lee snapped a photo. In profile, her face radiated calm thoughtfulness.

Death was not the thing Lynne feared most. Adults had made it out of the C-5A crash alive, Lee said. The worst possibility, to Lynne, would be living when children died.

————

Adult arms formed a firemen's chain on the tarmac. Doctors, nurses, ground staff, and escorts passed the babies from one set of arms to the next. Men balanced infants in the crooks of their arms. The older children walked from the buses onto the plane, their legs twiggy against the gray of the tarmac. Pan Am station chief Al Topping stood a full head above the South Vietnamese police around him. As a tall, wide-shouldered Black man, Topping had grown used to sticking out in Vietnam. Between rounds of patting down the children, he pushed his aviator sunglasses farther up on the bridge of his nose. He could not be too careful; if someone had bombed a military transport filled with orphans, an explosive device on a child was not out of the question.

Their tiny bodies were unbelievably hot, Karen thought as a set of hands passed her an infant, then a second and a third. Karen stood inside the plane, moving through the warmer air near the door into the cool of the plane once, twice, six times, eleven times, carrying infants. Her arms were full and a child with no leg had lost his crutches in the crush, so he hobbled down the aisle. The babies in her arms screamed as Karen placed each inside the nearest cardboard bassinet. She straightened and reached for another baby. Her eyes met those of the woman handing her the child. Both of the women's eyes brimmed.

Tori stood in the galley taking stock. She counted heads, then lost count. The women were performing perfectly. She walked back down the steps to the tarmac.

"Ma'am," a doctor said, approaching her. "We'd like to bring our nurses."

The Seventh-Day Adventist hospital had three nurses, he explained, young Vietnamese women who wanted to leave before the Communists arrived. They had no visas. They had no documentation at all. But the doctor would vouch for them, he said. The women stood behind him.

Tori looked at the women, calculating. There was a low chance they were capable of sabotaging a plane full of war orphans. Something similar, though, might have happened to the previous day's plane. But the adults were so outnumbered by the wave of needy children. Extra hands, trained hands, would help. "I can't authorize that," she said. "I'll ask the captain."

The doctor nodded and turned away.

"Strip-search them and lock them in the lav," the captain instructed Tori when she asked about the nurses.

Tori returned to the doctor and the nurses by the plane. One by one, she patted the women down. She ran her hands across their white uniforms, behind their legs, under their armpits, around their necks, under their hair. She led them onto the plane.

"Just stay in the bathroom until we're cruising," she said as she locked the door.

Karen continued up and down the aisle, two infants at a time. In the galley, she saw a Vietnamese immigration official leaning over the adoption forms. As he walked out, she overheard a volley of dialogue between two adoption agency workers.

"Well, you've got to fill this in somehow . . ."

"I don't know . . ."

"Give him a new name."

She reached out toward a new duo of infants, scooped them into her arms. The knowledge that not all the children were orphans did not appear in a single moment, with the agency staffers' dialogue; rather, it had grown with an accretion of details. At thirty-one, Karen had been anguished over the possibility of not having children. She understood being a mother was the most essential and powerful thing a woman could do, a human experience she did not want to miss. She knew maternal love to be fierce, sacred. She tucked one infant and then the other into bassinets. The scope of the present disaster—the fear that could drive a mother to hand her infant over to an unknown future—overwhelmed her. Empathy became anger as she moved down the aisle. *What the hell did we do to these mothers that they're sending their babies away?* she thought.

The women organized the children on the plane by age and health.

The youngest babies went into first class, where the escort-to-infant ratio was highest. In the main cabin, older babies went two to a bassinet. Children who could sit up were in the middle of the plane, with bassinets under their short legs, and the oldest were in the rear. The ill or injured would go upstairs to a makeshift sick bay in the lounge. The doctors assessed their needs. Some infants required IV fluids, but a razor was needed to shave a patch of their scalps where the needle would enter. Tori nodded and again sought out the pilot, then the flight engineers. One of the men had to have a safety razor handy. But no. She moved through the plane, flagging down any adult male, and eventually she found a razor. She had not known that infant IVs went into veins in their scalps.

Finally the children were settled in their seats. Al Topping stepped into the plane momentarily before locking it up. The din and the scent of the frightened children was unbelievable. He could not imagine being on the flight. The second plane was in the air above Saigon, ready to swoop toward the runway for a second load of children. He headed back to the airport to give the order for it to land.

From the front of the cabin, the seats appeared empty, as if the plane were a ghost ship, nothing but sound and smell. As Karen walked through the aisle, she saw older children pressing their faces against the windows or reaching for babies. She went to her jump seat and strapped herself in.

Once the plane had reached cruising altitude, Tori began to circulate. A few of the children spoke French. She could communicate with the older ones. She checked their bracelets, which carried a combination of Vietnamese and Anglo names, destinations, and medical conditions. These facts were the barest of clues to the chaos from which each child had been sent. A child bound, eventually, for Luxembourg might wear a scribbled name tag reading *Lux Enbollrg;* a baby named Ne Tuan might bear a note reading *loose stool*. Tori carried those children whose bracelets indicated an illness upstairs to the sick bay.

IV lines crisscrossed the first-class lounge. The doctors moved around the room, attending to the survivors of the previous day's crash and to the sickest of the children. There were cases of hepatitis, meningitis, and chicken pox. In an attempt to keep diseases from flooding the plane, all sick children were to remain upstairs.

Tori found a little boy with chicken pox in the general cabin; she gripped his hand and walked him upstairs, then returned to checking on the others. Within minutes a French-speaking little boy tugged on her skirt. The sick child had gone back downstairs to be with his friends, he told Tori.

"Take me to him," Tori said. Together they found the little boy. Tori walked him down the aisle and back up the stairs.

Karen watched men — volunteer escorts from Hong Kong — changing diapers expertly on aisle-seat tray tables. They had probably never changed their own children's diapers, she thought, but here they were. She admired their dexterity and lack of fuss.

In the aisle, a snowdrift of torn paper gathered. Escorts had passed out coloring books, colored pencils, and small toys indiscriminately. The smaller children had ripped up the coloring books and then torn apart emergency pamphlets, airsick bags, magazines.

A young teenager, one of the volunteers — Karen saw him as a California-surfer type, with his long hair and easy gaze — offered an arm to the injured boy who had lost his crutch. In his other arm he carried an infant. Karen continued down the aisle, stepping over children, on her way to the galley for a bottle of milk. She folded down a jump seat and sat to try to feed a baby, but he would not take the bottle. He moved his face back and forth as she chased his moving mouth with the bottle's nipple. His nose was incomprehensibly small. Behind her sat a little girl. When she thought Karen was not looking, she reached out to touch the American woman's blond hair.

"Have you seen that fourteen-year-old with long hair in row twenty-three?" a flushed woman asked Karen as she stood for another bottle. Karen nodded. "That's my son. He's becoming a man tonight," the woman said proudly.

The French-speaking little boy tugged on Tori's blue skirt again. Again his friend had escaped, he said. And he had to use the toilet, but he was not tall enough.

Tori found a box for him, waited outside the lavatory, and then they found the escaped child again. *Everyone, absolutely everyone,* Tori thought grimly, *will have chicken pox by Guam.*

Lynne leaned over seats, holding a bottle in each hand, trying to feed two squalling infants at once. When they each latched on, she leaned the bottles against the bassinet, grabbed more bottles from the galley, and moved on to the next set of babies. She hoped the pilots would find the cleanest, clearest airstreams. Turbulence would frighten the older children and rock the precarious bottles from the mouths of the younger ones.

Lynne attended to the babies who were wet or hungry or both. She handed hamburgers to the older children. Lynne felt gratitude and respect for the competence of the women with whom she worked. No one needed Tori to tell them what to do. They responded to the need they saw with instinctive direction and authority. Men waged war with no consideration for the disastrous consequences, she thought. Across industries and professions, they sought ugly power. And women worked together to clean up the mess.

Tori began to understand what had occurred to Karen: Some of the children had parents. Some tiny wrists wore no medical bracelets. They could not be identified as orphans. She lifted her feet above the debris and the toddlers now crawling through the aisles while pasting a smile on her face for the older child whose wrist she now examined.

By the time they landed in Guam, it would be night. For the time being, the stewardesses reached over children and lowered the window shades, hoping that the darkness would signal sleep for at least some. It worked. Karen moved through the cabin with a flashlight, checking for moving rib cages. She pressed her hand against scrawny bellies, making sure the small bodies had cooled as the plane's temperature stabilized.

Tori settled into the first seat in business class, bulkhead space in front of her, so that her crew knew where to find her. Volunteers brought her a rotation of infants who would not take bottles, and Tori tried to coax them to eat.

Joanie looked at her watch. She'd been on her feet for nearly eighteen hours, she realized. A little girl had all but attached herself to her, following her around the plane as she changed diapers and swapped empty bottles for full. They sat together on a jump seat now.

As Karen carried trays back to the galley, she saw a little girl leaning over a crying baby boy. Karen smiled at the girl as she picked her way around them. Heartwarming. She watched as the little girl raised her hand in a closed fist and then punched the baby.

Karen dropped the trays in a sharp clatter and grabbed the child's shoulders. She raised her own hand, ready to slap the girl, then stopped herself. Her face felt tight. She picked the girl up and handed her to the fourteen-year-old volunteer. She brought the baby, now screaming, up the stairs. The teenager and child followed.

"He looks fine," a doctor said as he ran fingers across the baby's tiny face. The little girl's name was added to the list of children with special requirements.

The stewardesses were quietly making do amid the overwhelming need. There was a perverse gorgeousness at work, Lynne thought as she looked around. Tori was in the bulkhead surrounded by a cluster of children. Joanie was still trailed by the little girl. Karen was shining her flashlight into bassinets. Paula, ever animated, was telling the older children stories. The civilians too had found their tasks.

The plane began its descent. Another crew would board the plane and steward the children on to Honolulu, then San Francisco. With nowhere near enough seats, Tori now sat on the floor in front of the seats in which she had strapped children. A few of the older kids with whom she had been speaking French sat next to her. She wrapped her arms around all the children she could, and then the plane was on the ground. The pilots had performed marvelously, she thought.

Tori remained on the floor as the doors opened, as the rest of the women stood to brief the oncoming crew. Karen watched their faces as they walked aboard, the widened eyes, the incongruity of their starched uniforms set against the disorder. Lynne went down the stairs, as did Karen. The stewardesses gathered on the tarmac.

Tori did not want to leave. "The new crew is just like me," she tried to reassure the children. "You see? The same uniform, different faces, but the same kind of people."

Joanie sniffed as she hugged the little girl goodbye.

Cars waited outside to take the crew to the hotel. Tori climbed into one and began to cry.

19

The Most Incredible Scene

WHEN THE FIRST CIVILIANS WALKED UP THE STAIRS OF ONE of the two 747s that landed in the United States, they were presented with "the most incredible scene of deprivation and illness I've ever seen," said the medical director of the orphan reception center in San Francisco. "The staff of about fifteen or so were so exhausted that many of the women could barely stand."

In the first chaotic weeks of the babylift, flights removed children from the country in fits and starts, hundreds of them per plane. Three planes took off from Saigon, went to Guam, and continued on to the United States, but then flights were halted. By April 11 they had resumed. By April 17, nearly two weeks after Tori, Karen, and Lynne's flight, 1,650 children had landed in the United States, but questions over their legality pushed the Immigration and Naturalization Service to stop further flights. Discrepancies began to emerge even before all the children had arrived. Numbers and names varied across official documents. On April 18, the agency announced the flights could continue until the total permitted number of children, two thousand, had arrived. Over a three-week period, 2,242 children were flown to the United States on a succession of chartered flights on various airlines, World and Pan Am included. *Playboy* magnate Hugh Hefner, sensing a public relations opportunity, donated the use of his "bunny plane" to fly one group of orphans from San Francisco to New York; a few off-duty Playboy Bunnies volunteered to fly with the children.

But news articles had begun to reflect a more conflicted tone concerning the evacuations. An informal conference of two hundred fifty aid workers, congresspeople, and Immigration and Naturalization Services officials convened in early April to speed the airlift of orphans, the meeting punctuated by challenges to the presumption that the Vietnamese children, especially of Black American servicemen, would be better off in the U.S. than in Vietnam. "Do you think they'll be allowed in the South Boston schools?" one attendee asked, referring to the highly publicized school busing conflicts playing out in this all-white enclave. A Yale psychologist called the children "pawns." An MIT political scientist asked who the real orphans were, the children or Vietnam? "We're trying to prove that we are not really abandoning these people," he said. "We want to know we're still good, we're still decent." A Vietnamese anthropologist living in California told the reporter that she was "livid." "What is this terror Americans feel that my people will devour children?" she asked.

Karen called her parents from the airport. The women had been told to take two weeks of paid time to quarantine; having been exposed to so many diseases, they could not handle food on a flight. With no one waiting for her back home in Missoula, Karen wanted to spend the time with her family.

Down in Whittier everything was the same, including the junky Oldsmobile she parked in her parents' driveway, the broad, sunny streets with cars extending diagonally from the storefronts of low buildings, and the low suburban houses.

Karen told her parents about the flight's feeling of unreality, the weight of the tiny infants in her arms—too light—and the little girl who punched the baby. She had prayed at takeoff—to which God she was unsure.

Now Karen moved around her parents' house from one room to the next, her aimlessness a reflection of the sudden lack of direction in her life. She felt more than ever that she wanted to have children, but she was afraid that she had no path to them.

Her friends had noted how the physical distance between Karen and Alan kept them together. Their incompatibilities had less time to rise to the surface with weeks and even years separating each segment of commitment, with Alan in the navy and Karen flying for large chunks of time. "I knew you had to marry him to get him out of your system," her mother said when they divorced. But Karen did not regret marrying Alan. Even though he had broken her heart, Alan made Karen smarter, more daring, she thought. She would eventually talk about him with a complicated blend of exasperation and gratitude.

After watching Karen mope around the house for two days, her mother approached her. "You've always wanted to be a writer," she said. "Haven't you? Why don't you write this up? This is the perfect story for *Reader's Digest.*"

Her parents got the *Los Angeles Times* every morning; few articles related the status of the children. On April 8, one, "Drama and Tragedy: Last Flight on Its Way in Operation Baby Lift," briefly reported on the situation. There was an op-ed, sharply critical of the endeavor: "The United States Is Still Sure That It Knows Best." Then there was "'Operation Babylift' Closes Shop." Karen agreed with the suspicion about her government's interests, but to her, real people had still been doing real things to try to help other real, frightened people, no matter how confused it had gotten.

She sat down every day at the typewriter her mother had set up on a desk in her brother's old bedroom. Karen recalled the details of the flight, stitched them together into a cohesive story: The teenage volunteer who looked like the surfers she had grown up with, his proud mother. The doctors scrambling to keep up with the sick children. The overwhelming quantity of need, the feeling of trying.

By the time she finished, the quarantine was done too. Karen had developed no symptoms of any illness. "War Comes Aboard," she titled the piece. She pressed the pages into an envelope and sent it off to *Reader's Digest*. She began to fly again. Her wanderlust had acquired a new edge. Karen's determination to roam was now as much intellectual as physical.

In California, no one asked Lynne any questions about the refugee flight. If her life were a staged play, she thought, she would have just leaped from her Manhattan Beach–based theater to an entirely different stage, performed three full acts, and then jumped back again mid-scene into her own play. The beginning, middle, and end of the orphan flight had taken place at a remove from her life, and the arc of its story felt disconnected from her own.

Back home, Lynne never read a news article about the babylift. If there was television coverage of it, she had been watching other programs. Alex had gotten the job in Hong Kong; they would move across the Pacific in a few months. Lynne spent time dismantling their apartment and organizing their possessions into boxes. For now she continued to fly. But Lynne felt her loyalties split between her husband and Pan Am.

Later Lynne would consider how the play-within-the-play had shaped the larger production of her life. It would occur to her that in parallel with the babylift—an enormous, definitive rupture in the life of every single child on the plane, a change that would be scrutinized for many years, that would come to define the futures of the children as they grew into adults—she was going through a much smaller yet still significant change. Her own life was fracturing into a before and after. She had spent years out in the vast, imperfect world; now she turned toward the domestic sphere. Los Angeles to Hong Kong, Pan Am to her family.

When Lynne told her supervisor she'd made her decision, she heard her own thoughts echoed back to her: "I can't believe you're quitting. You love this job."

"I don't really have a choice," Lynne replied. She explained that she thought she was making the right decision.

"Nobody quits Pan Am," the woman said, shaking her head.

In a letter to her parents, she wrote that the world had seemed about to cave in when she quit. She flew on her last discounted ticket to meet Alex in Seattle, where they would be living temporarily before Hong Kong. Lynne felt "homeless, jobless, friendless, and moneyless." She went to dinner with Alex's boss, sewed herself a dress with fabric from India, and cleaned and packed and ironed clothes for the move. Lynne had been learning basket-weaving to have an "occupation." And as she wrote her parents, "Alex has been hinting about a family but not yet until I get settled maybe in 10 years or so!"

By that summer, she and Alex had set up a home in Hong Kong. She tried to do work for Pan Am with Austin Lee, the public relations man she'd met on the babylift flight, but it did not become a career. Lack of interest in Chinese culture among the expatriates she met in this former British colony repelled Lynne. With her science background, she volunteered at the Grand Aquarium, observing and assisting the trainers. She wore plain clothing; she walked everywhere; she made Chinese friends. Soon she got pregnant. She and Alex returned to Seattle to live after a year and a half in Hong Kong, and after she gave birth, the task of reentering the workforce as a woman and mother turned out to be more difficult than she had imagined. It was Lynne's knowledge of China that would lead to her second career.

Within twenty-four hours of Tori's arrival in Newport Beach, she received a call from her base manager. Would she go back for another load of orphans? She had already been exposed to their illnesses. Tori flew immediately to Guam; her quarantine meant only that she could not crew on a plane, not that she could not deadhead on one. But when she arrived at the Guamerica Inn, she was told that the orphan airlift had been canceled. She would be kept on the island on standby. The State Department, she was told, would foot the bill to keep two crews and two 707s on the island until the evacuation from Saigon was complete.

Tori waited on Guam. Saigon's fall was imminent. Bribes, threats, and covert operations proliferated. In classified advertisements, a "fairly pretty high-school girl . . . from [a] well-to-do family" asked to pose as a daughter or bride; a Vietnamese economist offered ten thousand dollars to any American man who married his pregnant wife. Lumpy walls of sandbags strung with concertina wire blocked access to the airport. The embassy pressed Pan Am station manager Al Topping to increase his flights out of the country to halt rising panic.

A flight into Vietnam would leave Guam by three p.m. or it would not leave at all. It was too dangerous for a plane to be on the tarmac at Tan Son Nhut at nightfall. One of the stewardesses decided that the women waiting on Guam formed a club of sorts—the "Mortar Magnets," she called them. Each day, as the clock ticked past three, they gathered around the pool or at the bar to drink the tension away.

Pan Am's sole Vietnamese stewardess had also volunteered for the flights. She hoped to sneak her four sisters out of South Vietnam while the country still existed. Stewardesses always traveled with an extra uniform, and she began to borrow them from anyone with a small frame. Tori handed her skirt and jacket over.

At the end of the month, three flights took off from Guam days before the North Vietnamese took over Saigon. The State Department charter flew to Saigon and returned with a meager two dozen government employees. On another 707, Tori flew to Clark Air Base in the Philippines to pick up a load of people who had left Vietnam by crowded boat. She brought the gaunt refugees, as subdued as the children had been noisy, to Guam, where they joined twenty thousand others waiting for processing.

And on Pan Am's final flight out of Saigon—the last commercial American airplane to enter and then exit the city for three decades —a stuffed planeload of employees and dependents, including four teenage girls in borrowed Pan Am uniforms, left the country. An American government agent had seen the women at the airport, "floating in their skirts," "spraining their ankles in high-heeled shoes." He watched as they approached the airplane. At the base of its stairs, one of the women took off her shoes and scaled the steps two at a time. In a very different context from that of so many stewardesses before them, the women raced away from the past in light blue uniforms.

All for one, Tori thought. *One for all.*

20

The Only Lonely Place
Was on the Moon

I N THE UNITED STATES, THE AMERICAN SOLDIERS WHO HAD RE-
turned from war—Tori's "boys," the ones who had, as Karen had
instructed them, come home safe—struggled to find a place for
themselves. Even if they were welcomed home, their stories were not
wanted. The country wanted to move on. As the North Vietnamese
moved through Saigon, a scene representing unvarnished U.S. defeat,
the tone of some American media verged on triumphant. A protest
movement led by the young people expected to wage war had helped
to bring about its end. Where this left the men who had fought it—the
men who had died for it—was unclear.

It was also unclear where the war's end left the thousands of stewardesses who had bought the men to and from combat and the few
—Tori, Karen, and Lynne among them—who had brought the war's
consequences straight home to the country's consciousness. By the
numbers, stewardesses had formed one of the largest groups of civilians to contribute to the Vietnam War. Nearly all of the hundreds of
women employed at Pan Am's Los Angeles and San Francisco bases
had taken war charters. Some women had flown soldiers in during

troop buildup and out during the war's final withdrawal—nine full years in and out of combat theater.

In the weeks and months following the babylift, the event continued to capture the American imagination. "Many people in the United States, and the government itself, wanted a happy ending to the war which lasted twelve years for the Americans. They wanted to feel we had won something," wrote journalist Gloria Emerson in her National Book Award–winning *Winners and Losers.* "In the spring of 1975 it was the arrival of two thousand Vietnamese children, described as orphans, who were rushed here just before the Communists prevailed . . . we needed something alive to forget the dead."

But across the country, feature articles and opinion pieces continued to detail the muddied ethics of the endeavor from start to finish. The first C-5A crash, it soon emerged, had not been caused by sabotage. A rear cargo door blew out at twenty-three thousand feet. The military had apparently long been aware of such mechanical malfunctions on the craft.

Soon the lawsuits began. A sister of one of the escorts who'd died in the crash charged the Lockheed Aircraft Corporation with negligence. A class-action lawsuit on the part of Vietnamese mothers of evacuated children named "Henry Kissinger et al." as defendants. It cited the Paris Peace Accords and the Geneva Conventions in which three articles laid out orphan protocols, none of which had been followed. Among other stipulations, it stated that orphans' education should, "as far as possible, be entrusted to persons of a similar cultural tradition."

There was a far more serious breach: Immigration and Naturalization Service investigations found that 263 children, 10 percent of the evacuees, had never been eligible for adoption. Plaintiffs pored over INS documents and claimed the number was much higher: 1,511. Birth mothers arrived in the United States asking for their children. Many adoptive families dug in. One couple facing a lawsuit from a birth mother who had arrived in the States would delay the trial of their case for nearly a year. Throughout the following year, individual lawsuits by Vietnamese mothers present in America nearly all found in favor of the mother. The refugees and their children became new American families. The class-action lawsuit, though, unraveled as soon as case files opened; the children's situations were tremendously varied. "If ever there were a 'Frankenstein monster posing as a class action lawsuit,' this is it," the judge said.

Independent considerations of the children's adoptive situations revealed further complications. One official estimated that 325 Black Vietnamese American children, all up for adoption, had been placed with white parents. Of forty Black families approved for adoption, only five had been selected by adoption agencies. "We believe that these children can best survive the racism in America and achieve a healthy identity through adoption by Black families," said a representative of the Black Child Development Institute at a press conference alongside two other social service agencies.

The children had been taken from the country in chaos and haste by individuals whose intentions were overwhelmingly good. But this act of national catharsis after a devastating war was twisted through bureaucratic mistakes that revealed profound and damaging biases. A decade earlier, perhaps, such carelessness and prejudice might have passed with less immediate resistance, but that time was gone.

At the start of the jet age, the number of passenger-miles in the United States—a standard measure of industry growth—was thirty-one billion. In 1975, the same statistic hit one hundred and twenty billion. Air travel continued to grow, pushed up and up by a value-minded American public who were now flying for vastly different reasons than they had two decades earlier. No longer were airplanes the near-exclusive province of businessmen and the jet set. Airplane seating configurations reflected the change: a first-class cabin that had once consumed up to a third of a jet's cabin had shrunk in proportion to the growing economy class. People traveled to visit family and friends and to vacation. College students headed to campus on a plane rather than in a car. Unthinkably, more passengers wore jeans than pearls. In the twenty-first century, passenger-miles have risen to over five hundred billion.

By many accounts, it was the 747—its huge passenger load and investment—that began the end for Pan Am. Between 1969 and 1976, the airline lost $364 million as its debt rose to $1 billion. And then there was a fatal crash, still among the worst in history: in 1977 in Tenerife, a KLM jet taking off hit a taxiing Pan Am plane on the runway; 567 passengers died.

Pan Am tried to adapt to the changing needs of its customers by buying National, folding that airline's routes and its Nancy-, Margie-, and Barbara-named planes into the Pan Am fleet. But in 1978, the Airline Deregulation Act was passed and the reasons for the acquisition were no longer relevant, as rules around where Pan Am could and could not fly dissipated. Fares, too, were no longer regulated. Airfare prices had previously been set by the Civil Aeronautics Board according to the distance a passenger traveled, not what the purveyor of airplane and crew wanted to charge. But now fare competition began. The era of Pan Am's protective relationship with the U.S. government had ended at the worst possible time: interest rates and fuel prices were high, there was growing inflation, and in 1980, a recession began.

The airline began the long, slow process of selling off its assets to stay in business. The InterContinental Hotel Group was put on the block, as was the Pan Am Building on Park Avenue, the last New York skyscraper with legal rights to display its brand name in huge lettering. The sign soon spelled MET LIFE. The subsidiary Falcon Jet Corporation was sold. The Pacific Division and the entire swath of the world that had been, half a century earlier, the final link in the airline's ability to encircle the globe were gone by the mid-1980s. In 1991, the airline declared bankruptcy. Pan Am, TWA, Braniff, Eastern—within a decade, none would exist.

Pan Am's last flight landed in Miami on December 4, 1991. On the tarmac, the plane taxied beneath the arc of a fire truck's water cannon. Imagine rainbows dappling the warm air. Among the pilots and passengers, the assembled ground crew, and the police standing in an almost military row on the tarmac, few eyes were dry.

Change wasn't confined to Pan Am or even the airline industry. Throughout the mid-1970s, across business, government, media, and sports, the sense of what women could or should do was shifting. Women journalists brought lawsuits against *Newsweek* and the *New York Times,* pointing to the scores of men under them who had been promoted. Billie Jean King beat aging tennis star Bobby Riggs at his own game after Riggs had proclaimed that "women belong in the bedroom and the kitchen, in that order." Restrictions on prescriptions for the pill were now illegal, as was banks' discrimination against women, thanks to the 1974 Equal Credit Opportunity Act. Women went out to dinner in groups now. They appeared in rising numbers in the halls of medical and law schools.

As a result of a 1973 lawsuit Northwest Airlines was ordered to do away with its ban on eyeglasses and weight monitoring for its female cabin attendants. The verdict, according to one newspaper editorial, was "another in the lengthening series of decisions which insist that corporations abolish the obsolete, artificial distinctions between men's professions and women's work." Lawsuits would continue into the 1980s as former stewardesses sought to dismantle restrictions around pregnancy and appearance and to claim reassignment and back pay.

And yet, many of the women who had labored to bring about such changes, whether through lawsuits or their mere presence in the face of often overwhelming discrimination, still stared at stagnant job titles. Diplomat Alison Palmer would eventually spend about $150,000 leading a class-action lawsuit against the U.S. government; it started in 1976 and did not reach resolution for well over a decade. "It was a matter of principle. I saw the State Department—as well as the women —being injured by the terrible waste of talent," she later said. Finally, the court found in favor of Palmer and the other members of the suit, and the State Department eventually sent letters to 601 women to notify them that they might be eligible for reassignment.

A 1972 suit brought against Pan Am by a man who had applied to be a steward and was rejected gained speedier results. The airline argued that it was, as a profit-driven corporation, simply meeting its passengers' preferences by hiring women for the job. A psychiatrist explained the emotional reactions behind such preferences. A woman passenger might find a male steward's service intrusive or inappropriate. An apprehensive male passenger, he testified, would be either emasculated or repulsed by a fellow man's reassurance, depending on whether he saw the steward as more or less masculine than himself. Only a woman could effectively, by her "nature," calm both sexes. The judge hearing the case was not convinced and ordered Pan Am to "cease and desist from refusing to hire males as flight cabin attendants on the basis of their sex." The era of flight service as the near-exclusive domain of women was over.

By the late 1970s, a new cohort of crew used the flexibilities of the job to attend graduate school. Degrees in hand, thousands of women slipped into male-dominated fields. They worked as attorneys, psychiatrists, and bankers. They started small businesses and took their places on the mastheads of newspapers and magazines in increasing numbers. Having been initially unable to gain access to the professions and industries in which they had hoped to work, craving something that would afford more freedom for less friction, some stewardesses had sought refuge serving on planes that would take them around the world until the public position of women back home shifted enough to accommodate their ambition.

In the midst of these changing times, they would struggle to claim the respect they rightly deserved within and outside the industry. "Every time I see girls in slacks, it reminds me of China," former President Nixon had said in 1973 before asking a female reporter to turn her pants-clad behind toward him. Although, in the wake of the Watergate scandal and Nixon's 1974 resignation, Gerald Ford now sat in Nixon's office, and the prohibition on women in pants in the White House was lifted, it would not be until the 1980s that pants would be an option for flight attendants' uniforms. Epaulettes and slacks on female flight crews, one airline found in the 1980s, reduced in-flight assaults on attendants. Yet management believed that passengers might see such uniforms as "too military." On a few airlines, women would be required to wear makeup and skirts well into the twenty-first century.

Many women continued to fly for decades. Over the years, they flew out of one title for the job they performed and into the next. The term now is *flight attendant.*

Other women moved into management and had long and rewarding careers. Though they no longer made up a flight crew, their connections to one another only strengthened as they climbed company ranks together. "I think they'd all been just as determined as I," Clare Christiansen said of the women in the Manhattan flight service office. As a result of one particularly satisfying promotion, she took charge of upgrading stewardesses into management positions, helping women make the exact leap toward which she had struggled years earlier.

Diversity on the airlines increased too. Hazel Bowie would, for her forty-year career in flight, remain in the minority, but over the years she collected a strong network of African-American and Latina stewardess friends and acquaintances, some of whom left stewardessing and found huge success in business or academia. Flying had generated lists of contacts around the world and helped them, as young women, grow comfortable among all kinds of people. "[Flying with Pan Am] let me assert myself, my African-ness, wherever I am," said Alice Dear, the first Black woman appointed executive director of the African Development Bank in the 1990s. Hazel took her mother—who had once been so afraid for her daughter's safety as an adventurous young Black woman—to Bangkok and Hong Kong, out through San Francisco and over the Pacific and back through Europe with stops planned in various cities. For the first time in her life, Hazel saw her mother in total awe. The look of wonderment on her face at the Bangkok flower market, in Hazel's opinion, was a masterpiece that rivaled any she ever saw in the museums of Rome.

In the constant revision of history to reinsert marginalized individuals into scenes in which they always existed, the women have slowly gained recognition for their contributions to the American war in Vietnam. In 1993, Diane Carlson, a former army nurse, dedicated the Vietnam Women's Memorial, located on the National Mall across a winding path from Maya Lin's stark Vietnam Veterans Memorial wall of names. Approximately eleven thousand women were stationed in Vietnam during the war. The tally of two hundred sixty-five thousand working women and volunteers commemorated by the Women's Memorial includes stewardesses. Carlson said of the memorial she founded, "We tried to recognize that everybody had a job to do and we were part of a big team. What would we have done without those wonderful flight attendants who offered us all some comfort?"

A very few of the stewardesses, especially those who crewed the more dramatic and dangerous flights, self-identify as veterans of war. Relatively few place their work in historical context or speak openly with civilians about the job's more difficult moments. It is too much effort to address the disconnect between the perception of the job as all glamour and access amid the optimistic globalism of the 1960s and its actual context, which also entailed objectification and misunderstanding, war and danger—the dark side of that globalist vision.

Airline alumni organizations launched in the 1950s still serve as essential community for large numbers of women—along with increasing numbers of men—who understand one another, they say, like family. Many of these women still wear pearls from Hong Kong and Italian shoes purchased in Milan rather than in New York department stores. The women gather for reunions and yearly luncheons that pull together hundreds of former stewardesses and continuing flight attendants in conference hotels and on cruises. They still have fun together. Their conversation never stops, but it gets either louder and funnier or quieter and more intimate as the time passes. As Clare Christiansen says of her management cohort in retirement, some of whom she speaks to on the phone three times a week, "I would die without my girlfriends."

People who know these former stewardesses like to talk about them. A daughter elaborates on the places her mother visited and tells stories of movie stars and politicians she served and the refugees she comforted. Nieces and nephews pass on the family lore about the colorful aunt who brought them the best Christmas gifts from around the world. Neighbors and friends hearing about a war flight after a few bottles of wine have made their way around the table at a former stewardess's home don't forget it.

After the babylift, Tori, Lynne, and Karen went their separate ways. From a certain perspective, the flight they had served on was a harbinger for the coming years. Millions of human lives continued to sweep on around the circumstances that drew or repelled airlines. The global movements of the next decades—the dismantling of the USSR and changes in laws governing legal immigration resulting in increased arrivals from Asia and Latin America—would continue to send hundreds of thousands of refugees and immigrants on planes toward a new life in the United States with new challenges.

But at thirty-five thousand feet, challenges were usually straightforward. The crews who served the plane's passengers—refugees and businesspeople, rock stars and diplomats, college students and tourists—performed the same movements they had since the start of the jet age. Arms reached to pick up a tray. Eyes scanned the rows. Hands offered pillows as one passenger reclined a seat, then another, then another, all the way to the back of the cabin. Stewardesses were always one step ahead, anticipating movements, making them happen, creating a force felt on the ground below.

EPILOGUE

Success can only be measured in terms of distance traveled.
— MAVIS GALLANT, *GREEN WATER, GREEN SKY*

TODAY, ANYONE VISITING EITHER LYNNE OR KAREN MUST GET on a very small plane, the kind that requires passengers to load their own rolling suitcases onto a rack beside the belly, the kind that anyone over five nine has to duck to enter.

Visiting Tori doesn't involve a small plane. She still lives in Orange County, save for a few months every summer when she retreats to her family's yellow cabin on the Oslo fjord. Her nieces and nephews come down on the weekends and they grill out on the deck, sit on the porch, eat, and walk along the rocky outcroppings that separate the small clusters of summer homes. Tori is as quick as they are with a light and friendly commanding air—she knows what she is doing—and a true laugh. When her family leaves in the early evening to get back to their Oslo homes, the sun is still as high in the sky as it is at three p.m. in California.

Tori rose in the ranks at Pan Am. She spent a year in Hawaii training recruits in the late 1970s, then returned to Los Angeles, where her seniority allowed her to choose her every flight. She would never again fly at the whim of the airline except during the single month of the year that every stewardess was required to spend on standby. When Pan Am sold its Pacific routes to United in 1986, Tori left Pan Am for United in order to stay with the routes. She never married. As her seniority grew at United, she could be picky with her flights, keeping up with an enormous network of friends scattered around the world, tracing the ways the cities she had known so well for so long changed rapidly over the course of the 1970s, 1980s, and 1990s.

By accident and by design, the course of Tori's life continued to bump into the era's conflicts. During the Lebanese civil war, she watched violence unfolding against the familiar façade of the Phoenicia InterContinental hotel during one of the bloodiest battles of the war, the so-called Battle of the Hotels. During the Gulf War, Tori volunteered to fly troops to Kuwait for Operation Desert Storm. The faces in the cabin reflected an older army, now that there was no draft, with more women and career military officers.

After a long treatment for lung cancer, Tori retired at age sixty-five. She goes on cruises with her stewardess friends and attends the reunions of World Wings International, the association of former Pan Am flight crews. These conventions usually draw between three hundred and eight hundred attendees to cities many of the women know well: Paris, Stockholm, Bangkok, where the Siam InterContinental was torn down in 2002. Tori still serves tea in the delicate cups she bought for her first New York apartment, the thin porcelain decorated with gray branches and pink roses. She talks about the diplomatic incidents of foreign countries of decades past as if she had discussed them over a martini with a prime minister the previous day. She smiles like she really means it. She does.

For years, Lynne came down with the flu every April on the anniversary of the babylift. She never got sick otherwise.

When she and Alex returned to Washington State in 1976, Lynne could not find a job—flying, which she had quit the year before, was the only job on her résumé—so she volunteered at the Seattle Asian Art Museum. She dived back toward her comfort with the international, her tenacious interest in cross-cultural communication. At the museum she met the two Chinese-language professors at the University of Washington who led her to her career in international relations. She worked first as an international student adviser at the University of Washington, helping students from 105 countries study in the United States. During the Iran hostage crisis she attended campus rallies with the Iranian students; she was pregnant with her second daughter at the time. When she picked up newspapers the next day, she thought immediately of her own student days—of how crowd assessments did not describe her own observations on the ground and how the actions of complex people were often reduced to stereotype.

She and her family spent a few years in Germany when Lynne's two daughters were young and then they moved to Massachusetts, where Lynne worked at a high school. She spent some years staying home with her children—she loved motherhood unwaveringly—and others pursuing jobs in education. Her skill for cross-cultural communication adapted particularly well to the school environment, with its high stakes and the emotions of nervous parents. She especially enjoyed working on college campuses for their youthful energy and for the close vistas they gave her onto the protest movements of the day. The students liked her. Lynne is reflexively maternal, easy with encouragement, and organized, and she wields quietly fierce and informed opinions about international politics. The students at the University of Washington said that Lynne understood them as no one else in the administration did. She had been to nearly all of their home countries.

Today Lynne lives on an island of the Bahamas, a short, beautiful flight from Nassau. She and Alex bought the place in the late 1990s. The house in the tropics would be their retirement home, or so they thought. Within a month a hurricane had stripped the ranch house nearly down to studs. They began to rebuild, beam by beam, tile by tile, themselves; when it became clear that the task was too large to fit into vacations, they quit their jobs and moved down. Their college-student daughters came to help on school vacations. Lynne and Alex have rebuilt the house twice now. Alex answers the phone with a single phrase: "It's a beautiful day in the Bahamas."

To drive with Lynne across the island on its windswept, potholed roads is to hear the backstories of many of its residents. Lynne can no longer quiz Pan Am passengers on their lives, so she learns of the people around her. At restaurants she talks to the owners about the new hours, how they're doing, who their customers tend to be; she tells them about the mutual friend who hurt his back and she buys a loaf of bread to drop at his house on her way out because he is probably in too much pain to shop for himself. Lynne is a nexus for information that does not stray toward gossip. Her small frame has become birdlike in her older age and she walks with compact confidence. She wears her silver hair long and twisted up in the back. Her daughters live in Northern California and London and both work in international relations, one in business, one in the nonprofit sector. Lynne taught them everything she knows about travel: how to move as a woman through the world with curiosity and confidence and deference for local perspectives and customs and how, whether she is near or far from home, that stance erases fear.

"My mother," her elder girl says, "has no fear of the other."

Reader's Digest rejected Karen's article on the babylift, but her local paper, the *Missoulian,* gave her columns of page space. She presented a detailed, nuanced, and rounded account of the flight and wrote that the experience had changed her forever. A year later, *Reader's Digest* published the story.

Her last two years at Pan Am were, as she says today, riding the gravy train. She spent the considerable capital she earned for the public boost she had given the airline picking and choosing her favorite routes and taking as many weeks off between flights as she could. During those weeks, she was in Missoula, hiking, fishing, and swimming.

She quit flying in 1978 on a whim after a first-class passenger on a South America flight snapped his fingers at her. *Nope,* Karen thought, and she was done. She bought a suitcase full of San Blas Indian textiles and flew home. Soon the *Missoulian* offered her a column. Karen went on to cover an enormous range of topics, from rising crime among well-off teenagers to how Hollywood researched word-of-mouth approval of movies.

She met a tall, handsome rancher with a fierce sense of humor and a quiet generosity. As it turned out, he read her columns. When he brought Karen to his family ranch, she saw that this was exactly what she had traced from the window of the 747 on the polar route all those years before: a place just outside of town, five hundred acres up a winding road. They married; she and her husband began to grow and sell organic alfalfa and bean sprouts that eventually supplied all of western Montana, and Karen had the baby she had wanted for years, a little boy. She loved, absolutely loved, being a mother. She continued to write, though less often. Then a combination of restiveness and financial need took her down yet another path: Karen began a business to vet and place home-care aides. Eventually, her son took over the business. She and her husband raised sheep and alfalfa on a ranch an hour and change outside of Missoula until Karen's husband died in 2019.

In 2000, at the twenty-fifth anniversary of Operation Babylift, she appeared on *Good Morning America* and on the cover of *Reader's Digest* with one of the orphans who had ridden on her plane, the daughter of Massachusetts congressman William Delahunt. This new visibility sparked a new phase in Karen's life; now it was filled with invitations to weddings and baby showers and travels across the country to spend time with the children she had helped bring to the United States. Two American adults believe themselves to be the infant in a sepia-toned photo Karen keeps on her mantle, her "Vietnamese baby." Karen says they are both her babies.

Today, Karen possesses a variety of Montana grit laced with intro-spection. When she flies, she chooses window seats but can't get used to having to stay seated. She misses the cockpit and perching on the jump seat with her magazines.

As individuals, stewardesses shared an instinct to roam that propelled their personal and professional growth, each woman in her own way. As a group, stewardesses forever shifted the American woman's place in her country and the world.

To say that travel is different today than it was in the years of the jet age is a dramatic understatement. Still—occasional accidents and terrorism puncture a largely well-regulated industry whose speed and safety has rendered accessible pockets of the world that to most peo-ple once felt distant. The overabundance of tourism now may keep humans from places as distinct as the Louvre and Mount Everest, and the environmental impact of the airline industry contributes hugely to the existential threat of climate change. An interconnected world, as refugee crises, financial market crashes, and the swift movement of disease have made clear, brings complications as well as opportunities. Internationalism is newly controversial. And still, to many, it is a sig-nifier of sophistication, a moral imperative, a representation of human progress. "Fluidity, mobility, illusoriness—these are precisely the qual-ities that make us civilized. Barbarians don't travel. They simply go to destinations or conduct raids," writes Nobel laureate Olga Tokarczuk.

Amid all that has changed, flight attendants' movement around and knowledge of a multitude of geographies still gives them an elusive fascination to both the grounded and frequent fliers alike. Latter-day versions of *Coffee, Tea, or Me?*—now written by actual flight atten-dants—describe both the aggravations of crewing on present-day planes with high passenger loads and minimal airborne perks and the still-appealing flexibility and access of the job. Look through nearly any magazine even glancingly concerned with travel today and you will find flight-attendant packing tips or a favorite travel outfit. The purveyors of advice are still overwhelmingly female and the advice skews toward the aesthetic. The composition of the perfect suitcase today still bears a strong resemblance to the arrangement recommended by Pan Am training books of the 1960s.

Former Pan Am stewardesses have continued to fly for other airlines, and they have become doctors and mothers and national heroes. In India in 1986, a Pan Am stewardess was fatally shot while helping passengers, including several children, escape during a terrorist attack. She won the nation's highest medal for bravery, the first woman in history to do so. One former Pan Am stewardess, Patricia Ireland, served as president of NOW for a decade. Another founded Voters for Choice, the nation's biggest nonpartisan PAC, with Gloria Steinem. Former Pan Am stewardesses have worked as diplomats, made documentaries and Hollywood television shows, and written bestselling books — Mary Higgins Clark began her working life as a Pan Am stewardess.

Former stewardesses have stayed in touch with one another. And they have continued to travel, together and alone, using their ex-employee benefit cards to the fullest, visiting old haunts and continuing to buy pantyhose in Paris, shoes in Italy. They have thoroughly mapped the ins and outs of standby — the earliest flight is the best bet, especially in cities with a good nightlife, since at least one passenger will not show up in the morning. A sold-out flight is never actually sold out. Not for them.

ACKNOWLEDGMENTS

The women in these pages and many thousands more were deeply committed to being in the world. So many stewardesses and then flight attendants striding purposefully through airports in uniform, visiting foreign cities alone—insisting on this one aspect of physical freedom —made room over decades for the women of my generation to move with more ease through more of the world than women ever had before. The space that stewardesses inhabited and the comfort they earned in motion allowed me, today, to take my own satisfaction from travel, and for that I am grateful.

My thanks first to Lynne Rawling, Karen Walker Ryan, and Tori Werner, who invited me into not only their memories in so many long and winding interviews, treading the same ground from different angles, but also into their homes and their families. Thank you to Clare Christiansen and Hazel Bowie, who answered similarly repetitive questions with candor and grace. They are all remarkable women, and I am grateful both for their time and to know them.

Many people have given me time and information again and again. This list will likely be incomplete, and I apologize to anyone I have overlooked. Edward and Roberta Trippe, Pamela Taylor, Jan Wollett, and Rebecca Sprecher, my pseudo-hippie-godmama, were especially generous, patient, and supportive of this work. In no order at all, my deepest thanks to Paula Helfrich, Laurien Nuss, Dian Stirn Groh, Joan Policastro, Bronwen Roberts, Alex Rawling, Nicole Rawling, Felicia Fairchild, Don Cooper, Helen Davey, Lee Trujillo, Karen Van Es, Myron "Rosie" Rosenstein, Nancy Hult Ganis, Kristina Kiehl, Renate Van Kempema, Margret Ives, Phyllis Johnson Siudy, Elke Etling, Theresa Webber, Valerie Lester, Donna Lively, Holly Borowiak, Mary Ann Mercier, Anne Sweeney, Tania Anderson, Al Topping, Alice Dear, Gail Jennings, Ingrid Templeton, Jane Fujioka Noe, Joan Carnell, Nellie Avillez, Melanie Camp, Diane Carlson Evans, Helen Hegelheimer, Jill Snow, Jim Trullinger, Marci Levine, Micki Voisard, Mindy Kammeyer, Peter Bennett, P. J. Rimson, Kathy Flora, Sabine Renard, Sam Wessling, Siv Adams, Sheila O'Brien, Suzanne Neal Perkins, Carla Manley, Carol Young, Helga Rohrs, Hildegaard Niepal, Marion Semler, Jeanne Jackson, Annmari Ryan, Tom Money, Tim Walker, Nick and Sandy Javaras, Alan Reynolds, Robert Dorsey, Doug Miller. Thank you to the veterans of the United States armed services who answered my questions on Veterans Day weekend 2018: Ann Kelsey, Andrea Beal, Judy Jenkins Gaudino, Marc Leepson, Jack Devine, Jim Ottman, Bat Murtha, Marione "Dino" Lawrence, Robert Lee Delawer, Kurt Sandusky, Bill Gray, Susan Miller, Karen Arndt, and Ann Mitchell Kilty.

World Wings International conventions and luncheons, Pan Am Historical Foundation events, and Internal German Service reunions allowed me to steep in the social environment of the Pan Am family. It is a remarkable network, and its leadership—especially Nancy McAllister and Leslie Manning at World Wings—opened many doors for me. There is much that I have learned in casual conversations with women at conventions in Bangkok, Savannah, and Berlin, and though it would be difficult to trace out exactly who helped me in what way, when, and how, I am grateful for the opportunity to crash their parties.

Three books provided a robust foundation for the research for my own: Kathleen Barry's *Femininity in Flight: A History of Flight Attendants,* Victoria Vantoch's *The Jet Sex: Airline Stewardesses and the Making of an American Icon,* and Jenifer Van Vleck's *Empire of the*

Air: Aviation and the American Ascendancy. I am indebted to their scholarship.

Thank you to the editors who worked with me on the first pieces of writing to come out of this material: Katia Bachko and Seyward Darby at the *Atavist*; Paul Reyes and Alison Wright at *Virginia Quarterly Review*.

Thank you to W. Ralph Eubanks, whose perspective on what these women could show the world matched my own from the start; to Lauren LeBlanc and Ashley Patronyak, whose eyes and minds helped refine initial, very rough drafts; and to Dartmouth's Ed Miller, who let me sit in on his excellent Vietnam War class. The University of Miami's archivists Christina Favretto and Nicola Hellman-McFarland helped orient me, and researcher Jeiddy Lopez got elbows-deep in files when I could not do so myself.

Friends and colleagues were so very generous with their time and their intellects. Their keen eyes, unwavering enthusiasm, and honesty were critical at many junctures. Alyona, Nicole VanDeventer, Megan Foley, Kathy Beaird, Tara FitzGerald, Spencer Bailey, Farah Hussain, fact-checker Angely Mercado, and—may our work together continue forever—Artis Henderson, Suzanne Mozes, and Tanya Paperny. Your attention and fellowship are a buoy and a boon.

My agents Zoe Pagnamenta and Alison Lewis have helped steer me toward what I want to do even before I know it sometimes. This book could not have found a more sensitive editor than Deanne Urmy, who has known exactly when and how to direct me. Thank you to Jessica Vestuto and everyone at Houghton Mifflin Harcourt.

Thank you to my mother, Joan Cirillo, and father, Roger Cooke. My mother moved around the world so eagerly and confidently with my sister and me in tow—in no small part thanks to the flight attendants who helped her care for the two of us in transit—and she still takes such pleasure from deep, honest immersion in places that are not her own. My father told me when I was young that a feminist is anyone who believes that men and women are equal. He also played so much Connect Four and gin rummy with me on so many plane rides that for me, flight has always been something to look forward to. I owe my mother and father very much, but travel and conviction are the two things I thank them for now.

Last, always, and forever, every day, thank you to Patrick Proctor, without whom none of this would exist in the first place.

NOTES

Interviews with Hazel Bowie: October 2, 2018; October 19, 2018; January 10, 2019; April 12, 2019.

Interviews with Clare Christiansen: April 20, 2017; May 21, 2018; April 8, 2019; March 4, 2020.

Interviews with Lynne Rawling: July 6, 2017; July 12, 2017; July 18, 2017; July 26, 2017; August 2, 2017; August 16, 2017; August 23, 2017; August 31, 2017; September 20, 2017; November 1, 2017; November 9, 2017; November 30, 2017; May 25, 2018; October 25, 2018; February 5, 2019; February 6, 2019; February 7, 2019.

Interviews with Karen Walker Ryan: February 12, 2015; December 11, 2015; February 15, 2017; March 24, 2017; April 13, 2017; April 20, 2017; May 12, 2017; May 18, 2017; June 19, 2017; February 22, 2019; February 23, 2019; February 24, 2019; February 25, 2019; October 20, 2019; November 15, 2019.

Interviews with Tori Werner: October 23, 2015; November 30, 2016; January 11, 2017; January 20, 2017; April 4, 2017; April 6, 2017; May 29, 2017; May 30, 2017; November 26, 2018; November 27, 2018; October 10, 2019; November 4, 2019; May 12, 2020.

1. A JET-AGE JOB

page

3 *"How can you change":* Boston Globe, June 2, 1970.

"Why don't you join": Periscope Films, "Pan Am Airlines 1969 Ad Campaign," November 23, 2016, https://www.youtube.com/watch?v=uUzjkIFow8g.

5 *Around the country:* Mark Kurlansky, *1968: The Year That Rocked the World* (New York: Ballantine, 2004), 54.

6 *what President Eisenhower: Public Papers of the Presidents of the United States: Dwight D. Eisenhower, 1954,* April 7, 1954, 381–90, https://history .state.gov/historicaldocuments/frus1952-54v13p1/d716.
From one angle: Heather Stur, "Why the U.S. Went to War in Vietnam," Foreign Policy Research Institute, April 28, 2017, https://www.fpri.org/ article/2017/04/united-states-went-war-vietnam/.
From another: "Manifesto of the Eighteen," *Pentagon Papers* (Boston: Beacon Press, 1971), 316–21.

7 *the shopkeepers and bartenders:* "35 Color Photos That Capture Every-day Life of Rome in 1970," *Vintage Everyday* (blog), September 22, 2017, https://www.vintag.es/2017/09/35-color-photos-that-capture-everyday.html.
Airline press releases: Victoria Vantoch, *The Jet Sex: Airline Stewardesses and the Making of an American Icon* (Philadelphia: University of Pennsylvania Press, 2013), 105.

8 *"Sadie in New York":* Louise Bargelt, "An Air Hostess Looks at Life —and Finds It Pleasing," *Chicago Sunday Tribune,* April 26, 1936.

9 *"The passengers relax":* Francis Vivian Drake, "Air Stewardess," *Atlantic Monthly* 151 (February 1933).
Front-page articles: "Air Heroine Tells Her Part in Fatal Wreck," *Chicago Tribune,* April 8, 1936.
"Air Hostess Finds Life Adventurous": "Air Hostess Finds Life Adventurous," *New York Times,* April 12, 1936.
Sadie Ericson was: Bargelt, "An Air Hostess Looks at Life."
Prices were stabilized: Laura Holson, "Pan Am Remains Grounded. In Culture, That Is," *New York Times,* October 26, 2019.

10 *In New York City:* Meredith L. Clausen, *The Pan Am Building and the Shattering of the Modernist Dream* (Cambridge, MA: MIT Press, 2004).
"Marvel or Monster": Ada Louise Huxtable, "Marvel or Monster?," *New York Times,* January 24, 1960.
Pan Am gave women: Kathleen Barry, *Femininity in Flight: A History of Flight Attendants* (Durham, NC: Duke University Press, 2007), 40.
United Airlines hired: SFO Aviation Museum and Library, "United We Stand: Female Flight Attendant Uniforms of United Airlines," https://www.sfomuseum.org/exhibitions/united-we-stand-female-flight -attendant-uniforms-united-airlines/detail#5.
Other airlines enlisted: Vantoch, *The Jet Sex,* 106.
An upper crust: Arthur Herzog, "It's the Innest, It's the Jet Set," *Sunday New York Times Magazine,* October 28, 1962.

11 *constituted 64 percent:* Barry, *Femininity in Flight,* 41.

In the 1960s: Virginia Postrel, *The Power of Glamour: Longing and the Art of Visual Persuasion* (New York: Simon and Schuster, 2013), 194.

French-speaking Jackie Kennedy: Postrel, *The Power of Glamour,* 196.

Americans sympathetic: Paul Vitello, "Erwin Harris, Ad Executive Who Seized Cuban Assets, Dies at 91," *New York Times,* March 18, 2013.

Hijackings as yet: Brendan I. Koerner, *The Skies Belong to Us: Love and Terror in the Golden Age of Hijacking* (New York: Crown, 2013).

12 *pay was commensurate:* Barry, *Femininity in Flight,* 29.

In the 1950s: Betsy Israel, *Bachelor Girl: A Secret History of Single Women in the Twentieth Century* (New York: HarperCollins, 2002), 184.

14 *square granite:* Clausen, *The Pan Am Building,* 112.

eighty-by-forty-foot sculpture: Clausen, *The Pan Am Building,* 151.

2. HORIZONS UNLIMITED

15 *She was a little suspicious:* Karen Walker Ryan, letter to her parents, March 18, 1969.

16 *The four pages:* Pan American World Airways records, series 1, box 14, folder 134, Otto G. Richter Library, University of Miami Special Collections.

18 *two hundred fifty thousand American troops:* Maria Höhn and Martin Klimke, *A Breath of Freedom: The Civil Rights Struggle, African American GIs, and Germany* (New York: Palgrave Macmillan, 2010).

"*I don't see how":* Roy Reed, "Alabama Police Use Gas and Clubs to Rout Negroes," *New York Times,* March 8, 1965.

19 *A Department of Defense:* "U.S. Military Race Relations in Europe —September 1970," Frank Render, Department of Defense, U.S. Assistant Secretary of Defense, Manpower and Reserve Affairs, Memorandum for the Secretary of Defense.

the color photographs: Richard K. Popp, *The Holiday Makers: Magazines, Advertising, and Mass Tourism in Postwar America* (Baton Rouge: Louisiana State University Press, 2012), 84.

When her money: Karen Walker Ryan, letter to her parents, April 9, 1966.

20 "*In our advertising":* Horizons Unlimited, 1963, Pan American World Airways records, box 2, folder 3.

Paragraphs of text: Horizons Unlimited, 1963, Pan American World Airways records, box 2, folder 3.

21 *sections on hijackings:* Pan American World Airways records, box 11, folder 5.

23 *Illustrations in the manual:* Victoria Vantoch, *The Jet Sex: Airline*

Stewardesses and the Making of an American Icon (Philadelphia: University of Pennsylvania Press, 2013), 116.

24 *Management's approval:* Vantoch, *The Jet Sex,* 248, footnote 85.

26 *had risen into the dozens:* Brendan I. Koerner, *The Skies Belong to Us: Love and Terror in the Golden Age of Hijacking* (New York: Crown, 2013), 44–45.

3. A WOMAN IN UNIFORM

27 *The jacket:* Cathleen Dooley, "Battle in the Sky: A Cultural and Legal History of Sex Discrimination in the United States Airline Industry, 1930–1980" (PhD diss., University of Arizona, 2001), 113.

Pan Am called it: Long Beach Press-Telegram, March 14, 1965.

the writer George Sand: Janet Wolff, *Feminine Sentences: Essays on Women and Culture* (Berkeley: University of California Press, 1990), 41.

28 *Clad in an authoritative uniform:* Valerie Steele and Claudia Kidwell, eds., *Men and Women: Dressing the Part* (London: Booth-Clibborn Editions, 1989), 72.

former British colonizers: Meredith Coffey, "Ethnic Minorities and the Biafran National Imaginary in Chukwuemeka Ike's *Sunset at Dawn* and Chimamanda Ngozi Adichie's *Half of a Yellow Sun,*" in *Writing the Nigeria -Biafra War,* ed. Toyin Falola and Ogechukwu Ezekwem (Rochester, NY: Boydell and Brewer, 2016), 267.

countries used seizing: Marc Dierkx, *Clipping the Clouds: How Air Travel Changed the World* (Westport, CT: Praeger, 2008).

29 *In Vietnam:* "Military and Civil Aircraft Vie at Busy Saigon Airport," *New York Times,* January 30, 1966.

An ex-navy pilot: Robert Dorsey, interview with the author, November 5, 2018.

Braniff sent its stewardesses: Kathleen Barry, *Femininity in Flight: A History of Flight Attendants* (Durham: Duke University Press, 2007),180.

a model languidly: Ad Classics, "Braniff Airways—the Air Strip," YouTube video, March 19, 2013, https://www.youtube.com/watch?v=7TZX ryuhSMg.

American Airlines introduced: Marylin Bender, "Airlines Are Going Sky High for Fashionable Stewardesses," *New York Times,* August 23, 1967.

Executives swapped them for: Tania Long, "Airways Turn to High Style in Bid for Business," *New York Times,* April 2, 1967.

One group of GIs: William Prochnau, "Stewardesses Love Their Job, but It Punishes Them Emotionally," *Seattle Times,* January 11, 1968.

30 *Vetting began in hiring:* Victoria Vantoch, *The Jet Sex: Airline*

Stewardesses and the Making of an American Icon (Philadelphia: University of Pennsylvania Press, 2013), 112.

the average U.S. airline stewardess: Flora Davis, *Moving the Mountain: The Women's Movement in America Since 1960* (Chicago: University of Illinois Press, 1999), 17.

31 *second-largest:* Matthias Hühne, *Pan Am: History, Design, and Identity* (Berlin, Germany: Callisto, 2016), 282.

The airline retained: Harriss v. Pan Am. World Airways, Inc., 437 F. Supp. 413 (N.D. Cal. 1977).

"We don't fly for love": Barry, *Femininity in Flight,* 33.

"Sex is neutral": Gloria Steinem, "The Moral Disarmament of Betty Coed," *Esquire,* September 1, 1962.

A poll of: Betsy Israel, *Bachelor Girl: A Secret History of Single Women in the Twentieth Century* (New York: HarperCollins, 2002), 210.

32 *interspersing photos:* Vantoch, *The Jet Sex,* 57.

"blowsy blonde": Donald Bain, interview with the author, February 17, 2015.

33 *"stew zoos":* Rachel Jones and Trudy Baker with Donald Bain, *Coffee, Tea, or Me?* (New York: Penguin, 2003), 71.

"The way she describes": Margo Howard, "Fun Loving Rachel," *Chicago Tribune,* October 8, 1970.

In 1968 alone: "The People's Choice," *New York Times,* February 16, 1969.

"Our first run movies": *Long Beach Independent,* Monday, January 11, 1965, https://www.newspapers.com/newspage/17627841/.

4. PIPELINE TO PARADISE

34 *three hundred thousand:* "Timeline: Vietnam War and Protests," PBS.org, http://www.pbs.org/wgbh/americanexperience/features/two-days-in-october -vietnam-battlefields-and-home-front/.

In the mid-1960s: "Military and Civil Aircraft Vie at Busy Saigon Airport," *New York Times,* January 30, 1966.

35 *first months of 1966:* "More Rest Trips for GI's Sought," *New York Times,* December 26, 1965.

For four months: "Background Information R&R Development Chronology," 1967, World Wings International records, box 281, folder 19, Otto G. Richter Library, University of Miami Special Collections.

36 *Pan Am had garnered:* Richard Witkin, "45 Jets Ordered by Pan American; Cost $269,000,000," *New York Times,* October 14, 1955.

37 *Anti-American demonstrations:* "Telegram from the Embassy in Vietnam

to the Department of State," Department of State, Central Files, POL 27 VIET S. Secret; Immediate; Nodis; LOR, https://1997-2001.state.gov/about _state/history/vol_ii/46_55.html.

38 *When the call sounded:* Clare Christiansen, interview with the author, April 20, 2017.

its dollar-a-month: World Wings International records, box 281, folder 19.

Pan Am also contracted: "Pan Am Sells Two 727s to Growing Air Vietnam," *Clipper,* World Wings International records, series 1, box 637, folder 3.

spring of 1966: Edward Hausner, "Pan Am Profit Gets off Ground," *New York Times,* May 4, 1966.

39 *a press release:* "Pan Am Expects to Airlift 375,000 U.S. Servicemen in South Vietnam on Rest and Rehabilitation Leaves During 1967," Pan Am press release, World Wings International records, box 281, folder 19.

"No army has ever": "Recreation: Five-Day Bonanza," *Time,* December 22, 1967.

an uneventful flight: Author interviews with Helga Rohrs, October 23, 2015; Hildegaard Niepal, May 24, 2017; Carla Manley, March 3, 2017; Carol Young, May 29, 2018.

40 *they glanced: Between the Lines,* directed by Scott Bass and Ty Ponder (Pure Frustration Productions, 2008).

here's the war: Jack Devine, interview with the author, November 11, 2018.

Over the duration of the war: Alan J. Vick, *Air Base Attacks and Defensive Counters: Historical Lessons and Future Challenges* (Santa Monica, CA: Rand Corporation, 2015), 7.

At each base: Myron Rosenstein, interview with the author, November 6, 2018.

41 *During one stewardess's:* Rohrs interview.

Newspapers back home: William Prochnau, "7 Cities in Orient Are Bachelor Paradise," *Seattle Times,* January 10, 1968.

From Taipei: "Recreation: Five-Day Bonanza."

42 *one article observed:* "Recreation: Five-Day Bonanza."

"Stewardesses Love": William Prochnau, "Stewardesses Love Their Job, but It Punishes Them Emotionally," *Seattle Times,* January 11, 1968.

"Sixty very happy": San Jose Mercury-News, April 23, 1967.

some of the women: Author interviews with P. J. Rimson, March 27, 2017; Suzanne Neal Perkins, April 11, 2017.

the red seeped through: Young interview.

watched stewardesses' smiles: Bill Gray, interview with the author, November 11, 2018.

43 *the New York suburbs:* World Wings International records, series 1, box 257, folder 29.

servicemen on R&Rs: Prochnau, "7 Cities in Orient."

44 *One stewardess:* Rohrs interview.

45 *landing had acquired:* Anika Burges, "Remembering Hair-Raising Landings at Hong Kong's Kai Tak Airport," *Atlas Obscura,* July 21, 2017, https://www.atlasobscura.com/articles/kai-tak-hong-kong-airport-scary-landing.

Hong Kong earned: "Take a Tour of Hong Kong in the '60s," *South China Morning Post,* March 18, 2018.

46 *"fly such missions":* Edgar Ulsamer, "A Welcome Lift from the Airlines," *Air Force,* March 1968.

"HKG Crews Return": "HKG Crews Return for Reassignment," *Clipper,* World Wings International records, series 1, box 637, folder 3.

the mortuary: Gloria Emerson, *Winners and Losers: Battles, Retreats, Gains, Losses, and Ruins from the Vietnam War* (New York: W. W. Norton, 2014), 26.

"Your stewardesses are": "'Most Experienced' in Peace or War," *Clipper,* June 15, 1966, World Wings International records, series 1, box 637, folder 18.

47 *"often and clear":* Jim Reese, World Wings International records, series 1, box 637, folder 18.

most airlines enforced: Kathleen Barry, *Femininity in Flight: A History of Flight Attendants* (Durham, NC: Duke University Press, 2007), 123.

5. FOREIGN SERVICE

48 *Stewardesses who had peeled:* Margret Ives, interview with the author, July 21, 2017.

49 *Wallpaper made of:* "Roberts Field, Liberia," *Just an Old Pilot* (blog), October 29, 2011, http://justanoldpilot.blogspot.com/2011/10/roberts-field-liberia.html.

50 *Phyllis, a 4-H star:* Phyllis Johnson Siudy, interview with the author, April 12, 2017.

found herself struggling: Elke Etling, interview with the author, May 12, 2017.

51 *quasi-professional partners:* Molly M. Wood, "Wives, Clerks, and 'Lady Diplomats': The Gendered Politics of Diplomacy and Representation in the U.S. Foreign Service, 1900–1940," *European Journal of American Studies* 10, no. 1 (2015).

1.5 percent: Barbara Gamarekian, "Washington Talk; Women Gain, but Slowly, in the Foreign Service," *New York Times,* July 28, 1989.

53 *moved to withdraw:* "1967: De Gaulle Pulls France Out of NATO's Integrated Military Structure," NATO.int, March 3, 2009, https://www.nato.int/cps/en/natohq/opinions_139272.htm.

54 *Instructions suggested:* "Hints on Packing Suitcase," World Wings International records, box 14, folder 134, Otto G. Richter Library, University of Miami Special Collections.

55 *"The emancipation of":* Henry Kam Kah, "'Africa Must Unite': Vindicating Kwame Nkrumah and Uniting Africa Against Global Destruction," *Journal of Pan African Studies* 4, no. 10 (January 2012).
"subversive elements": "African States Accuse Ghana; Unity Group Seeks to Mediate," *New York Times,* June 11, 1965.
financial mismanagement: Tad Szulc, "U.S. Said to Spurn Ghana Loan Appeal," *New York Times,* April 14, 1965.
entourage abandoned him: David A. Apter, "Ghana's Independence: Triumph and Paradox," *Transition* 98 (2008): 6–22.

56 *underground presses:* Loni Klara, "During the Nazi Occupation of Norway, Humor Was the Secret Weapon," *Atlas Obscura,* August 9, 2016, https://www.atlasobscura.com/articles/during-the-nazi-occupation-of-norway-humor-was-the-secret-weapon.

57 *local teenage dancers:* Joyce Nyairo, "Fare Thee Well, Nairobi's Home of Song and Sin," *Daily Nation,* August 29, 2014.
sixty-three-cent martinis: New Horizons World Guide (New York: Pan American Airways Publications, 1968).

59 *"18 Guinean Officials":* "18 Guinean Officials and Minister Seized by Ghana at Airport," *New York Times,* October 30, 1966.

60 *he would free:* "18 Guinean Officials."
Movie theaters: United Press International, "US Envoy to Guinea Is Under House Arrest," October 31, 1966.
the Guinean president: "Ankrah Ridicules Charge," *New York Times,* November 1, 1966.
"piracy": "Ankrah Ridicules Charge."
"a fundamental principal": Pan American World Airways records, series 1, box 764, folder 1, Otto G. Richter Library, University of Miami Special Collections.

61 *the airline sponsored:* "Hotel Bristol in Conjunction with Pan American Airways Presents 'The New York Look' 1965 Spring and Summer Fashions," *New York Look to Scandinavia,* Pan American World Airways records, series 5, box 183, folder 1.

62 *eventually released:* "Ghana Releases Guinean Envoys," *New York Times,* November 5, 1966.

a juridical responsibility: "Ghana Releases Guinean Envoys."

State Department newsletter: "50 FSOs Attend Benjamin Guest Seminars in Beirut," *U.S. Department of State Newsletter* 72 (April 1967).

knew that some: Benjamin Welles, "Woman Winning State Department Case," *New York Times,* February 28, 1972.

63 *word of one critic:* Ada Louise Huxtable, "Idlewild: Distressing Monument to Air Age," *New York Times,* November 25, 1962.

recently completed terminal: Thomas Leslie, "The Pan Am Terminal at Idlewild/Kennedy Airport and the Transition from Jet Age to Space Age," *Design Issues* 21, no. 1 (Winter 2005).

64 *first bars ever:* Betsy Israel, *Bachelor Girl: A Secret History of Single Women in the Twentieth Century* (New York: HarperCollins, 2002), 220–21.

pioneer of the bunch: Richard West, "Looking for Love in So Many Places," *New York,* December 28, 1981, 24–31.

police barricades: Nicola Twilley, "How T.G.I. Friday's Helped Invent the Singles Bar," *New Yorker,* July 2, 2015.

6. PAN AM WAS THE AMERICAN FLAG

65 *Trippe began the company:* R.E.G. Davies, *Airlines of the Jet Age* (Washington, DC: Smithsonian Institution Scholarly Press, 2011), 14.

66 *the president called on Trippe:* Marylin Bender and Selig Altschul, *The Chosen Instrument: Juan Trippe, Pan Am, the Rise and Fall of an American Entrepreneur* (New York: Simon and Schuster, 1982), 332.

President Roosevelt announced: Jenifer Van Vleck, *Empire of the Air: Aviation and the American Ascendancy* (Cambridge, MA: Harvard University Press, 2013), 136.

Its Accra headquarters: Van Vleck, *Empire of the Air,* 143.

Listeners on four continents: Across the Pacific, Moreno/Lyons Production, https://filmmakerscollab.org/films/across-the-pacific/.

67 *the CIA at one point:* Jeff McConnell, "The CIA and Airlines: A 36-Year History," *CounterSpy* (December 1983–February 1984).

"Pan Am was": Bender and Altschul, *The Chosen Instrument,* 477.

a shadow State Department: Bender and Altschul, *The Chosen Instrument,* 477.

Thirteen of the top: Davies, *Airlines of the Jet Age,* 63, 108.

68 *Scrabbling at a level:* Davies, *Airlines of the Jet Age,* 65.

Thousands of small airlines: R.E.G. Davies, *Rebels and Reformers of the Airways* (Washington, DC: Smithsonian Institution, 1987).

"the most fascinating": Bender and Altschul, *The Chosen Instrument,* 13.

Daly launched World: Bender and Altschul, *The Chosen Instrument,* 66.

"mostly benevolent dictatorship": Cynthia Gorney, "King of the Cut-Rate Airways," *Washington Post,* June 25, 1980.

small U.S. military: Davies, *Rebels and Reformers of the Airways,* 129.

69 *The initial financial commitment:* Bender and Altschul, *The Chosen Instrument,* 503, 504.

7. UNEQUIVOCALLY IN THE WORLD

70 *Pan Am Flight 1:* Airline Timetable Images, http://www.timetableimages .com/ttimages/pa.htm.

"I must pinch myself": Amelia Earhart, "Amelia Earhart: 'I Am More Eager Than Ever to Fly Again,'" *New York Times,* July 13, 2017.

72 *sprung into being:* Peter Westwick, *Blue Sky Metropolis: The Aerospace Century in Southern California* (Berkeley: University of California Press, 2012).

doubled since 1950: "Aerospace: The Industry That Built the South Bay," *Easy Reader News,* October 17, 2013, https://easyreadernews.com/aerospace -chronicles-industry-built-south-bay/.

74 *an extravagant network:* Jenifer Van Vleck, *Empire of the Air: Aviation and the American Ascendancy* (Cambridge, MA: Harvard University Press, 2013), 269.

"travel deficit": "Text of President's Statement on Balance of Payments Problem and Steps to Meet It," *New York Times,* January 2, 1968.

"to get through 1968": Christopher Endy, *Cold War Holidays: American Tourism in France* (Chapel Hill: University of North Carolina Press, 2004), 189.

"Americans, traveling more": "Annual Message to the Congress on the State of the Union," LBJ Presidential Library, January 17, 1968.

75 *"probably his most":* Endy, *Cold War Holidays,* 197.

"Really seeing America": Van Vleck, *Empire of the Air,* 270.

"the very essence": "The Very Essence of Our Free Society," *Chicago Tribune,* January 5, 1968.

"Fly American": Van Vleck, *Empire of the Air,* 270.

In private in 1966: Marylin Bender and Selig Altschul, *The Chosen Instrument: Juan Trippe, Pan Am, the Rise and Fall of an American Entrepreneur* (New York: Simon and Schuster, 1982), 505.

contracts approaching: Seattle Times, September 30, 1968.

"somewhere between": Najeeb E. Halaby, Pan Am Management Club, International Hotel JFK, December 16, 1968, Pan American World Airways records, box 1, folder 2, Otto G. Richter Library, University of Miami Special Collections.

76 *May's annual meeting:* Bender and Altschul, *The Chosen Instrument,* 513.

"Peace will not": Lyndon B. Johnson, "Remarks at the National Reactor Testing Station," Arco, Idaho, August 26, 1966, http://www.presidency.ucsb.edu/ws/index.php?pid=27806.

a way toward: "Peace Aim Is Seen in U.S.-Soviet Step," *New York Times,* October 5, 1966.

77 *"Pan Am does":* Bender and Altschul, *The Chosen Instrument,* 484.

"With this great instrument": Halaby speech to management, Pan American World Airways records, public relations and marketing, box 1, folder 2 934 13 + 1 39 7, Otto G. Richter Library, University of Miami Special Collections.

lease for a two-story: "Flights to Soviet Will Start Today," *New York Times,* July 15, 1968.

a full-page ad: "Pan Am Running an Ad in Moscow," *New York Times,* July 15, 1968.

"We want tourists": Jerry Hannifin, "Challenge to the West for Global Business," *Life,* July 26, 1968.

professed the hope: "Aeroflot Leads on Moscow Run, but Pan Am Is Satisfied, Too," *New York Times,* July 7, 1969.

"more symbolic than": Holmes Alexander, "An Event to Remember," McNaught Syndicate, July 29, 1968.

"Blue Skies, Champagne": Victoria Vantoch, *The Jet Sex: Airline Stewardesses and the Making of an American Icon* (Philadelphia: University of Pennsylvania Press, 2013), 127, 251.

even as other headlines: David Binder, "A New Spy Scandal Develops in Bonn," *New York Times,* October 27, 1968; William Beecher, "Air Defense System Becoming Obsolete Against New Arms," *New York Times,* May 20, 1968.

Nuclear war felt: David Greenberg, "Fallout Can Be Fun," Slate.com, February 20, 2003.

"The enemy's hopes": Neil Sheehan, *A Bright Shining Lie: John Paul Vann and America in Vietnam* (New York: Vintage, 1989), 699.

coordinated strikes by: "What Happened in the Tet Offensive's First 36 Hours," *Military Times,* January 31, 2018.

78 *"What the hell":* Joel Achenbach, "Did the News Media, Led by Walter Cronkite, Lose the War in Vietnam?," *Washington Post,* May 25, 2018.

"the greatest purveyor": Benjamin Hedin, "Martin Luther King, Jr.'s Searing Antiwar Speech, Fifty Years Later," *New Yorker,* April 4, 2017.

He would bring: "President Nixon's 14 Addresses to the Nation on Vietnam," Richard Nixon Foundation, September 2, 2017, https://www

.nixonfoundation.org/2017/09/president-richard-nixons-14-addresses
-nation-vietnam/.

Twelve percent: Pan American Airways Annual Report for 1968, Pan
American World Airways records, printed materials, periodicals, box 2,
folder 33.

79 *"something a little more":* Braniff Pages, "End of the Plain Plane," You-
Tube video, November 10, 2006, https://www.youtube.com/watch?v=H3
_aNtQFsLk.

8. ONE, TWO, THREE, WHAT ARE WE FIGHTING FOR?

80 *wide windows:* "Designing the Luxury Hotel: Neal Prince and the Inter-
Continental Hotel Brand," New York School of Interior Design Library,
https://nealprince.omeka.net/.

81 *increased sixfold:* Porphant Ouyyanont, "The Vietnam War and Tourism in Bangkok's Development, 1960–70," *Southeast Asian Studies* 39, no. 2
(September 2001): 178.

Toyotas and Buicks: Hannah Beach, "The Capital of Gridlock," *Time,*
February 8, 2008.

military men exclusively: Ouyyanont, "The Vietnam War," 179.

82 *cars drove around:* "The 1969 Peace Rally," *Boston Globe,* October 17, 2012, https://www.bostonglobe.com/specials/insiders/2012/10/17/
bgcom-archive-peace/bH6RFGVYJ7Dg8u1fHAOFBN/picture.html?p1=
Article_Gallery.

"We won't creep around": Jerry Lembcke, *The Spitting Image: Myth,
Memory, and the Legacy of Vietnam* (New York: NYU Press, 2000), 54.

Young Americans for Freedom: "Nixon Supporters Planning War Rallies," *New York Times,* November 9, 1969.

Nixon was described: Marvin Kalb, *The Nixon Memo: Political Respectability, Russia, and the Press* (Chicago: University of Chicago Press,
1992), 207.

83 *a full-page ad: Waging Peace in Vietnam: US Soldiers and Veterans Who
Opposed the War,* ed. Ron Carver, David Cortright, and Barbara Doherty
(New York: New Village Press, 2019), 57.

84 *hundreds of thousands:* Joseph Lelyveld, "Protests on Cambodia and Kent
State Are Joined by Many Local Schools," *New York Times,* May 6, 1970.

four million students: Ken Burns and Geoffrey C. Ward, *The Vietnam
War: An Intimate History* (New York: Alfred A. Knopf, 2017), 451.

one thousand veterans: United Press International, "1971 Year in Review: Vietnam Demonstrations," April 22, 1971, https://www.upi.com/
Archives/Audio/Events-of-1971/Vietnam-Demonstrations/.

9. WHAT DO YOU WOMEN WANT?

89 *the same images:* Shatner Method, "International Press Response to Apollo 11 Moon Landing—ABC News—July 22, 1969," YouTube video, February 10, 2019, https://www.youtube.com/watch?v=PV1tQPKwzFg.

somewhere over the Pacific: Mindy Kammeyer, interview with the author, July 10, 2017.

91 *Acacia trees shot:* Travel Film Archive, "*New Horizons*—Morocco and Kenya, 1970," YouTube video, September 22, 2013, https://www.youtube.com/watch?v=mqMIqyduJBE.

92 *cheeky tourist guides:* "Travel: What to Do When the Hijacker Comes," *Time,* Friday, December 6, 1968.

"It was great": Brendan Koerner, "#29: Lawrence Rhodes," Skyjacker of the Day Tumblr Archive, http://skyjackeroftheday.tumblr.com/post/50989044105/29-lawrence-rhodes.

A skyjacker: Brendan Koerner, *The Skies Belong to Us: Love and Terror in the Golden Age of Hijacking* (New York: Crown, 2013), 49.

Planes from Iberia: Tad Szulc, "Craft from Lisbon Fly Men and Arms to African Rebels," *New York Times,* November 5, 1967.

a ragtag group: "'Peace Pilot' Leaves Lisbon to Aid Biafrans," *New York Times,* July 26, 1968.

94 *Respectable, middle-class:* Gail Collins, *When Everything Changed: The Amazing Journey of American Women from 1960 to the Present* (Boston: Little, Brown), 158.

95 *"Good girls go":* Carole Cadwalladr, "The First Cosmo Girl," *Guardian,* May 16, 2009.

in cities where: Frank Langfitt, "Suzie Wong's World Has All but Vanished," *Baltimore Sun,* June 30, 1997.

the outline of: "Roberts Field, Liberia," *Just an Old Pilot* (blog), October 29, 2011, http://justanoldpilot.blogspot.com/2011/10/roberts-field-liberia.html.

Dozens of new: Ada Louise Huxtable, "Down Town Blues," *New York Times,* April 16, 1967.

96 *A 1969 memo recommended:* Clark Mollenhoff, "Government Secrecy Cited in Sex Discrimination Case," *Des Moines Register,* July 2, 1971.

Among thirteen: Barbara Gamarekian, "The Heroine of the State Department's Women," *New York Times,* April 6, 1976.

the hotel group's newest: "Designing the Luxury Hotel: Neal Prince and the Inter-Continental Hotel Brand," New York School of Interior Design Library, https://nealprince.omeka.net/.

98 *near-absolute norm:* Betsy Israel, *Bachelor Girl: A Secret History of Single Women in the Twentieth Century* (New York: HarperCollins, 2002), 184.
doubling the approximately: "Divorce and Divorce Rates," U.S. Department of Health, Education, and Welfare, National Center for Health Statistics, Hyattsville, MD, March 1978.

10. I'M OKAY, YOU'RE OKAY

99 *Other Hong Kong stewardesses also:* Author interviews with Helga Rohrs, October 23, 2015; Hildegaard Niepal, May 24, 2017; Carla Manley, March 3, 2017; Carol Young, May 29, 2018.

100 *smuggle a newsreel:* Manley interview.
home at two: Pamela Taylor, interview with the author, November 19, 2018.

101 *some forty new InterContinental hotels:* "Designing the Luxury Hotel: Neal Prince and the Inter-Continental Hotel Brand," New York School of Interior Design Library, https://nealprince.omeka.net/.
"When you've seen": Matthias Hühne, *Pan Am: History, Design, and Identity* (Berlin, Germany: Callisto, 2016), 301.
eight stewardesses: Kathleen Barry, *Femininity in Flight: A History of Flight Attendants* (Durham, NC: Duke University Press, 2007), 131.
30 to 40 percent: Flora Davis, *Moving the Mountain: The Women's Movement in America Since 1960* (Chicago: University of Illinois Press, 1999), 19.
told a reporter: Henry LaCossitt, "Adventures of the Air-Line Stewardesses," *Saturday Evening Post,* June 26, 1954.

102 *Among the first:* Barry, *Femininity in Flight,* 144.
over 266,000 women: Victoria Vantoch, *The Jet Sex: Airline Stewardesses and the Making of an American Icon* (Philadelphia: University of Pennsylvania Press, 2013), 106.
By October of 1966: Davis, *Moving the Mountain,* 23.
"Men can carry trays": Barry, *Femininity in Flight,* 158.
One questioned: Barry, *Femininity in Flight,* 163.

103 *At the Miss America pageant:* Roxane Gay, "Fifty Years Ago, Protestors Took on the Miss America Pageant and Electrified the Feminist Movement," *Smithsonian,* January 2018.
"curvy, hazel-eyed coed": Judy Klemesrud, "There's Now Miss Black America," *New York Times,* September 9, 1968.
In Manhattan Betty Friedan: Sascha Cohen, "No Unescorted Ladies Will Be Served," *JSTOR Daily,* March 20, 2019.

104 *"However valid"*: Denis Binder, "Sex Discrimination in the Airline Industry," *California Law Review* 59 (September 1971).
airlines remained willing: Barry, *Femininity in Flight,* 160–64.

105 *in purposeful motion*: Barry, *Femininity in Flight,* 203.
pantsuit was ascendant: Valerie Steele and Claudia Kidwell, eds., *Men and Women: Dressing the Part* (London: Booth-Clibborn Editions, 1989), 72.

106 *Sex* plus *marriage*: Barry, *Femininity in Flight,* 164.
"led to impose": *Sprogis v. United Air Lines, Inc.,* 444 F.2d 1194.
a job that women: Barry, *Femininity in Flight,* 172.

107 *the peril of*: *Harriss v. Pan Am. World Airways, Inc.,* 437 F. Supp. 413 (N.D. Cal. 1977).
"By allowing a 'preggie'": Barry, *Femininity in Flight,* 205.
pilots circulated: Barry, *Femininity in Flight,* 200.

110 *"Stewardesses Get New Look"*: United Press International, "Stewardesses Get New Look at Pan Am," February 7, 1969.
the Manila Bulletin: Pan American World Airways records, personnel, flight attendants, box 4, 292, folder 17, Otto G. Richter Library, University of Miami Special Collections.
wrote directly to: Pan American World Airways records, personnel, flight attendants, box 4, 292, folder 17.

111 *"a slimming, longish proportion"*: Pan American World Airways records, personnel, flight attendants, box 4, 292, folder 17.
Halaby's leadership style: Marylin Bender and Selig Altschul, *The Chosen Instrument: Juan Trippe, Pan Am, the Rise and Fall of an American Entrepreneur* (New York: Simon and Schuster, 1982), 518.

112 *a flight to Amsterdam*: Robert Lindsey, "Airlines, in Flight of Fancy, Offer Under-26 Travelers Rock and Organic Food," *New York Times,* July 13, 1972.
"Au revoir": Pan American World Airways records, personnel, flight attendants, box 4, 293, folder 15.

11. OPEN SKIES FOR NEGRO GIRLS

113 *Najeeb Halaby hoped*: Christine Yano, *Airborne Dreams: "Nisei" Stewardesses and Pan American World Airways* (Durham, NC: Duke University Press, 2011), 22.
largely the children: Yano, *Airborne Dreams,* 22.

114 *executives openly admitted*: Victoria Vantoch, *The Jet Sex: Airline Stewardesses and the Making of an American Icon* (Philadelphia: University of Pennsylvania Press, 2013), 63–64.

"existing and potential": Richard Witkin, "Aviation: Stewardess," *New York Times*, December 29, 1957.

"Last year": James Rorty, "The First Colored Air Hostess," *Crisis* (June–July 1958): 339.

One applicant testified: Vantoch, *The Jet Sex*, 73–74.

115 *nearly one thousand*: Kathleen Barry, *Femininity in Flight: A History of Flight Attendants* (Durham, NC: Duke University Press, 2007), 120.

recruitment efforts stalled: Cathleen Dooley, "Battle in the Sky: A Cultural and Legal History of Sex Discrimination in the United States Airline Industry, 1930–1980" (PhD diss., University of Arizona, 2001), 110–11.

many recognized: Author interviews with Nellie Avillez, October 15, 2018; Alice Dear, March 5, 2020.

117 *violence had begun*: "The Four Days in 1968 that Reshaped D.C.," *Washington Post*, March 27, 2018.

a strained silence: Ben A. Franklin, "Capital Put Under 4 p.m. Curfew," *New York Times*, April 7, 1968.

"deepen the hatred": Matthew Siegfried, "Coretta Scott King Speaks! Solidarity Day at Resurrection City," YouTube video, February 7, 2017, https://www.youtube.com/watch?v=9Z-a4Yx5Y9c.

118 *crowd around her*: Aaron Moselle, "Poor People's Campaign Seeks to Revive MLK's Vision," Whyy.org, May 14, 2018.

Negro Motorist Green Book: New York Public Library Digital Collections, *Travelers' Green Book: 1966–67 International Edition: For Vacation Without Aggravation*.

119 *entire towns could pose*: James W. Loewen, *Sundown Towns: A Hidden Dimension of American Racism* (New York: Touchstone, 2006).

12. SHE'S SO BUSY BEING FREE

123 *was not ready*: Alan Reynolds, interview with the author, November 18, 2019.

could not really afford: Tim Walker, interview with the author, November 18, 2019.

125 *ship was dilapidated*: "Sailing Ship Towed After Engine Trouble," *Port Angeles Evening News*, July 23, 1969.

see its weight: Tom Money, interview with the author, October 27, 2017.

A guidebook: *New Horizons World Guide* (New York: Pan American Airways Publications, 1965), 546.

Few tourists: Tom Buckley, "Fiji Fears Tourism but Can Hardly Wait," *New York Times*, July 19, 1970.

126 *"Some recklessly romantic":* Travel Film Archive, *"New Horizons*—Fiji and New Caledonia, 1970," YouTube video, June 18, 2009, https://www.youtube.com/watch?v=3aOhQcPVnUU.

127 *The Manhattan Beach courts:* Dave Hall, "Manhattan Tourney, the Wimbledon of Volleyball: '68 Match Called 'Most Famous' of All Time," *Los Angeles Times,* June 30, 1989.

128 *explained his cold feet:* Reynolds interview.

129 How to Make: Kathleen Barry, *Femininity in Flight: A History of Flight Attendants* (Durham, NC: Duke University Press, 2007), 185.

130 *met a Playboy bunny:* Barry, *Femininity in Flight,* 185.
In five-second intervals: Ultra Swank, "I Got 747's to Miami!—National Airlines," YouTube video, November 29, 2011, https://www.youtube.com/watch?v=XawRcZWgBPw.
National Airlines: Barry, *Femininity in Flight,* 177–78.
dared passengers to: Susanna Schrobsdorff, "Sexist, Silly, Sublime: Era Ads," *Time,* April 24, 2012.

131 *"Skirts were up":* Alix Kates Shulman, "Sex and Power: Sexual Bases of Radical Feminism," *Signs: Journal of Women in Culture and Society* 5, no. 4 (Summer 1980): 590–604.
"There are lots": "Anything Goes: Taboos in Twilight," *Newsweek,* November 13, 1967, 67.
Southwest Airlines stewardesses: Barry, *Femininity in Flight,* 177–79.
"We like flirtations": Barry, *Femininity in Flight,* 186.

132 *a raised eyebrow:* Betsy Israel, *Bachelor Girl: A Secret History of Single Women in the Twentieth Century* (New York: HarperCollins, 2002), 210.
"a liberated woman": "Gloria Steinem: A Liberated Woman Despite Beauty, Chic and Success," *Newsweek,* August 16, 1971, 51–55.
"The single working girl": John Nordreevier, "Vacation and the Single Girl: Tireless Pursuit of a Dream," *New York Times,* July 29, 1970.
"Do not dare": Israel, *Bachelor Girl,* 234.
"A study": Israel, *Bachelor Girl,* 211.
"No unescorted ladies": Georgia Hickey, "Barred from the Barroom: Second Wave Feminists and Public Accommodations in U.S. Cities," *Feminist Studies* 34, no. 3 (Fall 2008): 382–408.
An unmarried woman: Rose Evelth, "Forty Years Ago, Women Had a Hard Time Getting Credit Cards," Smithsonian.com, January 8, 2014.
refused to wear: "The Nation: Fly Me," *Time,* November 15, 1971.

133 *Friends would later:* Nick Javaras, interview with the author, October 2, 2019.

13. SPLENDID CAPITALIST AIRPLANES

137 *20 percent less:* Marylin Bender and Selig Altschul, *The Chosen Instrument: Juan Trippe, Pan Am, the Rise and Fall of an American Entrepreneur* (New York: Simon and Schuster, 1982), 515–24.

In January of 1970: "First Lady Christens First 747 Jet," *New York Times,* January 16, 1970.

annual losses reached: Robert Lindsey, "Pan Am Decline Began with Order for 747's," *New York Times,* August 24, 1974.

Pan Am had launched: Jenifer Van Vleck, *Empire of the Air: Aviation and the American Ascendancy* (Cambridge, MA: Harvard University Press, 2013), 272–73.

138 *"locked in":* Bender and Altschul, *The Chosen Instrument,* 517.

"Not the sort": Jon Swan, "We Have Met the 'Enemy' and Found Them Human—Tourisme Engagé," *New York Times,* June 6, 1971.

"try James Bond": James F. Clarity, "Letter from a Friend: Moscow," *New York Times,* September 20, 1970.

All Aeroflot stewardesses: Victoria Vantoch, *The Jet Sex: Airline Stewardesses and the Making of an American Icon* (Philadelphia: University of Pennsylvania Press, 2013), 142.

139 *bought a samovar:* Author interviews with Joan Policastro, March 3, 2015; Holly Borowiak, March 30, 2017; Mary Ann Mercier, September 14, 2015.

On the ground: Policastro, Borowiak, and Mercier interviews; author interviews with Donna Lively, March 24, 2017; Siv Adams, October 16, 2019.

"Shake the KGB": Adams interview.

140 *Mike Wallace:* Lively interview.

a bottle of champagne: Tania Anderson, interview with the author, August 10, 2015.

141 *"My husband thinks":* Kathleen Barry, *Femininity in Flight: A History of Flight Attendants* (Durham, NC: Duke University Press, 2007), 119.

Some nonwhite stewardesses: Sheila Nutt, "Travel Back in Style: Pan Am Black Bird," *Huffington Post,* April 4, 2012.

Some wore their hair: Miriam Birigwa, "Building a Spirit of Inclusion: Pan Am and the Cultural Revolution," *Boston Hospitality Review,* October 1, 2014.

Let me make it: Alice Dear, interview with the author, March 5, 2020.

"Who sat in this": Dear interview.

142 *"allowed me to be":* Dear interview. Dear went on to earn an MBA while flying, which led to a long career in international finance. She credits the West African contacts she cultivated on layovers in Monrovia with influencing her later work as President Bill Clinton's appointee to the African Development Bank.

Small waves: Julia Ioffe, "The History of Russian Involvement in America's Race Wars," *Atlantic,* October 21, 2017.

144 *American Airlines stewardess:* Vantoch, *The Jet Sex,* 128.

Yves Saint Laurent: Kate A. Baldwin, *The Racial Imaginary of the Cold War Kitchen: From Sokol'niki Park to Chicago's South Side* (Hanover, NH: Dartmouth College Press, 2015), 144–58.

the corps spinning: Richard Nixon Presidential Library, "Soviet Union, Part 2, May 23–26, 1972: Moscow, Red Square, Signing Ceremonies, Bolshoi Ballet," YouTube video, September 14, 2018, https://www.youtube.com/watch?v=Z2Kvl7A3PCI.

145 *Lenin had nationalized:* Glenn Collins, "The Moscow Circus: Vaudeville That Delivers a Nationalistic Message," *New York Times,* September 11, 1988.

Iron Feliks: Sabra Ayres, "Russia Had Its Own Version of the Confederate Monument Problem. The Solution: A Sculpture Park in Moscow," *Los Angeles Times,* August 28, 2017.

Gellhorn could not wait: Martha Gellhorn, *Travels with Myself and Another: A Memoir* (New York: Putnam, 2001), 282.

146 *"a Russian peasant's dream":* Eugene Lyons, *Assignment in Utopia* (New Brunswick, NJ: Transaction, 1991), 451.

station chief's wife: George Hambleton, interview with the author, March 25, 2015.

14. DE FACTO FEMINIST

148 *the 747's bar lounge:* Thomas Leslie, "The Pan Am Terminal at Idlewild/Kennedy Airport and the Transition from Jet Age to Space Age," *Design Issues* 21, no. 1 (Winter 2005).

a square-rigger's: Pan American World Airways records, photographs, aircraft, airplanes, Boeing 747, box 4 (interior shots).

149 *bests and worsts:* Calvin Trillin, "U.S. Journal: NY/LA/NY: A Traveling Person on a Beautiful Place," *New Yorker,* April 4, 1970, 66–77.

150 *throughout the 1960s:* Victoria Vantoch, *The Jet Sex: Airline Stewardesses and the Making of an American Icon* (Philadelphia: University of Pennsylvania Press, 2013), 105.

151 *song for the occasion:* "NOW Demonstration," *New York Times,* March 1, 1972.

two Iranian passengers: "Why Stewardesses Are Up in the Air," *New York Times,* December 17, 1972.

"The airline hostess": Laurie Johnson, "Airlines Assailed by Steward-esses," *New York Times,* December 13, 1972.

152 *"I don't think of":* Kathleen Barry, *Femininity in Flight: A History of Flight Attendants* (Durham, NC: Duke University Press, 2007),195.

"revolution waiting to happen": Gloria Steinem, "Gloria Steinem on How Female Flight Attendants Fought Sexism in the Skies," CNTraveler. com, March 25, 2016, https://www.cntraveler.com/stories/2016-03-25/gloria-steinem-on-how-female-flight-attendants-fought-sexism.

Future Stewardesses for: Barry, *Femininity in Flight,* 193.

Two issues of Ms.: Barry, *Femininity in Flight,* 193.

153 *Feminist activism felt:* Barry, *Femininity in Flight,* 190.

whose volunteer endeavors: Liza Williams, "Airline Stewardess: Time Off for Good Behavior," *Playgirl,* February 1, 1974.

"I've always thought": Barry, *Femininity in Flight,* 207.

155 Let's ridicule: Alex Rawling, interview with the author, February 7, 2019.

157 *royal hat:* "Landmark to Be Torn Down," *Bangkok Post,* June 30, 2002.

15. A MATTER OF SERIOUS AND CONTINUING CONCERN

158 *women who had worked:* Dana Sachs, *The Life We Were Given* (Boston: Beacon Press, 2010), 13.

American commentators debated: Winthrop Rockwell, "Efforts Grow to Bring Here Babies that GI's Left in Vietnam," *New York Times,* January 3, 1972.

Estimates of their numbers: Tad Szulc, "Embassy in Saigon Calls Babies of GI's 'a Serious Concern,'" *New York Times,* July 26, 1971; T. Grant Call-ery, "Children of War: The Problems of Amerasian Children in Vietnam," *Case Western Reserve Journal of International Law* 6, no. 1 (1973).

159 *stewardesses who had flown:* Author interviews with Jane Fujioka Noe, March 30, 2017; Gail Jennings, May 2, 2017; Anne Sweeney, April 24, 2017.

Sixty percent of Americans: Mark Gillespie, "Americans Look Back at Vietnam War," Gallup poll, November 17, 2000.

"a matter of serious": Szulc, "Embassy in Saigon."

on the black market: Heather Marie Stur, *Beyond Combat: Women and Gender in the Vietnam War Era* (Cambridge: Cambridge University Press, 2011), 178.

The U.S. government called: "Another Way the U.S. Has Left Its Mark on Vietnam," *New York Times,* April 30, 1970.

160 *Actor Dick Hughes:* Gloria Emerson, "Until They Found the Shelter, Their Home Was Danang's Streets," *New York Times,* August 3, 1970.

A few hundred orphans: Rosemary Taylor and Wende Grant, *Orphans of War: Work with the Abandoned Children of Vietnam, 1967–1975* (London: Collins, 1988).

An orphanage director: Taylor and Grant, *Orphans of War,* 33.

An Air France stewardess: Rockwell, "Efforts Grow."

One Pan Am stewardess: Sam Wessling, interview with the author, July 14, 2017.

a stewardess told: Mindy Kammeyer, interview with the author, July 10, 2017.

16. AN EXTENSION OF THE AIRLINE

162 *Hollywood Park racetrack:* Hadley Meares, "The Glitz and Glamour of Hollywood Park," *Curbed,* September 20, 2018.

163 *wider social unrest:* Mike Davis and Jon Weiner, *Set the Night on Fire: L.A. in the Sixties* (New York: Verso, 2020).

One 248-unit complex: "Housing: Pads for Singles," *Time,* August 26, 1966.

164 *the Swede made:* Siv Adams, interview with the author, October 16, 2019.

improvised: Adams interview; Sheila O'Brien, interview with the author, May 25, 2017.

165 *They played hearts:* Sabine Renard, interview with the author, March 22, 2017.

only five thousand tourists: Robert F. Rogers, *Destiny's Landfall: A History of Guam* (Honolulu: University of Hawaii Press, 1995), 222.

"forever summer latitude": *New Horizons World Guide* (New York: Pan American Airways Publications, 1965), 548.

166 *middle of the island:* Rogers, *Destiny's Landfall,* 213.

operational base: Rogers, *Destiny's Landfall,* 228.

167 *Guidebooks recommended:* *New Horizons World Guide,* 548.

sent in secret: Anthony Lewis, "Menu for Disaster," *New York Times,* October 4, 1976.

a stewardess had watched: Karen Walker Ryan, interview with the author, April 20, 2017.

168 *one scholar later argued:* Jerry Lembcke, "The Myth of the Spitting Antiwar Protester," *New York Times,* October 13, 2017.

worked toward an understanding: David J. Morris, "The VA Treated My PTSD All Wrong," *Washington Post,* November 11, 2016.

washed over men: Ken Burns and Geoffrey C. Ward, *The Vietnam War: An Intimate History* (New York: Alfred A. Knopf, 2017), 583.

"The country doesn't": "Transcript: Kerry Testifies Before Senate Panel, 1971," NPR.com, April 26, 2006.

169 *so collectively dirty:* Gloria Emerson, *Winners and Losers: Battles, Retreats, Gains, Losses, and Ruins from the Vietnam War* (New York: W. W. Norton, 2014), 162.

one in five soldiers: Bernard C. Nalty, *Air War Over South Vietnam 1968–1975* (Washington, DC: Air Force History and Museums Program, 2010), 319.

once collected two: Adams interview.

Another stewardess told: Mindy Kammeyer, interview with the author, July 10, 2017.

began to bring dogs: Nalty, *Air War,* 318.

171 *"I walked out":* *The Vietnam War,* episode 9, "A Disrespectful Loyalty," directed by Ken Burns, September 27, 2017, PBS.

Defense Attaché Office: William E. LeGro, *Vietnam from Cease-Fire to Capitulation* (Washington, DC: U.S. Army Center of Military History, 1985).

Whether its operations: Indeed, declassified military documents establishing the DOA show the words *U.S. military presence* crossed out and replaced with *Department of Defense presence* throughout. See "Defense Attaché Office: Saigon," Central Intelligence Agency, sanitized copy approved for release December 26, 2012, https://www.cia.gov/library/readingroom/docs/CIA-RDP80R01720R000800010040-5.pdf.

newspapers decried: "Cease-Fire," *New York Times,* January 28, 1973.

at least: These numbers would increase dramatically in the two decades following the war. "In 1995, the Ministry of Labor, War Invalids, and Social Affairs released an estimate of 1.1 million Communist military deaths and almost 2 million civilian deaths due to war-related causes from 1954 to 1975." Charles Hirschman, Samuel Preston, and Vu Manh Loi, "Vietnamese Casualties During the American War: A New Estimate," *Population and Development Review* 21, no. 4 (December 1995): 783–812.

one and a half million: "Vietnam War Casualties," *New York Times,* January 24, 1973.

fresh unrest: William Warren, "Letter from Bangkok," *New York Times,* February 10, 1974.

172 *a new constitution:* Giles Ji Ungpakorn, "1968 and the 'Thai Seventies,'" VersoBooks.com, May 17, 2018. https://www.versobooks.com/blogs/3823-1968-and-the-thai-seventies.

American corporations reaping: Douglas Karsner, "The Real Bottom

Line: A History of Business Executives Move for Vietnam Peace," *Essays in Economic and Business History* 31 (2013).

"Does Pan American": Pan American World Airways records, series 1, box 637, folder 3, Otto G. Richter Library, University of Miami Special Collections.

stewardesses were trained: Soviet stewardesses, at least, were certainly agents for their own country. A CIA memo on tradecraft from 1960 outlines Soviet stewardesses' techniques for keeping American foreign agents distracted in the air with menus and magazines. See Thomas W. Wolfe, "Obstacle Course for Attachés," *Studies in Intelligence* 4, no. 3 (1960).

173 *"a pseudo-private airline"*: "The Covert War," *New York Times*, June 13, 1971.

"the servant of": Richard Halloran, "Air America's Civilian Facade Gives It Latitude in East Asia," *New York Times*, April 5, 1970.

"I take it": Barbara Gamarekian, "The Heroine of the State Department's Women," *New York Times*, April 6, 1976.

it was "a rank-ridden": Gamarekian, "The Heroine."

174 *All money-losing flights*: Marylin Bender and Selig Altschul, *The Chosen Instrument: Juan Trippe, Pan Am, the Rise and Fall of an American Entrepreneur* (New York: Simon and Schuster, 1982), 521–22.

Braniff stewardesses too: Michael Magers, "Inside the Sisterhood of Braniff Flight Attendants," *Condé Nast Traveler*, August 31, 2018.

17. EVERYTHING FLYABLE

179 *Kissinger assuring Congress*: Thomas E. Ricks, "Setting the Record Straight on the End of the Vietnam War (2): How It Really Ended," Foreignpolicy.com, April 15, 2015.

eight hundred million: David K. Shipler, "Vast Aid from U. S. Backs Saigon in Continuing War," *New York Times*, February 25, 1974.

Rumors spread: Michael Maclear, *The Ten Thousand Day War: Vietnam, 1945–1975* (New York: Avon, 1982), 321.

Thousands of vehicles: Bernard Weinraub, "Refugees Tell of Attack on Their Caravan," *New York Times*, March 21, 1975.

"Convoy of Tears": Maclear, *The Ten Thousand Day War*, 322.

180 *Half of Saigon*: David Butler, *The Fall of Saigon: Scenes from the Sudden End of a Long War* (New York: Dell, 1985), 23, 313.

Communists and mountain tribes: Cited in Butler, *The Fall of Saigon*, 92, 97.

Rumor had it: Dana Sachs, *The Life We Were Given* (Boston: Beacon Press, 2010), 12.

Terrified mothers left: Sachs, *The Life,* 56.

orphanage workers rushed: Sachs, *The Life,* 45.

To do so even: Sachs, *The Life,* 42.

combination of forces: Rosemary Taylor and Wende Grant, *Orphans of War: Work with the Abandoned Children of Vietnam, 1967–1975* (London: Collins, 1988).

181 *Pan Am's passenger lists:* Al Topping, interview with the author, October 10, 2019.

citizens jamming: Malcolm W. Browne, "Tensions Grow in Saigon; New Coup Plot Reported," *New York Times,* April 4, 1975.

Vietnamese woman claw: Topping interview.

air force major: "4 in Saigon Seize C-130 and Fly 52 to Singapore," *New York Times,* April 5, 1975.

One flight with: "Old DC-3 Rescues 98 Vietnam Orphans," *New York Times,* March 24, 1975.

"Everything flyable": "Old DC-3 Rescues."

An East German would: Malcolm W. Browne, "A Deep Bitterness Toward U.S.," *New York Times,* April 5, 1975.

182 *When Daly asked:* Butler, *The Fall of Saigon,* 148.

an air traffic controller: Larry Engelmann, *Tears Before the Rain: An Oral History of the Fall of South Vietnam* (Oxford: Oxford University Press, 1990).

saw thousands: Jan Wollett, interviews with the author, December 13, 2018, and September 30, 2019.

183 *Human bodies dropped:* Butler, *The Fall of Saigon,* 158–64.

"As calm fell": MrGlb2012, "The Last Flight from Da Nang, Vietnam 1975," YouTube video, September 28, 2011, https://www.youtube.com/watch?v=pzcWZ7j1iTg.

184 *Among Juan Trippe's arguments:* Marylin Bender and Selig Altschul, *The Chosen Instrument: Juan Trippe, Pan Am, the Rise and Fall of an American Entrepreneur* (New York: Simon and Schuster, 1982), 505–6.

flying a first: Sachs, *The Life,* 49–50; Patricia Murphy, "Flight Attendant on Saigon Evacuation: You Wanted 'to Help Every Child,'" NPR.com, April 28, 2015.

he would pay: "Airline to Fly Orphans from Vietnam," *New York Times,* April 2, 1975.

military and medical supplies: Andrew H. Malcolm, "U.S. Cargo Plane Lands in Saigon, but Whether It Is Start of an Airlift Is Unclear," *New York Times,* April 2, 1975.

deputy prime minister wrote: Butler, *The Fall of Saigon,* 220.

185 *"I can't guarantee":* "Transcript of President's News Conference on Foreign and Domestic Matters," *New York Times,* April 4, 1975.

"It is the President's obvious intent": Sachs, *The Life,* 89.

186 *Orphanage workers, escorts:* Taylor and Grant, *Orphans of War,* 168–72; Rachel Martin, "Remembering the Doomed First Flight of Operation Babylift," NPR, April 26, 2015.

many dozens: Butler, *The Fall of Saigon,* 227; Defense Intelligence Agency, "Remembering the First Operation Babylift Flight," https://web.archive.org/web/20130927194734/http://www.dia.mil/history/features/operation-babylift/.

Anyone resisting arrest: Browne, "Tensions Grow in Saigon."

187 *had mortgaged his Connecticut:* Donna Greene, "Solo Effort that Led to Worldwide Relief," *New York Times,* April 27, 1997.

Another agency: Sachs, *The Life,* 90.

no Vietnamese airport staff: Topping interview.

18. WAR COMES ABOARD

188 *"The Great Retreat":* *Newsweek,* March 31, 1975.

190 *Ingrid heard:* Ingrid Templeton, interview with the author, June 5, 2018.

twenty airlines: Kathleen Barry, *Femininity in Flight: A History of Flight Attendants* (Durham, NC: Duke University Press, 2007), 205.

193 *snapped a photo:* "Interview with Karen Ryan," YouTube video, May 21, 2015, https://www.youtube.com/watch?v=VWQYBm1LUL8.

196 *bracelets, which carried:* Rosemary Taylor and Wende Grant, *Orphans of War: Work with the Abandoned Children of Vietnam, 1967–1975* (London: Collins, 1988).

19. THE MOST INCREDIBLE SCENE

201 *"the most incredible scene":* Douglas Kneeland, "Many Children Found Ill on Arrival from Vietnam," *New York Times,* April 5, 1975.

By April 11: "Airlift of Children Resumes in Saigon," *New York Times,* April 12, 1975.

1,650 children: Philip Shabecoff, "Airlift of Young Vietnamese to Resume," *New York Times,* April 18, 1975.

Discrepancies began: Robert D. McFadden, "Non-Orphans Reported Among Airlifted Children," *New York Times,* April 11, 1975.

Numbers and names: Dana Sachs, *The Life We Were Given* (Boston: Beacon Press, 2010), 204.

the agency announced: Shabecoff, "Airlift of Young Vietnamese."

2,242 children: Sachs, *The Life,* 207.

Playboy *magnate Hugh Hefner:* Rosemary Taylor and Wende Grant, *Orphans of War: Work with the Abandoned Children of Vietnam, 1967–1975* (London: Collins, 1988), 191.

202 *punctuated by challenges:* Richard D. Lyons, "Washington Meeting on Children's Airlift Is Jarred by Charges of Racism and Elitism," *New York Times,* April 8, 1975.

A Yale psychologist: Richard Flaste, "Controversy Is Growing," *New York Times,* April 9, 1975.

A Vietnamese anthropologist: Flaste, "Controversy."

203 *"Drama and Tragedy":* David Lamb, "Drama and Tragedy: Last Flight on Its Way in Operation Baby Lift," *Los Angeles Times,* April 8, 1975.

"The United States": Bob Greene, "The United States Is Still Sure That It Knows Best," *Los Angeles Times,* April 11, 1975.

"'Operation Babylift'": United Press International, "980 in U.S.: 'Operation Babylift' Closes Shop," *Los Angeles Times,* April 15, 1975.

206 *Bribes, threats:* Ed Lavalle, *Last Flight from Saigon* (Washington, DC: U.S. Government Printing Office, 1978), https://media.defense.gov/2010/Sep/28/2001330140/-1/-1/0/last_flight_from_saigon2.pdf.

In classified advertisements: Fox Butterfield, "A Saigon Question: Stay or Flee?," *New York Times,* April 21, 1975.

a Vietnamese economist: Fox Butterfield, "Panic Rises in Saigon, but the Exits Are Few," *New York Times,* April 24, 1975.

Lumpy walls: George Esper, "Evacuation from Saigon Tumultuous at the End," *New York Times,* April 30, 1975.

The embassy pressed: Wolfgang Lehmann, interviewed by Robert Martens, "The Association for Diplomatic Studies and Training Foreign Affairs Oral History Project," May 9, 1989, https://www.adst.org/OH%20TOCs/Lehmann,%20Wolfgang%20J.toc.pdf.

One of the stewardesses: Rebecca Sprecher, interview with the author, May 15, 2020.

Tori flew: "8,000 Reach Philippines," *New York Times,* April 28, 1975.

twenty thousand others: Andrew Malcolm, "Refugee Airlift to Guam Resumes," *New York Times,* April 28, 1975.

207 *"floating in their skirts":* Oliver Todd, *Cruel April: The Fall of Saigon* (New York: W. W. Norton, 1990), 320.

20. THE ONLY LONELY PLACE WAS ON THE MOON

208 *By the numbers:* Sarah Rose, "Flight Status," *Washington Post Magazine,* May 13, 2020.

209 *"Many people in"*: Gloria Emerson, *Winners and Losers: Battles, Re-treats, Gains, Losses, and Ruins from the Vietnam War* (New York: W. W. Norton, 2014), 37.

The military had apparently: Dana Sachs, *The Life We Were Given* (Boston: Beacon Press, 2010), 77.

A sister of one: "Lockheed Is Sued for $200-Million in 'Babylift' Crash," *New York Times*, June 15, 1975.

investigations found: Sachs, *The Life*, 208.

Plaintiffs pored over: Sachs, *The Life*, 206.

210 *individual lawsuits*: Sachs, *The Life*, 204.

One official estimated: Nancy Hicks, "Black Agencies Charge Injustice in Placing of Vietnam Children," *New York Times*, April 19, 1975.

hit one hundred and twenty billion: Bureau of Transportation Statistics, "U.S. Passenger-Miles," https://www.bts.gov/content/us-passenger-miles.

211 *it was the 747*: Robert Lindsey, "Pan Am Decline Began with Order for 747's," *New York Times*, August 24, 1974.

buying National: Josh Barbanel, "President Gives Final Approval to Pan Am and National Merger," *New York Times*, December 23, 1979.

worst possible time: R.E.G. Davies, *Airlines of the Jet Age* (Washington, DC: Smithsonian Institution Scholarly Press, 2011), 162–63.

selling off its assets: Davies, *Airlines of the Jet Age*, 162–63.

212 *Among the pilots*: "December 4, 1991: The Last 'Clipper' Flight," *Airways*, December 4, 2016.

Riggs had proclaimed: Gail Collins, *When Everything Changed: The Amazing Journey of American Women from 1960 to the Present* (Boston: Little, Brown, 2009), 246.

"another in the lengthening": Kathleen Barry, *Femininity in Flight: A History of Flight Attendants* (Durham, NC: Duke University Press, 2007), 170.

Lawsuits would continue: Jean Thompson, "Maternity Suit Flight Attendants and Ground Workers Win $1.9 Million in Back Wages After Challenging National Airlines' Mandatory Maternity Leave," *South Florida Sun-Sentinel*, July 16, 1987.

Diplomat Alison Palmer: Barbara Gamarekian, "Washington Talk; Women Gain, but Slowly, in the Foreign Service," *New York Times*, July 28, 1989.

213 *The airline argued*: Barry, *Femininity in Flight*, 167.

214 *"Every time I see"*: Collins, *When Everything Changed*, 241–42.

the prohibition on: "White House Lifts Ban on Women in Pants," *New York Times*, November 26, 1973.

Yet management believed that: Valerie Steele and Claudia Kidwell, eds., *Men and Women: Dressing the Part* (London: Booth-Clibborn Editions, 1989), 72.

particularly satisfying promotion: Clipper 23, no. 4 (February 14, 1972).

215 *Approximately eleven thousand women:* "History of the Vietnam Women's Memorial," Vietnam Women's Memorial Foundation, http://www.viet namwomensmemorial.org/history.php.

"We tried to recognize": Diane Carlson Evans, interview with the author, November 1, 2018.

EPILOGUE

218 *Battle of the Hotels:* Rita Daou, "Beirut Eyes Future for Famed Hotel Turned Civil War Relic," *Times of Israel,* May 4, 2014.

During the Gulf War: Charles Imbriani, "Civilian Involvement in the 1990–91 Gulf War Through the Civil Reserve Air Fleet" (PhD diss., Florida State University, 2012).

222 *"Fluidity, mobility, illusoriness":* Olga Tokarczuk, *Flights* (New York: Riverhead, 2007).

actual flight attendants: Heather Poole, *Cruising Altitude: Tales of Crashpads, Crew Drama, and Crazy Passengers at 35,000 Feet* (New York: William Morrow, 2012).

nearly any magazine: Hillary Reid, "Why Do Almost 400 Flight Attendants Own This $24 Jumpsuit?," NYMag.com, November 21, 2019; Aislyn Greene, "How to Pack a Suitcase," Afar.com, January 17, 2019.

223 *the nation's highest medal:* Aditi Malhotra, "'Neerja' Film Tells Story of Pan Am Flight 73 Attendant Who Saved Passengers in Hijacking," *Wall Street Journal,* February 17, 2016.

INDEX